D0850059

# Endings and Beginnings

# Endings and Beginnings

## On the Technique of Terminating Psychotherapy and Psychoanalysis

Herbert J. Schlesinger

THE ANALYTIC PRESS

2005      Hillsdale, NJ          London

Published by The Analytic Press, Inc.
101 West Street, Hillsdale, NJ  07642
www.analyticpress.com

Some material in Chapter 7 was originally published as "Diagnosis and Prescription for Psychotherapy," *Bulletin of the Menninger Clinic*, 33:269-278, 1969, and appears here by permission of The Guilford Press.

An earlier version of Chapter 10 appeared as "Technical Problems in the Analysis of the Mourning Patient," in *Three Faces of Mourning*, edited by Salman Akhater. It is adapted here by permission of Jason Aronson Publishers.

Typeset in Palatino by Laserset, Hancock, NY 13783

**Library of Congress Cataloging-in-Publication Data**

Schlesinger, Herbert J.
    Endings and beginnings : on the technique of terminating psychotherapy and psychoanalysis / Herbert J. Schlesinger.
        p.    cm.
    Includes bibliographical references and index.
ISBN 0-88163-413-1
1.    Psychotherapy—Termination. 2. Psychoanalysis—Termination.
    I. Title: On the technique of terminating psychotherapy and psychoanalysis. II. Title.

    RC489.T45S34 2005
    616.89'14—dc22

                                                                    2005045230

Printed in the United States of America
10 9 8 7 6 5 4 3 2 1

\* \* \* \* \*

*I dedicate this book to my wife, Ann H. Appelbaum, M.D. In countless ways that only the heart knows, she served as resident muse and in that vital capacity, inspired, reassured, and exemplified patience, all at no small cost to her own writing. I hope she finds the book rewarding; she is not one to disappoint lightly.*

\* \* \* \* \*

*Or say that the end precedes the beginning,*
*And the end and the beginning were always there*
*Before the beginning and after the end*
*And all is now.*
—T. S. Elliot, "Burnt Norton," in *Four Quartets*

# Acknowledgments

As this book is in every sense a continuation of *The Texture of Treatment* (*TAP*, 2003), the acknowledgments in that earlier installment are still current. I shall not repeat them other than to note that, once again, Stanley Goodman was the friend every author longs for, a sternly benevolent reader and critic who even welcomed the imposition to read first drafts. Once again, he exercised his gift for puncturing pretentious phrases. He searched out and scoured the mud from many a construction.

Paul Stepansky also read an early draft with pencil in hand. He not only smoothed out some rough places, he engaged with the ideas and his marginalia enriched the text. And once again, Eleanor Starke Kobrin used her red pencil lovingly and to good effect so that every line finally passed muster.

Thanks to Stanley, Paul, and Lenni, my position has been made nakedly clear; you may agree with my ideas or not, but you will not be in doubt about what I meant to say.

I also want to thank the many friends, colleagues, and students who encouraged me to get on with this project. Now, with book in hand, they can argue with me in private without fear of rebuttal.

# Contents

# Preface

It may seem counterintuitive to begin a book on endings and beginnings of psychotherapy and psychoanalysis that will be useful for beginners as well as for old hands by asserting that ending is what psychotherapy is all about. After all, beginners are worried mainly about how things will go or not go with their first cases, and they express their concern with heroic efforts to seduce and hold on to the patients assigned to them. They fear that the patients will take one look at them, recognize them as neophytes, and leave, confirming their not-so-secret fear that their lack of experience shows and that it implies incompetence. The ability to hold on to a patient became a mark of competence.

You will note the irony that a would-be therapist would want to hold on to a patient rather than help him get the services he needs and move on, but we must recognize that while the fear is excessive, it is not baseless. After all, how can we fault a therapist who wants the patient to remain long enough to get the services he came for, however long or short that time might be? Therapy is a process and processes do take time. But there are less reasonable factors at play that support beginners'self-comforting belief that retaining one's patients is a sign of competence.

The faculty of training clinics, many of whom hold a generally psychodynamic point of view, expect that,even with skilled therapy, all patients need a good deal of time to "get well." "Normal" therapy for all patients thus is of indefinite duration. "Brief psychotherapy," if recognized at all, may be regarded dismissively as a special variety of minimal treatment suitable for the not-very-sick or not-very-interesting patient. Hence the suspicion that, if a patient leaves before attending for a respectable period of time, it must be because the therapist lacked the skill to hold the patient and the loss counts as his failure. I was brought up in this tradition. When I was young in the field, the only students who were offered jobs in the clinic were those whose patients remained with them throughout the training year. The commonsensical idea that it ought to be our business to help patients get what they came for as rapidly as feasible so that they can do without us somehow had acquired an odor of disreputable haste and a willingness to short-change patients.

The source of these now strange ideas, which seem to equate duration with quality of treatment, is, of course, an odd remnant of the aura that still surrounds psychoanalysis. It once was the dominant ideology in American psychotherapeutics and still is an important influence on the contemporary scene. Psychoanalysis is a powerful method of psychotherapy, and many of us believe that, in certain instances, nothing else will do. It is not a panacea, however. In its native format, psychoanalysis has limited application.

Several adaptations of psychoanalysis, the various psychodynamic psychotherapies, have extended the therapeutic reach of psychoanalytic ideas. Some of these applications are marred by an unfortunate residue of the great respect that psychoanalysis retains, including the overvaluation of the duration of therapy; since psychoanalysis takes a long time, taking a long time must be a universal good. The current nonspecific imitation of psychoanalysis is even named "long-term psychotherapy." Sadly, the defining characteristic of a therapy so named is that therapists are led to expect that nothing useful will result in finite time. I have discussed this issue and how and when change occurs in psychotherapy elsewhere (Schlesinger, 1988, 2003) and discuss it again in this book as it is vital to the issues around ending and termination.

Describing matters in this way, of course, highlights the absurdity of measuring the success of treatment and the competence of the treater by how much time the the treatment took. I am not making a case for "short-term therapy" or time-limited therapy, although both of these offshoots of psychoanalysis have useful applications. All therapy, like all processes of whatever description, takes time. The question of how much time is enough for an adequate therapy is a core issue that must be addressed, taking into account the psychopathology and circumstances of the individual patient. It is not an issue that can be settled by fiat, as with the faulty assumption that only "long-term" therapy is honorable. That declaration brings me back to my original assertion that ending treatment is what it is all about and the question whether it is sensible or not to thrust the idea on a beginner whose mind is set on how to make such a solid beginning that he will not lose his patient.

If my motive were only to distract beginners from their beginning worries and, like an evangelist, preach about ultimate things, the task would be both pointless and fruitless. But a concern about ending is much broader than planning for ultimate discharge, useful as that planning is. Ending also refers to a state of mind. The patient entering therapy naturally will be concerned about who his therapist will be, how "good" the therapist is, and whether they will get along. But he also bring with him into this new beginning the baggage of his prior failures, his inability to manage his life, and the sense of being at the end of his rope. We could say that, while the therapist is at the beginning of this opening treatment, the patient is somewhere in the middle of his treatment. Having failed at self-treatment, he is about to start again, hoping to do better with professional help.[1]

It is especially clear that doctor and patient begin at different starting points when, as is often the case in training clinics, the patient is not newly admitted but is a "transfer," one left stranded by a student who rotated off service, leaving the patient to be "picked up" by a member of the next class. The lesson here is that when one begins a therapy, or anything else, the necessary implication is that one has ended something else. For beginning therapists, the lesson is that they should consider and explore the significance of the patient's recent experience of failure, or perhaps partial success, abandonment, and ending as both therapist and patient overlap their immediate concerns to get to know each other well enough to decide about beginning a new therapy. In its most general form, the lesson is that experiences of ending and beginning permeate each other, an idea that informs much of what is to follow in this book.

The approach I advocate does not subscribe to any political or social ideology but does share the general humanistic concerns of all psychotherapy. It is a commitment to the worth of the individual and to the relief of unnecessary suffering. It takes a generally developmental point of view toward life and appreciates the validity of individual differences. It holds that honest communication facilitates personality growth and smoothes the progress of psychotherapy. It recognizes that maturity implies a concern for others as well as for the self and holds that assuming responsibility for oneself is the basis for moral and healthy behavior.

Finally, as I warned readers of my earlier book (Schlesinger, 2003), you will not find here a comprehensive review of everything written on ending and termination. I have drawn instead on some 50 years of practice, teaching and supervising psychotherapy and psychoanalysis and now think I have some idea of what works and why.

The major ideas I offer about the technical aspects of beginning and ending psychoanalysis and dynamic psychotherapy are:

---

[1] When the word patient is used, analysand also applies. When "he" or "him" is used, "she" or "her" also applies. When the word therapist is used, analyst also applies. When the word analyst is used, the reference may be exclusive. I will address this special problem of usage in Chapter 5.

1. The ending of psychotherapy is the most important part of the treatment. In a major sense, any treatment is about ending it; it is about how to obviate the need for the therapist. When the time comes for the actual ending, if the analyst handles it sensitively and skillfully, he helps to ensure that the gains of the treatment are enduring (so called, structural change).

2. While the word termination is commonly used as if it were the only proper way to refer to the closing down of treatment, I hold that termination and ending are not synonyms. Treatments may end in any number of ways—including the patient's quitting in disgust, eloping out of fear, breaking off in order to attend school, or quitting as matter of course because, "I got what I came for." I reserve the term termination for the process of bringing the treatment to an end electively and with the agreement of both parties that the maximum expectable benefits have been obtained. Its distinctive features are that it is planned and gives full consideration both to a review of the treatment and its accomplishments and disappointments and to the problems associated with ending, particularly those associated with separating from the therapist, especially freeing the patient's gains from the fantasy that they depend on remaining a patient. A common form of this not always conscious fantasy is that the gains are on loan; they belong to the therapist, and to continue to enjoy them, one must stay in the therapist's good favor. It follows that both therapist and patient should allow sufficient time, following the agreement to stop treatment, to "work through" these implications of the impending separation, that is, to terminate the treatment to the extent possible.

3. The experience of separating from the analyst has much in common with separations in all significant relationships, including those that are brought about by the death, divorce, loss of job, and graduation. It differs from most other important separations in that ideally it is both voluntary and planned, so that the parties remain together to understand the process until the agreed upon ending date. This separation does not (generally) result from anger or disappointment, although these feelings, among others, are likely to emerge during the process of working through.

   Unlike at the separation occasioned by death, there are no cultural arrangements to help the patient deal with the sense of loss of the therapist and therapy. The therapist must be fully acquainted with the "natural history" of human relationships and the common phenomena related to mourning significant losses.

4. Beginning and ending refer not only to the actual opening and closing of treatment. Throughout treatment, patients have experiences that feel to them that in some odd sense they once again are "at a beginning." In the same way, at times they may experience feelings that would be expected at a significant ending, the fear that one is about to lose something important, perhaps even that one is about to be abandoned. Such feelings, of course, are expectable if the actual ending of treatment is imminent while the patient feels unready. But such "ending-phase" phenomena also appear whenever the patient achieves some portion of a goal, even a minor portion, since the least of achievements predicts that treatment will end some day whereas the sense of loss is felt now. The therapist then has the opportunity to help the patient appreciate the significance of these feelings, why they "belong" in the context of achievement and why the awareness of success carries with it, paradoxically, a bit of sadness. Such periods of "working-through" serve as "miniterminations," as rehearsals for the work that will be required around the eventual ending of the treatment. The therapist can use these ending and beginning phenomena as landmarks to locate where he and the patient are in the process of treatment

5. During the diagnostic evaluation, the therapist should estimate from the patient's history the difficulty the patient is likely to have eventually in ending the therapy: will he be willing to engage in a phase of termination, even if the ending is instigated in part by an external exigency? We should expect patients to end treatment in a way consistent with the way they experience relationship. We should not expect every patient to end therapy with a recognizable termination phase. Some go through the "mad-sad-glad" paradigm we analogize to grieving and mourning. We can easily fit this pattern into the most desirable mode of ending, a termination based on working-through.

   Other patients are so reluctant to feel the pain of separating, or so fear abandonment, that they decamp before the therapist can take up the topic; they are likely to quit as soon as they sense or fear that ending is "in the air." Some patients have never had the experience of ending a regular connection to another person while remaining in a positive relationship. Some of these people can separate only by devaluing the therapist and the therapy in a paranoid way. Still other patients do not seem to enter a "whole" personal relationship with the therapist; they relate themselves mainly to the healing function of the therapist as a "part-object."

It is important that the therapist have the proper expectation of how patients tolerate the painful feelings that arise when one ends a significant relationship.

6.  Few therapists had any experience ending a therapy electively during training. Training clinics do not encourage students to end and terminate treatments; these clinics prefer that students "transfer" patients to members of the next class. However, even when external circumstances, such as the therapist's limited tenure at the clinic, seem to determine when treatment must end, the therapist can work with the patient to end electively and terminate to the extent possible at an earlier point when he notices that ending phenomena are present. In this way, he can help the patient to deal with the loss of himself, rather than leaving this vital aspect of treatment to his successor. Of course, it is assumed that more treatment is immediately called for, other than for the despair at having been abandoned. The conscientious therapist may be spared the trauma of feeling forced to abandon the patient he has become so attached to. Ending the current episode of treatment is a matter separate from deciding that the patient needs more treatment, and the decisions should not be conflated, as they frequently are.

7.  People differ in how they experience time passing, and they locate themselves differently in time. The polar examples are that some are chronic beginners, always facing even familiar situations as if nothing in life had prepared them for this moment. Everything is new and either exciting and inviting or uncertain and dangerous, depending on other factors. Others are chronically at a point of ending. They expect to leave imminently and fear being prevented from getting away or being left by someone important to them. For them, there will not be enough time to do whatever they have in mind. Their main concern is how to put off the inevitable abandonment. Part of a thorough evaluation of a new patient is the assessment of his relationship to time, in addition to his relationship to work, love, death, other persons, success, failure, and morality.

8.  It is a common experience that, after some time with seeming progress, therapy seems to "get stuck." The tendency to stagnate belongs in a discussion of endings and termination. Frequently, a case reaches an "impasse" because of issues related to fear of separation or because other sensitive issues in the relationship with the therapist that have been avoided by both therapist and patient (the elephant-in-the-room phenomenon). Both parties may attempt

to avoid the pain inevitably associated with separating from a valued other by becoming caught up in a transference–counter-transference bind. Impasses that persist because the analyst does not understand, or is reluctant to interpret, the dynamics of the situation ultimately may acquire the dire label of "interminable analysis." Here I discuss the phenomena of the impasse and seeming interminability in terms of the presence of an unanalyzed "transference neurosis" and how the parties may extricate themselves so that treatment may continue or termination may be accomplished.

I commend these ideas to you and suggest that you try them in your practice before coming to any conclusion about them.

# A Little History and Some Definitions

This chapter contains what I generally skip when browsing, the boring explanation of why the author feels that the common language has failed him and he must devise a new vocabulary to express his unique views. Still, I judge the risk of confusing you to be greater than the risk of boring you, and so I hope for your indulgence. If you are at all interested in what I have to say and still skip the next few pages, you may have to return to them when you are in a much less receptive mood. Be warned. If you have read this far, you will have noticed that I refer to beginning and ending rather differently than other writers do; it is time to make those differences explicit.

The fog that surrounds so many discussions among analysts results in part from the casual, not to say whimsical, way we often abuse the ordinary terms of discourse. It is as if, once we graduate as analysts, we are no longer slaves of the common language but are its masters—free, Humpty Dumpty-like, to use words as we please. In that dismal tradition (but I hope you will agree with better reason), allow me to attempt to clarify the use of several familiar terms: ending, termination, phase, process, time, and structure.

## Ending and Termination

Analysts, as well as psychotherapists in general, tend to refer to all matters having to do with ending treatment as "termination," as if ending and termination were synonyms; indeed our tradition encourages it. As I discuss in Chapter 2, there are many ways in which an arrangement between consenting adults, treatment included, may come to an end. English is rich in terms to describe those ways: stop, finish, quit, flee, interrupt, discontinue, elope, drop out. We use all these words discriminately in the clinic to capture the particular way a patient left an episode of treatment.

But, if a former supervisor asks you why the patient you once consulted him about is no longer in analysis and you answer with a shrug and say, "Because it ended," he is certain to follow up with, "But was it successfully terminated?" Analysts do seem to have something special in mind about that word and do not consider "end" to be a synonym. If you inquire tactfully of the former supervisor (and let us assume he is one of the more patient ones) what he means by his question, you may hear a reasoned reply; he hopes that the ending came about through mutual agreement, that it preferably was not driven by some exigency or a competing preference in the patient's life or in yours, and that you took enough time to work through the implications of ending.[1]

I believe it is fair to say that in recent years a consensus has formed among analysts that an analysis should end as that supervisor described. It was not always so; early in our history, an analyst would decide that a patient had had enough and announce it to him. (I discuss these aspects of ending and termination in Chapter 3). Holding those preferences amounts to our taking the position that the ending/termination of analysis is a serious matter. But those preferences do not prescribe what a seriously engaged analyst and patient should be doing as they go about bringing the analysis to a close.[2]

So the puzzle remains. Since "ending" and "parting" are adequate ways to refer to the separating of people, including therapist and patient, and with so many other terms to specify the particulars of how and why they took diverging paths, why do we need to recruit a new term, termination, one not previously used in connection with human relationships?

A review is in order of the relatively brief history of the term termination in psychoanalysis. It first appeared in the psychoanalytic literature in English in 1937 when Joan Riviere, then an analysand of Freud, at Freud's request translated his just completed article, "*Die Endliche und Die Unendliche Analyse*" (Freud, 1937a) as "Analysis Terminable and Interminable" (Freud, 1937b). Both the English and the German versions appeared in the same year. Riviere's translation was later reprinted in *The Collected Papers of Sigmund Freud* (Freud, 1950), and James Strachey slightly modified that translation in *The Standard Edition* (Freud, 1937c). Strachey wrote a lengthy and informative introduction to the paper but

---

[1] Sad to acknowledge, however, this ideal is rarely reached in practice. As Novick (1982, p. 331) noted, the vast majority of analyses reported in the literature ended unilaterally.

[2] For a good review of this literature, see Bergmann, 1997.

did not comment on Riviere's strange choice of words to translate Freud's *endliche* and *unendliche*.

Since then, termination has become a term of art, seemingly the generic and only proper way to refer to the ending of psychotherapy as well as psychoanalysis. Oddly, the word termination has no roots in the German language in which Freud wrote. An indication that the term was not in common usage at that time is that it does not appear in the first edition of a standard psychiatric dictionary (Hinsie and Schatsky, 1940). But "termination" is included, with its current meaning but without comment, in the eighth edition of that dictionary (Campbell, 2004).

The *Freud Encyclopedia* (Erwin, 2002) has no entry for "termination" but termination is discussed, in the now usual fashion, in the article on "Psychoanalytic Technique and Process" (Richards and Richards, 2002). We can no longer ask Riviere or Strachey why they thought it necessary to enlist "terminable" and "interminable" to translate Freud's *endliche* and *unendliche* with words that allude to ultimate finality, with dreary and funereal implications that Freud did not intend.

Freud's *endliche* and *unendliche*, as Leupold-Löwenthal (1988) pointed out, have connotations different from and richer than terminable and interminable. He proposed that finite and infinite translate Freud's intention better.[3] Note too that interminable has connotations of weariness, boredom, and even despair, which are altogether lacking in *unendliche*. Substituting, as Leupold-Löwenthal suggests, finite and infinite yields the altogether different meaning that others too have proposed (e.g., Hoffer, 1950; Kramer, 1959; Ticho, 1967; Loewenberg, 1988; and Blum, 1989), that when a patient leaves analysis, analyzing continues through self-analysis and becomes a process more like education, which has no logical or necessary ending point.

Even if we take this revisionist point of view, we still can recognize that Riviere and Strachey did us a favor. There is something about the experience of ending psychotherapy and psychoanalysis that is different from other kinds of endings in human affairs, a difference that is worth preserving and that needs a distinguishing term.

There are several reasons to preserve the term termination to capture what is special about bringing an analysis to a close. There are also reasons to retain "end" to refer to the generic aspects of concluding treatment and to draw, as needed, on its many more-or-less synonyms to particularize endings. By reserving "termination" to refer to the unique aspect of a beneficial ending of a psychoanalytic treatment, whether psychoanalysis or psychotherapy, we can focus on the special concern of

---

[3] *Webster's Collegiate Dictionary*, fifth edition, gives infinite as a synonym for unending.

analysts, that when a patient leaves treatment, he should own the achievements he has made and take them with him. Analysts recognize that transference, which is the main focus of a psychoanalytic treatment, can also impede termination of treatment even though it may speed the ending of treatment.

What distinguishes termination from other ways of ending is that the analyst provides the patient a sufficient opportunity to work through (Freud, 1914) his fantasies that the gains he made depend on the transference and thus do not "belong" to him, that at best, they are on temporary loan. I ask you to agree that a patient has terminated his analysis,[4] and not merely ended it, to the extent that he and the analyst have worked through this issue.

Let me underline some implications of the observation that, in the best case, the analyzing does not stop when the patient leaves the analyst; it permits us to analogize the process to his education, which also continued, one hopes, after he left school. This analogy has other important implications. It leads us to recognize also that even while the formal psychoanalysis is ongoing, something similar is going on: a kind of alternation between active analyzing and another state that we could describe, variously, as testing to see what the consequences might be of the sense of inner freedom that resulted from the previous period of analyzing; or "metabolizing" the changes that just occurred; or seeming to take a vacation in order to appreciate the value of what analyzing has just yielded. The experience may be too various to capture with a single term, but its thrust is educational.

Let me dwell a bit longer on the implications of this observation. When we use the terms end and ending in connection with psychotherapy, we may not be aware that we are committing ourselves to a particular model of human interaction, one that, for convenience, we might call the treatment model. The model is of an instrumental relationship that each party enters to accomplish a purpose external to the relationship. When that purpose has been accomplished, or it becomes clear to one or the other that it is not likely to be accomplished, we expect them to end their meetings.

Some human activities do not conform to that model, for example, marriages, parenthood, and friendships. Ideally at least, these relationships are expected to last "until death do us part." Education follows its own model. Its goals may be external to the process or internal and, ideally, may be lifelong in duration. Although formal education is parsed by such rites of passage as graduation, it has no natural ending point. We may speak of a person as having been educated, but without any implication that he has reached the end of what he might learn.

---

[4] That is, has terminated *this episode* of analysis.

In contrast, we tend to speak of persons who have undergone some psychoanalysis as "having been analyzed." Although Freud (1937a) recommended that analysts undergo reanalysis periodically, the expression, "He was analyzed" suggests that having been with an analyst for a sufficient duration should do for all time. Some authorities agree with Freud when he referred to psychoanalysis as "after-education." They hold that analysis does not conform to the treatment model, as it is not so much a treatment as a form of education.

My position is that psychoanalysis (and psychotherapy) may be viewed from the vantage point of either model, depending on our immediate purpose and provided that we do not place education as necessarily occurring in a school or analysis as occurring only on a couch. Autodidaction and self-analysis capture the idea that the essence of both education and psychoanalysis is that they are lifelong processes of growth and development that need not be directed or conducted by an authority.

As my present interest is in the technical aspects of ending and terminating psychoanalysis and psychotherapy, however, I remain mostly within the model of an instrumental relationship as a treatment that ought to end when its purpose has been achieved. But within any particular psychoanalytic treatment, the model of education will seem to fit better. And that awareness will add to the koan of thinking about how to end an activity that in practice seems to have no natural ending point.[5]

When a person enters analysis or psychotherapy, usually it is because he wants treatment, typically to obtain something he feels is missing in his life or to get rid of some alien element, perhaps something that by courtesy could be called a "disease process." His initial expectation is that when he has achieved that purpose, treatment will stop. But this simplistic formula takes no account of the common experience that psychoanalysis functions as much as a goal-finding procedure as a goal-reaching procedure. While a person may begin psychoanalysis with one wish, typically he finds that in the course of achieving it, much more has happened than he expected. He is no longer quite the same and in ways that are not easy to define. At the very least, he is no longer satisfied simply to be free from whatever discomfort motivated him to enter treatment. His expectations have risen and his horizons have broadened, much as they do in the course of a good education.

Patients typically are driven to analysis by pain or discomfort so that their search for health is well within the medical model. In addition to all the expectable beginning worries, a patient's initial thoughts will also

---

[5] I refer to the dual nature of psychotherapy, including psychoanalysis, as a treatment and also as a form of education throughout this book, especially when the duality complicates the problem of ending it.

include the worry, "But how long will this take?"[6] The beginning patient devoutly wishes for speedy deliverance. But, before long, the patient may find that the pain is mostly gone or is bearable while the motive to seek relief has been replaced by an altogether different motive; excited curiosity has been aroused and is fed by the discoveries he is making about how his mind works. No longer concerned about speedy deliverance, the patient has become involved in the analysis for its own sake. Clearly, when this point is reached, the treatment model no longer fits what is going on. Probably without full awareness, the patient has become engaged in an educational adventure, one that is "inward bound."

I am simplifying matters here, of course, for while the newly minted student-of-self explores how his mind works, or looks around the landscape of his mind with his newly opened eyes, the analyst will continue to regard himself as a clinician working with a patient. Even though the patient may realize that he no longer presses for relief or discharge, he may remain haunted by fears that derive in part from the abandoned treatment model; from time to time, he fears that he no longer deserves the analyst's attention because he no longer is in pain. The analyst will also recognize that another force, in addition to intrinsic interest, that is, transference dependency, tends to hold the patient in the analysis while the fear of being dropped as unworthy serves as a new source of resistance. For a considerable time, the process will alternate between analysis as treatment and analysis as adventure as the patient works through the implications of his deepened understanding and the conflict between his desire to know and his reluctance to find out.

And there is the further complication I alluded to earlier: the patient senses that with his increasing mastery over his life he may no longer be able to justify his analysis as a needed treatment. A side effect of his improvement is the weakening of his claim to patienthood, a status he has come to value for its own sake and that he is unwilling to give up. Among his fears is the dark thought that maybe he is only fooling himself about being well. Maybe the gains are illusory, or perhaps they are only on loan, as it were, from the analyst and will have to be surrendered if he leaves.

One of the main tasks of termination, analyzing the patient's fearful transference fantasy that achievement inevitably will lead to losing the relationship to the analyst, is not solely a preoccupation of the patient at the literal ending of an analysis. That fear emerges throughout the analysis

---

[6] Freud (1913, p. 130) noted, wryly, that a patient so reluctant to begin may become one who refuses to leave.

whenever the patient accomplishes, or fears he is about to accomplish, some piece of analytic work.

## *Phase*

In its most common usage, phase refers to a period of time. In analysis, we speak of the beginning phase or the ending phase to allude to a period of indefinite duration around these points of interest in the *chronology* of a treatment. But "ending" and "beginning," like termination, can be delinked from any chronological implication and be used to refer to the *state of mind* one is in when one feels, perhaps without being aware of it, that one is facing a new situation or is leaving a familiar one. We often observe, typically after a period of intense investment in some issue, that the patient suddenly, and for the moment unaccountably, is experiencing the analysis as if the situation and the analyst were strangely new and unpredictable. Every therapist can recall a patient who has been in treatment for some time coming into a session and remarking in a puzzled tone of voice, "Have you always had that picture on the wall?" or "Have the walls always been this odd shade of yellow?" The décor has not changed, but the patient has, and he feels for the moment that he has never been here before. We may say that the patient is once again in a beginning phase.

Perhaps less commonly, we may recognize that a patient seems to be at an ending phase; he suddenly slows down, glumly loses interest, says or acts out the message, "What's the use? It will all come to nothing." Both observations, when we notice that the patient is at a new beginning or at a perhaps premature ending, are, of course, occasions for analytic inquiry. In Chapter 3, I discuss the dynamics that give rise to these odd experiences, the typical phenomena that mark their emergence, and how an analyst can use such observations as "landmarks" to locate himself within the process of the treatment.

Another implication of these observations is that at the inflection point when analyzing yields temporarily to "metabolizing," or when, after a period of useful analyzing, the patient wants to give up, he may be beginning a period of working through, and that process also amounts to what we could call a "minitermination." Thus, we can think of termination as a process that may occur in distributed fashion throughout the analysis, not just as a singular "phase" at the end of treatment.

Of course, we may still speak of the patient nearing the end of analysis as being "in *the* termination phase," now using phase in the chronological sense. At that ultimate time, the patient will be engaged in working through the implications of separating from the analyst in actuality as well as in fantasy.

*Process*

As I have discussed elsewhere (Schlesinger, 2003), analysts use the phrase "psychoanalytic process" to refer to what they believe to be the presumed distinctiveness of what goes on in a psychoanalytic treatment. Leaving aside the question of whether or not process in analysis is unique, I use the term process mainly to emphasize that the phenomenon under consideration takes place over time rather than as an event that takes place all at once. Thus, viewing interpretation as a process implies that the interpretation develops gradually in the interaction of analyst and patient rather than occurring as an announcement when the analyst "gives the patient an interpretation."

One might think that the concept of process should imply not only continuity but also smooth progression and homogeneity. Anyone who has been there will snort in disbelief. The course of psychotherapy, like the course of true love, is not smooth but bumpy, more discontinuous than fluid. Although, conventionally, we divide psychotherapy into units of sessions, sessions merely are units of convenience and have no necessary functional significance. Most writers make use of the concept of phase to capture these discontinuities and may define the term differently to suit their purposes. I refer to "beginning phase" and "ending phase" as marking the successive ways the patient experiences the treatment as it progresses helically on its bumpy path (see Chapter 3).

Consistent with the process view, I use beginning phase and ending phase to refer, not to the chronology of treatment but to the patient's experience of it. They are not categorical, mutually exclusive terms; aspects of both phases often will be present simultaneously. It can be highly useful to help the patient understand the ways in which he is both ending his concern about one issue while simultaneously beginning another. After all, we have no difficulty considering the same ceremony as commencement or graduation. Thus, in this version of the process view, psychotherapy passes through many beginning and ending phases. I believe you will find that this usage applies in many contexts when you are discussing psychotherapy.

Implicit in this usage is a methodological position I must make explicit. I have used such terms as transference as substantives, as if they referred to phenomena "out there," as matters located in the patient. That familiar usage may do for casual conversation, but we would do well to recognize that it seduces us into the methodological and practical sin of reification. We may avoid sinning, and inadvertently speaking nonsense, if we consider transference, as well as other familiar concepts, including resistance, defense, and development as referring to processes (see

Schlesinger, 1981, 1995, 2003) rather than substantives, but also as "points of view," as methodological vantage points or perspectives from which we may profitably view the phenomena going on "out there" in the therapeutic relationship and within the patient.

If we keep clear the methodological distinction between a phenomenon and the point of view we take toward it, we gain both clarity and considerable explanatory power. Keeping this distinction in mind, a therapist can avoid the error of reifying aspects of the therapy, such as by referring to "the transference." Instead, he can consider the unconscious fantasy from which transferential attitudes, behavior, and conflicts derive, or what particular feeling, position, conflict, defense against anxiety, or other attribute the patient is transferring just now, and to which transference object and at which phase of development he is transferring it. Notice that I have switched from referring to transference as a noun, as something the patient *has*, to referring to its verb form, as something the patient *does*. In what follows, I shift among several points of view (e.g., adaptive, genetic, dynamic, countertransferential, reality based) to conceptualize the phenomena of psychotherapy and demonstrate the increased understanding and heightened explanatory power that accrue to a therapist who can switch among the various conceptually compatible points of view as needed. Indeed, the therapist's ability to shift his point of view, which depends on his ability to maintain the therapeutic split as both participant and observer (Sterba, 1934; Schlesinger, 2003) provides much of the sense of empowerment that we call "therapeutic leverage."

The term process, which so often is used as if it were synonymous with psychotherapy itself (as in, "the process of psychotherapy"), can also have the status of a "point of view." When we view psychotherapy from the point of view of process, we agree to view phenomena as they change over the course of time.

## *Time*

Time has several senses, and we need all of them to conceptualize psychotherapy. Chronological time ("real time" or clock time) is linear and irreversible. Time as it refers to the unfolding of a process ("process time") is also linear and irreversible but is interruptible and variable in tempo. Time as experienced ("psychological time") is neither necessarily linear nor irreversible; memories, dreams, and fantasies demonstrate the mind's capacity to linger in time, to reverse time, and to repeat experiences endlessly. Anxiety shrinks time; depression expands it. Pleasure speeds it and pain drags it.

Psychotherapy takes place in real time while the experiencing of it takes place in psychological time. As in all other activities in the world, the passage of time in psychotherapy is governed by the sad fact that real time is linear and irreversible. Thus psychotherapy, from its very inception, quite properly is directed toward ends and toward its own ending. To an outsider, it might seem strange that there would be any need to remind the participants in such a goal-directed activity as psychotherapy to keep their goals and the pressure of time in mind. But it is the usual experience of the participants in psychotherapy that they become so fully absorbed in their interaction that they tend to lose touch both with the passage of time and with the purposes that brought them together. In contrast, at other times, both patient and therapist may feel oppressed by how long it seems to be taking to reach the goals of therapy, which seem to dangle just out of reach. We can think of goals as another point of view from which to examine the phenomena of psychotherapy.

We may also view the way one experiences the passage of time as having "organizing power," the ability to center one's mind or to feed one's preoccupation with one or another aspect of the treatment. The power of time as an organizer[7] can be seen most dramatically in time-limited psychotherapy (Mann, 1976) in which the patient may be reminded each session about the time that is left. Greenson (1992) noted the same phenomenon when an analytic patient has a premonition of ending. As Samuel Johnson quipped about the condemned prisoner, the awareness of impending execution "concentrates the mind." Promoting awareness that therapy will not go on indefinitely is also a feature of other planned, "brief" psychotherapies (Malan, 1963, 1976; Davanloo, 1980).

The effects of feeling under the pressure of time are not limited to such obvious situations. Indeed, even in an "open-ended" therapy, it is essential, at least for the therapist, to keep goals and time in mind as one anchoring point for his thinking and activity. If the therapist fails to do so, he invites a run-on therapy,[8] that is, he allows the essential nature of the relationship to change from an instrumental one to another, which, like a marriage or a vocation, is its own reward and justification. It is an important part of the therapist's initial diagnostic evaluation and his subsequent and continuous diagnostic efforts to assess the likelihood of achieving acceptable goals and what it will take for the patient to own the gains he makes and to free them from dependency on the therapeutic

---

[7] The term organizer I owe to Spitz (1955), who borrowed it from embryology.

[8] Although I am reluctant to describe it as "an interminable therapy" for reasons that must be clear by now, that is the common epithet (see Chapter 9).

relationship. This idea captures the main sense of therapy's being "terminable," that is, can be ended through a process of termination.

To return to the idea that one's relationship to the passage of time may serve as an organizer of one's experiencing, consider the following examples of the ways that patients experience time passing and how they locate themselves in time. The polar examples are that some, chronically, are beginners; they face even familiar situations as if nothing in life had prepared them for this moment. Everything is new and either exciting and inviting or uncertain and dangerous, depending on such other facets of character as whether they are bold or timorous. Others are chronically at a point of ending; wherever they are and whatever the situation, they seem to be expecting to have to leave momentarily. There will not be enough time to do whatever they have in mind. They may seem fearful about getting away before it is too late; they might miss the train. Or they may behave as if fearful that they are about to be left by someone important to them; for some, the main concern is how to put off the inevitable abandonment.

Part of a thorough evaluation of a new patient is to assess his relationship to time, in addition to his relationship to work, love, health, death, other persons, success, failure, morality and spirituality, or reason for being. These matters may not help the clinician to assign the patient to a recognized diagnostic category, but understanding the patient in such terms does facilitate psychotherapy.

## Structure

I am discussing psychotherapy not only from the point of view of process, its "flow," but also from a seemingly opposite point of view, that of the structure of the psychotherapeutic situation. I have adopted a point of view I developed elsewhere (Schlesinger, 2003), which places less emphasis on the regulatory power of what is sometimes called the "frame"—that is, the explicit arrangements for the treatment set up by the therapist—than on the regulatory power of the implicit mutual expectations of patient and therapist.

These implicit expectations are based on the culturally defined roles of doctors and patients as these roles are refined, distorted, and amplified by the patient's neurosis and by the unspoken wishes of the therapist. A patient's breaches of these implicit expectations, ranging from asking questions to prolonged silences to paying late, even more than so-called violations of the frame, have immense diagnostic value if the therapist understands them as important, tendentious communications couched in a regressive form, in action or action-language rather than merely in words. In this connection, my earlier discussions of action and acting out, as well as "resistance," as modes of communication and interpretation are relevant. These modes are vital not only for translation of content or to point to a genetic source, but also in raising the level of communication from action and action-language to symbolic speech (Schlesinger, 2003).

## More About the History of Ending and Termination

Even a cursory reading of the scanty literature on the topics of ending and termination will reveal that there is no established or agreed-upon technique for ending psychoanalysis. As the Richards (2002) remind us, in our earliest tradition, an analyst would decide when a patient had had enough and would announce that decision to the patient. When Glover and Brierley (1940) distributed a questionnaire about technique among British analysts, they found as much variability in practice around ending (called by them "termination," of course) as in other areas of analytic practice. In recent years, analysts seem to have recognized that there is (or ought to be) a termination phase that requires some special analytic consideration, but they have not reached consensus about how to conduct the analysis during that phase, other than relating it to the goals of treatment.

Ticho (1972) reminded us that the goals proper to psychoanalysis might not coincide with the life goals of the patient. Some writers (e.g., Stone, 1961) have proposed a kind of weaning by altering the frequency of appointments or offering group therapy to encourage the patient to have a more realistic view of the analyst. Others (e.g., Kubie, 1968) assert that it would be best for the patient to go to another analyst to resolve the transference to the first one. Still others maintain that the analysis should continue as usual through the last hour. Analysts also disagree about when a date should be set for ending, if indeed a date needs to be set at all (Goldberg and Marcus, 1985) and, if it does, who should set it. Opinions also vary about how much time is necessary to complete the "work" of termination.

In what follows, I discuss how therapists may discover from their understanding of the process of therapy when a therapy may be ended and how to deal with the several sources of problems that interfere with ending and termination.

# Patterns of Ending Psychotherapy

Ending is the most difficult and most important part of psychotherapy. Like the surgeon, the therapist should be as concerned about "getting out" as about "getting in." I have never known a conscientious psychotherapist who did not have trouble with endings. In part, the trouble is attributable to the fact that separations are the most difficult of human experiences. Another source of trouble is that many therapists have wrong expectations about ending, considering it to be a uniform process. To speak of "patterns" of ending psychotherapy implies that there is more than one way in which psychotherapy may end. There are in fact several, the choice determined mostly by the character of the patient but also by how the therapist treats him. While the "principles" that govern the activity of the therapist, particularly around endings, are the same for all psychoanalytically inspired treatments, whatever the nature of the patient, the application of these principles will differ depending upon the personality and pathology of the patient (Schlesinger, 2003). It follows that the therapist should be prepared for the way the patient is likely to anticipate and experience the ending of treatment.

The major dimension of character that has importance for ending has to do with the patient's ability to make and sustain strong interpersonal attachments. I do not distinguish, for the moment, between attachments based on conscious or unconscious fantasy and attachments based on more realistic considerations, for that issue falls within the subject matter of the treatment itself. All patients, whatever their problems in development and however much or little they are disturbed, have some capacity to make attachments and to sustain a sense of relatedness even when their resources are stressed.

People differ, of course, in how their ways of relating may regress under stress. For instance, to consider only one dimension along which relatedness might regress, the poles might be clinging dependency or

13

defensive withdrawal.[1] For some patients, it is particularly stressful to sense that an important relationship is changing. Once it has taken a comfortable form, they feel the relationship should remain fixed. They have little tolerance for the inevitability that relationships develop and change as a function of personal growth, mutual experience, and circumstance. Many of us experience the change in the quality of relationship positively as relationships deepen, become more significant and more mutually rewarding. In time, however, a relationship may change so much that one or both of the parties may feel they have outgrown it, and perhaps with mixed sadness and relief they agree to surrender it. But for the sicker of our patients, an important relationship changing to any significant degree may arouse so much anxiety as to be unsustainable, and they may feel impelled to break it off unilaterally.

Clearly, a patient's ability to remain in a relationship and to tolerate, or, better, to appreciate, change, tells us about the patient's psychological structure. Patients with a more intact psychological structure (and who, not incidentally, have had more conventional developmental histories) generally have considerable ability to form and sustain attachments. They can experience conflict without severe regression; have managed to surrender archaic attachments, fantasies, and illusions; can grieve and mourn actual losses; and form new attachments. At the other end of the continuum are persons who, either because of constitutional deficiency or adverse life experience, have impaired ability to make or sustain attachments or to relinquish whatever partial or infantile attachments they have somehow once managed to attain. They may do so fitfully, with low object constancy, and may have personality structures too weak to permit them to experience conflict about or within a relationship without severe regression (Akhtar, 1994).

You will certainly have thought to yourself that there is another group likely to find ending difficult: those who seem to make deep and seemingly unshakable attachments. The pathology of attachment includes excess as well as deficiency. I am not certain if some vastly dependent and adhesive persons are best thought of as being at the other end of the continuum of attachment or as a variant of those whose pathology manifests itself in their being attachment-shy. Perhaps this variety of patterns is enough to support my recommendation that, to prepare for the ultimate ending of treatment, a therapist ought to evaluate how and to whom the patient has formed attachments (including, of course, to the therapist), whether the attachment is or is not sufficient to maintain the

---

[1] I will not discuss the obvious fact that people may differ in the kinds of persons, animals, or things to which they prefer to become attached.

treatment situation, and how the patient anticipates ultimately ending the treatment and separating from the therapist. An adequate understanding of these matters will be invaluable when the time comes to think about the ending phase of treatment. But this recommendation is not a simple one to carry out.

The principles of psychoanalytic treatment and the therapies that derive from it rest on the theories of psychosexual development (Freud, 1905) and the development of object relationships (Bowlby, 1979). One's emotional situation at the ending of a relationship is commonly analogized to the grieving and mourning that follows a loss by death and to the associated pathologies of depression and melancholia (Freud, 1917). It is an unfortunate consequence of the way these theories are generally taught that beginning therapists are led to expect that good treatment is inevitably lengthy treatment and that the ending of a psychotherapy invariably involves a process analogous to mourning, a prolonged and painful detaching of patient from therapist as they work through the significance of the relationship. I guess that most therapists would recognize two patterns of ending: the patients who agonize over it and those who don't stay around for it.

The major theory of ending is, to put it simply, that stages have been identified that are analogous to those of mourning following loss through death and analogous to the process of reconciliation to one's own impending death: denial, anger, sadness and depression, reconciliation and acceptance (Kubler-Ross, 1969). The expected stages in the ending of psychotherapy have been epitomized more crudely as "mad-sad-glad." This expectation holds up in general for most patients in psychoanalysis and also for the broad range of more or less analyzable patients seen in psychoanalytic psychotherapy who make strong attachments to their therapists. This phenomenon is not a function of the type of therapy, but rather of the kinds of patients who tend to self-select for these therapies.

For these patients the anticipation of finishing psychotherapy brings about special problems related specifically to the ultimate separation from the analyst or therapist as well as generically to every separation. The patient mourns the impending loss as if the therapist were dying or leaving or the patient were abandoning the therapist. As he anticipates the ending of therapy and the severing of the relationship, the patient generally experiences a revival of infantile conflicts that had long seemed settled, and, not incidentally, the experience provides both patient and therapist with a final chance to analyze those conflicts again under the impetus of imminent ending.

But these phenomena and expectations do not apply only to "analyzable patients"; they are aspects of human development in general. Therapists, by and large, come from the more mature and advantaged segments of the population. They tend to expect (until experience teaches them otherwise) that all their patients, ideally at least, experience the end of a significant relationship the same way they do—with a deep sense of loss, expressed in grieving and mourning and perhaps tempered by gratitude. But to put the matter generously, like most ideals in life, this one is only approximated. For many of our sicker patients, the degree to which they prove able to achieve even a modest degree of the ideal will depend on how well the therapist understands the difficulties the patient has in tolerating the pain and other implications of ending, and our skill in helping the patient to deal with the experience of ending within the limitations of their character and residual pathology.

### *Factors That Influence the Way Patients Begin and End Treatment*

Among the extracharacterological determinants of whether a patient will have difficulty separating from the therapist and thus will need special help with ending are the following:

1.  The degree to which transferences, particularly of a dependent, clinging kind, have developed and have not been sufficiently analyzed.
2.  The kind of expectations the patient had in coming to therapy, for example, to solve a problem, resolve conflicts, or find a protector or a substitute for a lost object.
3.  Both the kind of regression, that is, the position the patient regresses to, and its severity may make for special difficulty in ending therapy in a process of termination. When they reconstitute, some patients who had regressed more severely than is comfortable for them or who had regressed in a way that felt dangerous may insist on remaining under the protection of the therapist and refuse to consider ending at all. Others, believing that the treatment caused the regression, may find it difficult to remain in treatment long enough to work through sufficiently the implications of ending; they are eager to leave as soon as possible, fearful it could happen again.
4.  The length of time the patient has been with the therapist is not the most important factor either in forming attachments or in regressing severely. Susceptible patients may attach very quickly and in unexpected ways, especially if the therapist is not alert to the tendency and does not consider it from the outset.

The major determinants of difficulty around ending are charactero-logical, reflecting the developmental level reached by the patient, the degree to which he is object related and can make and sustain attachments. The way a person has generally reacted to losses and separations in life gives strong hints about how he will react to separations from the therapist, including the ultimate one at the end of therapy. The way the patient reacts to interim separations, including those at the end of sessions and at holidays, can help the therapist predict how the patient will react to intimations that therapy will end.

It is a truism that, other things being equal, patients will experience the ending of psychotherapy in ways congruent with their character structures and defensive styles. Obviously, patients also begin psychotherapy in ways consistent with these aspects of character. The way a patient will attempt to frame the ending psychotherapy may be foreshadowed by the way he began. In general, the way a patient enters and leaves other significant relationships will be consonant with his way of engaging with the therapist and his way of anticipating separating from the therapist. Thus, it is important that the therapist try to understand the patient's characteristic attitudes toward beginning and ending, not only for their own sake but also to plan for how the treatment is likely to end and to decide what he must do to ensure that the patient will have an opportunity to experience a useful degree of termination of treatment.

Consider the following examples:

*Example 1.* The patient comes to the therapist anxious about a problem that, as the discussion reveals, he had all but resolved by himself. With only a little further discussion and some legitimate reassurance, he feels comfortable about the decision he had arrived at and is ready to thank the therapist for his help and say goodbye.

Not a few patients present with such a focal difficulty. We may assume that the reason he was uncertain about whether or not he had made the right decision may lie in its resonance with an as-yet unseen conflict. However, even if that is the case, the patient does not feel troubled by that conflict and is not disposed to investigate it further. Such patients make a significant functional attachment to the therapist, but one that is realistic, temporary, and minimally regressive, much as they might with the family doctor they call upon when ill and leave when well. These patients leave with a friendly feeling toward the therapist and return when another need arises. Ending, obviously, is not a problem for them and the issue of a need for a phase of termination does not arise.

*Example 2.* Here is an alternative outcome of that interview with a patient who feels he has been helped and who is now ready to leave. Suppose he recognized, while discussing his problem with the therapist, that he had been in similar quandaries before and that there seemed to be a pattern to them. The way the therapist interacted with him struck him not only as helpful, but also as interesting in its own right. He asks the therapist if he might continue meeting in order for him to understand better the pattern itself; perhaps it is what has been making his life less rewarding than it might be. In that event, a new treatment of perhaps considerable duration may ensue. In the course of time a regressive attachment to the therapist develops for which a phase of termination will be indicated.

In contrast, consider:

*Example 3:* This patient requests "long-term psychotherapy." His "complaint" is that he has been in treatment at this clinic several times, becomes discouraged, and drops out, rather than waiting for reassignment, when his therapist rotates off service. He feels better when he is in treatment and believes that in "long-term psychotherapy" there would be no such interruptions.

From the little information we have about this patient, we may assume that, for him, being in treatment is the goal, not the means to a goal, and at this point, at least, he prefers an endless relationship to a focused treatment. With additional interviewing, the clinician will determine whether psychotherapy of any kind is indicated or if, perhaps, a socialization or resocialization program is called for.

Again, in contrast, consider these patients:

*Example 4.* The patient fears he is having a "heart attack" and may even be "going crazy." He is desperate and yet terribly fearful of doctors, especially "shrinks" who like to "put people away." He clearly needs help to stave off further decompensation and clings to the interviewer even as he denounces doctors.

*Example 5.* The patient requests an appointment with a psychologist or social worker, specifically not with a psychiatrist. He does not want medication or any foreign substance put into his body. He is fearful of being controlled and of having his alertness blunted.

Most therapists of any experience have met patients who present themselves in these problematic ways, ways that also foretell different and characteristic problems about ending. We expect that these patients, who characteristically have difficulty in making attachments or who are highly defended against dependency, will also tend to have difficulty in trusting the therapist. As I discuss in Chapter 6, some can accept help only when they can construe the relationship so that it fits within their system of paranoid or denial defenses. When they improve and feel better, they prefer to credit the medicine or other circumstance rather than anything that took place between them and the therapist.

A sensitive therapist will not challenge these defenses, which allowed the patient to enter treatment and then to restabilize. If the patient becomes restive about remaining in therapy past that point, the therapist will consider helping him to end treatment as he began, with his defense of denial intact, and will not insist that the patient recognize the importance of the therapeutic relationship. Although the therapist remains alert to possible changes in the patient's way of relating to him, he does not attempt to draw the patient into an explicit phase of termination. In such instances, the power of the therapeutic relationship does not depend on the patient's acknowledging it.

Some patients who present with specific problems may in time resolve their issues sufficiently that the therapist senses that, on the basis of results, the treatment may be brought to a close with a phase of termination. But as a function of the inevitable regression, in the patient's mind the problem has become supplanted as a reason for being in treatment by the importance of the relationship itself. The patient "has" his psychotherapist and he "has" his psychotherapy and these possessions have become the pillars of his life. The ceremonial regularity of visits becomes overridingly important to him. The therapist has become the central figure in his life, and the therapy has become a substitute for living rather than a medium for change. The patient clings tenaciously to the relationship for its own sake.

If the therapist is not alert to the metamorphosis from a treatment supported by a relationship to a relationship for relationship's sake, there will seem to be no natural end to the process. As I discuss in Chapter 9, such a situation ought not be referred to as an interminable therapy. What therapist and patient are doing ceased being a therapy some time ago when, unnoticed, it metamorphosed into a relationship that is its own reward, perhaps for both parties.

## Ending and Termination

Just as there are several characteristic ways in which patients begin psychotherapy, so are their also several ways of ending. There are at least the four styles of ending I have just sketched that correspond to the various meanings the relationship with the therapist has for the patient. While the conscientious therapist will do all he can to make the ending of any treatment a useful experience for the patient, he ought to plan for a "termination phase" only for patients such as those in Examples 2, 3, 4, who both were aware of the central importance of the relationship and who experienced it regressively. We should not expect to engage patients like those in Example 1. We could describe these patients as allergic to relationship and they should be allowed (or preferably helped) to leave treatment when the focal problem has been solved without focusing their attention on the relationship any more than is necessary.[2]

I just referred to *planning* for termination for the first time, although the idea has been implicit throughout earlier discussions of the ending of psychotherapy. I think that a good deal of the grief that therapists suffer when patients break off treatment, or when the therapist tries to engage the patient in what the therapist regards as the necessary work of mourning before ending psychotherapy, results from the therapist's misguided efforts to apply indiscriminately to all patients a uniform model of ending.

Many therapists assume that a period of acknowledged mourning, with frequent open discussions of the importance of the relationship and the patient's fears about surrendering it, is an essential part of a dynamically oriented therapy. They are dismayed at the reactions they get when they attempt to impose this model on patients who, during the treatment, showed no indication of being aware of the importance (if any) of the relationship or even that they were in a relationship. A therapy that was useful to that point, in part perhaps because the therapist did not require the patient to acknowledge the relationship, may go awry or end abruptly, as if the therapist had made an indecent proposal. (I discuss in Chapter 6 how one might end therapy with a patient for whom the relationship perhaps was therapeutically important but defensively unacknowledged.) A process analogous to the working-through of termination may ensue, but perhaps it needs a different name.

### What Do We Mean by Termination, Anyway?

I have noted that there are several possible models for the ending of psychotherapy and that only some of them involve the process we call

---

[2] There are forms of psychotherapy other than problem solving, of course, and issues of ending figure differently in them.

termination. Now our concentration is on those cases in which a phase of termination *is* essential. Moreover, understanding the process of termination in those cases is essential to mastering the ending phases of treatment of patients who do not seem to require a period of termination.

First a brief review: We recognize that in psychotherapy the relationship is instrumental; that is, it is brought into being in order to accomplish a task. The relationship is not an end in itself, as it is in, say, a marriage, in which the relationship is itself the purpose, maintaining it is a desired goal, and which ideally ends only with the death of one of the parties.

In psychotherapy, ending is implicit in beginning. The therapist and the patient get together to accomplish a task, and then, when the task is finished, they separate. On the face of things, one would expect them to separate happily as a matter of course when the task is done. In this ideal sense at least, psychotherapy may be said to follow the treatment model or the educational model but not the marital model. But it is every therapist's rueful experience that this cheerful scenario is not what happens. The separating of therapist and patient when they have done the work they got together to do is often a time of high anguish for one and often both parties and is anything but a matter of course.

I spoke of the ending of psychotherapy as being implicit in all beginnings, but I restricted the necessity for "termination" to only some endings. Let me now clarify the distinction, first by throwing in a few more terms. Curiously, we have several words that could be used to describe the closing chapters of psychotherapy. We have at least "ending," "stopping," "finishing," and "terminating." While we may use all of them interchangeably when speaking casually about psychotherapy, in formal usage therapists usually speak as if terminating is the only proper way to refer to the winding down of psychotherapy. When I have finished my argument, I hope you will agree that all these words are useful and necessary and have a place in your working vocabulary. If you do, you will find that the following paradoxical-sounding statements are all plausible:

1. The patient stopped coming but did not end· his treatment.
2. The patient ended his treatment but did not terminate the relationship with the therapist.
3. The patient ended the relationship but did not end the treatment.
4. The patient ended the treatment but did not stop coming to see the therapist.[3]

---

[3] Similar arrays of statements to fill out a matrix of paradoxes could be constructed for the synonyms "separating," "leaving," "quitting," "abandoning," and "parting."

Certainly all psychotherapy must come to an end. However, psychotherapy is not a unitary matter, and not all its aspects share the same fate. If that is the case, what do we mean when we say that all psychotherapy must come to an end? What ends when the psychotherapy ends?[4]

First, most obviously and most importantly, the patient stops visiting the therapist. The appointments stop and the fees stop. What else is there to account for? How about the tasks with which the therapist and patient occupied their time? Does the "therapeutizing" stop? Does the "work" (Schlesinger, 2003) of therapy stop? Clearly, these questions require careful consideration. For the moment, however, let me propose that the answer may be variable, sometimes yes and sometimes no. The therapy may stop when the visits stop (or even sooner) or it may not, and whether or not it stops may have important implications for the patient and his emotional health. This point is central to my conception of the nature of psychotherapy, but for the sake of continuity, I shall skip over it for the moment.

Is that all? How about the gains that the patient presumably accomplished in the course of the psychotherapy? What is their fate? Obviously, we hope that what the patient gained from the therapy outlasts the visits and most often it does. Still, it is commonly feared by patients, and occasionally by therapists, that, if they stop meeting, the patient will relapse and reveal for all to see that the "gains" were, in fact, dependent on a continuing relationship with the therapist and that, instead, the patient had lost his independence.

Here is another topic for extended discussion: what is the relationship of the gains of the therapy to the transference? Was it merely a "transference cure," or was something more substantial accomplished, perhaps a "structural change?" And what about the relationship between the patient and the therapist? Does the relationship end when the visits stop, or is the relationship transcendent? Here, too, the answer must be ambiguous.

For some patient and therapist pairs, the relationship with the therapist turns out to have been one of the most important in the patient's life. The patient is highly aware of its importance and is reluctant to give it up. A good portion of the later phases of the psychotherapy of such a patient is given to exploring the meanings of the relationship, the nature, sources, and purposes of the unwillingness to give it up, and what "giving it up" would mean, actually and in fantasy. And it is for just this process that the term termination is needed.

---

[4] The reader will note the parallel to Freud's (1937c) discussion of the end of analysis.

I am reserving the special term termination to refer to all the issues I have yet to define fully that have to do with the final separation of the parties in the psychotherapy, in particular the detaching of the gains the patient has made in psychotherapy from dependency on the patient's sense of relatedness to the therapist. Keeping in mind that "termination" is not a synonym for ending, I will use all the synonyms for ending as appropriate.

What could it mean that the relationship between patient and therapist may or may not end? A little thought makes it clear that the issue is not simple. Let us look at it from the vantage point of the general treatment model. Most of us have a personal physician, a family practitioner, or internist on whom we rely when we are ill and whom we call when we need him. We visit him when we are sick and stop seeing him when we are well once again. It does not occur to us that our relationship is weak because our visits are episodic. We still "have" a physician. We "know" he is there when we need him even though in fact he may be on vacation or ill himself. We would likely feel an acute sense of loss, however, even when we are not sick, should we hear that our internist might have relocated or even died. But our sense of relatedness, trust, and even dependency does not depend on regularity of visits. It may be so also between patient and psychotherapist.

The idea that regular visits should end quite naturally without fuss or tears when the parties have finished the therapeutic task, and that the relationship will sustain even though the parties are not meeting, might seem outlandish to some therapists. They would remind us that it is far more usual for the relationship with the therapist to take the place of the patient's problem as the reason for his continuing attendance. Rather than remaining instrumental in the service of the therapeutic tasks, the relationship to the therapist takes on a life of its own. When the therapist hints about discontinuing their visits because the patient has accomplished what he came for, the patient quickly lets the therapist know, perhaps verbally and often through depression, rage, or relapse, that it was an offensive, even unthinkable, idea.

### Problems Terminating Psychoanalytic Psychotherapy

The problems in ending a psychoanalytic psychotherapy with a phase properly called termination are of several kinds, both conceptual and practical. In a sense, ending is what psychotherapy is all about. The two parties get together so that they can eventually separate, their mutually agreed upon tasks completed. A concern of many patients considering undertaking psychoanalysis or psychoanalytic psychotherapy is the reputation of those treatment modes for lengthiness. Much as patients may later demonstrate ingenious reluctance to forestall ending, at the beginning patients typically are concerned about the possible endlessness of treatment. Indeed, if psychoanalysis were in practice unending, it would hardly qualify as a treatment—a way of life perhaps but not a treatment. Duration of treatment should concern the therapist also. A major focus of his initial study of the patient should be to assess terminability. Can he foresee this treatment as coming to a successful conclusion and the patient's being able to go on alone? To put the matter in cognitive terms, this question may devolve into whether or not the patient has learned enough about how to deal with himself and others so that he can apply his knowledge without the constant tutelage of the therapist. Thus, ending is, or should be, a concern of the therapist as well as of the patient from the very beginning (Edelson, 1963).

If a therapist heeds this admonition and is mindful of the eventual ending of the therapy and the way the patient is likely to experience it, how would he go about it, and what should he do with the information? What follows is a summary of some of the points for the ideal case, the patient each of us hopes to see some day. A sketch of such an ending may serve as a base from which to describe alternative patterns of ending.

This "ideal" patient has been in therapy long enough so that the obvious gains may reasonably be estimated to be enduring, not transitory. The treatment has been cruising along uneventfully for a while. The patient continues to attend regularly and on time, but his attention often turns to matters in his current life and to interests that are occupying him but that are minimally, if at all, problematic. Only occasionally does he turn his attention to how his mind works, as when he becomes irritated by the failing of a colleague at work. He can contrast how once he was tempted to lash out at him and forced himself to suppress his anger. Now he recognizes the temptation but no longer feels the impulse to punish. Both he and the therapist have noted the smoothness of his life and the absence of conflict in the therapy.

First in dreams and fantasies, then in associations, and finally in direct discourse, the patient hints at the possibility of stopping "some day." The therapist has been thinking along the same lines. Though still therapeutically interested in the patient and accustomed to the treatment, he agrees that it is time to consider stopping "some day." The patient is gratified that the therapist agrees with his self-evaluation. Together with the therapist, he proposes an ending date about six months hence.

The patient continues to attend regularly, his attention given to a review of how he was when he first came and what brought him to his improved state. For the most part, his current life continues to run smoothly, but both he and the therapist observe that, as he reviews some formerly painful matters, he experiences a mild recurrence of familiar symptoms. At first, these unpleasant reminders that he may still be as he used to be raise his doubts about the advisability of stopping at all, let alone "so soon." They yield quickly, however, to interpretations that relate their revival to the process of working through the ancient conflicts.

After about three months, the patient again notices that his life is just about where he would like it to be and that he continues to come to therapy because he and the therapist have agreed that he "needed" to spend another three months to terminate "properly." The therapist calls his attention to this revised construction of their agreement; the patient recognizes that his conservative estimate of the time he would need was excessive, and they discuss moving the date forward. The patient has a few anxious moments at his temerity in tampering with such an important decision and provides another opportunity to work through the magical implications of ritual observance, formerly an important issue for him. In discussions over the next few sessions, he concludes once again that he has, indeed, gotten what he came to treatment for—and more—and that he has no immediate need for additional treatment. When, shortly thereafter, the shock of that recognition wears off, he and the therapist agree to have their last appointment in about two weeks, after the second of the three scheduled sessions for that week.

On the date set to stop, the session begins as usual. Only after a while does the patient comment on how strange it suddenly seems that he will not be returning tomorrow. He pauses for a while and then says he has stopped himself from asking if it would be all right, if things didn't go as well as he expected, to call for an appointment. He adds that he realizes that his momentary anxiety is about ending and that he knows full well that he will be free to return if he feels the need. The session ends with a firm handshake and mutual good wishes.

Several matters in that example need discussion: how to estimate when a treatment is ready to end and how to confirm that estimate, how and when to set a date for ending and how firm that date-setting should be, and how to understand the process of working through and the significance of symptom revival in the course of termination. Note that setting a date for ending does not begin the process of ending and termination but rather is a fairly late, though significant, event (Rangell,

1982). Note, too, that some authorities propose that analysis can be terminated "naturally" without setting a date (Goldberg and Marcus, 1985). (I take up these issues in subsequent chapters.)

Let us now look at why I assume that this patient and the ending of his psychoanalytic psychotherapy were "ideal." Clearly, I do not mean "ideal" in the sense of unrealizable, for the process I summarized is quite ordinary, even optimal. I did not, however, mention some of the difficulties that I believe therapists frequently introduce when they misunderstand the phenomena generally present at endings and the way patients of various kinds experience them.

I trust you will agree that the patient was ideal at least in the sense that he was able both to sustain a therapeutic relationship and to acknowledge it. The therapist correctly estimated this capacity from the patient's history of relationships and then confirmed it in the way the patient was able to deal with interruptions of therapy occasioned by weekends and vacations and unscheduled breaks because of illness. For this account of the process, I did not mention the nature of the patient's complaints and underlying disorder or the expectable intrusions of transference, with overtones of homo- and heterosexuality and dependency. These expressions of unconscious dynamics threatened neither the continuity of the treatment nor the process of ending.

The ending was optimal, at least in the sense that the patient was able to make gains that reflected change in the way his inner life was organized. He could openly consider ending once he became aware that he had satisfied his reasons for coming. He was also able to deal with the implication that ending would mean separating from the therapist as well as with the anxiety that he might relapse. He could enjoy the gains he had made in therapy and could work through the hostile implications of voluntarily leaving someone who has been helpful, and he could mourn the losses implied in ending. Just as important, he could appreciate that his reluctance to end reflected both the real value he placed on the relationship with the therapist and the magical fear that he might lose what he had gained if he dared to leave the protection of the therapist.

To summarize the capacities of the patient for whom a process of termination is indicated at ending:

1. The patient can make and sustain attachments; he is capable of forming and maintaining realistic and enduring relationships.
2. The patient can tolerate the regressive pulls at play in therapy, including homo- and heteroerotic wishes, dependency, and the defenses against them.

3.  The patient can tolerate separation and loss and can surrender fantasized gratifications and accept real ones.

## Patients' Initial Reactions to Forced Endings

As I discuss in Chapter 5, even when the maximum duration of a treatment is dictated by the rotation schedule of trainees, it is possible for therapists to help patients end therapy electively at some point when the treatment is in an "ending phase." In many training situations, however, this option may be neither taught nor valued.

The conventional training clinic does not encourage trainees to end treatment when the patient may have been helped enough to get on without further therapy. Instead, the clinic relies on the administrative mechanism of "transfer" to pass "unfinished" patients on from one trainee to another. In the interests of full disclosure, trainees may be required to tell patients at the outset that they will be present only until a certain date. Nevertheless, when student therapists are finally forced by their supervisors to inform their patients that they will be moving to another service and so will have to interrupt treatment, the news generally comes as a shock to the patients. One then sees a distorted picture of how patients react to ending in general since this forced ending is unrelated to their need for therapy or to their progress in therapy. Their reactions are complicated further by the sense that they are about to be abandoned by a therapist toward whom they had developed some degree of trust.

Patients react to this unwelcome news about impending loss of the therapist in ways consistent with their character structure and to the degree that they became involved in the treatment relationship. Likewise, they react in a manner that reflects the meaning of "achievement" to them and to the extent that there are realistic opportunities to make use of what they have gained in therapy. The ability to mourn openly an anticipated loss is a developmental achievement that all of us, including our patients, arrive at to varying degrees (Zetzel, 1949; Mahler, 1961; Fleming and Altschul, 1963; Dewald, 1965). Part of that achievement is the ability and willingness to remain in a relationship that one has been informed will shortly end, the main ability or character attribute that terminating therapy calls upon.

As I noted earlier, to anticipate how the patient will deal with the eventual loss of the therapist, the therapist should take account of the way the patient has dealt with other significant losses. The initial reactions (catalogued later) are just that—initial reactions that, for the most part, call upon the emergency defenses of patients when they learn that their therapist is about to leave them. If the therapist is prepared to help the patient with those defenses, he will be in a better position to engage the patient in as much of a process of termination as is possible under the circumstances. We demand great maturity of young therapists in this situation to do what is necessary to help patients. And every young therapist is likely to be preoccupied with his own ending issues, perhaps sorry to leave a familiar service for a strange one, perhaps feeling resentful at the "system" that forces him to leave his patients, whom he probably has just begun to understand, as well as feeling guilty about abandoning them. Given that the therapist probably has had little, if any, instruction about endings, he will, even with the best of intentions, have a difficult time mustering the clinical skills to meet the needs of his difficult patients at this most difficult of times for both of them. (In Chapter 6, I discuss this problem in some detail.)

Even though the therapist may not yet have mentioned to his patient that treatment will soon have to stop, the atmosphere in the clinic may have become more tense as staff get themselves ready for a difficult time. Gossip among patients in the waiting room may alert the patient that bad news may soon be sprung on him. Of course, the therapist is not the only source of information open to the patient. If the therapist listens closely, he may hear metaphoric references to ending or the revival of previously settled issues that in the patient's character are linked to ending. These references reflect the patient's more or less conscious concern that loss and separation are imminent. This concern will organize the patient's thinking and feelings in the same way that concerns about beginning organized his associations at that time.

Whether patients arrive "independently" at the conclusion that their treatment will be interrupted or learn about it from the therapist's announcement, they will react idiosyncratically. We can recognize some common initial reactions patients have to being told their treatment will be interrupted for the convenience of the therapist:

*Flight*

Some patients are so reluctant to experience the pain associated with separating, or they may so fear abandonment, that they decamp even before the therapist brings himself to take up the topic; they are likely to quit as soon as they sense or fear that ending is "in the air." They sense the change in the therapist's manner as he struggles to invent a decent and humane way to tell his patients the bad news. It is a large order for the young therapist in this painful situation to prepare himself to understand that the subtle changes in the patient's behavior are reactive to the growing uncertainty and distancing of the therapist who is feeling guilty about withholding bad news.

For some therapists, the unannounced dropping out of a patient is the first inkling that they had been telegraphing the bad news wordlessly. To avoid the pain of separation, to help contain their anger about being abandoned, and possibly to retain a fantasy of having been in a relationship with a "good therapist," other patients may not show up for another session after hearing the news. It is especially important that the therapist of a patient given to flight be prepared for this reaction and inform the patient early enough in that session to have time to work with the patient about the temptation to call it quits at once.

*Withdrawal*

At the news, a patient may simply slump in the chair and become silent and seemingly unreachable. Again, the therapist should be prepared for such a response if, as is likely, it is a characteristic one that the therapist has had some experience in dealing with around that patient's earlier disappointments. It will take patience and persistence for the therapist to uncover the activity in the patient's seeming slump into passivity and to help him to verbalize it.

*Regression*

While all these initial reactions to the news of impending loss involve regression, I use the term here in the restricted sense of a return of symptoms or of a tendency to take refuge in a developmentally earlier emotional position. Patients with little tolerance for experiencing anxiety or who are unable to put strong feelings into words may express them in action. Again, the prepared therapist will be in a better position to help the patient find the least (self-) destructive way of expressing his feelings and to separate his justifiable reactions of anger and grief from the ancient reflexive pattern of reacting to hurt by hurting back, at whatever personal cost.

*Denial*

Most initial reactions include some measure of denial, at least to the degree that the patient tries to hold off reacting to the unwelcome information until he has had time to consider its implications. The therapist who has been expecting a blowup may be disconcerted if the patient acts as if he had not heard anything important, nods, and goes on with his own agenda. Again, the *prepared* therapist will be in a better position to help the patient by knowing when to allow the patient to face matters when he is ready to or perhaps by sensing in the patient's subsequent behavior some indirect or metaphoric reference to the "news."

The therapist must be alert to the temptation to feel relief that "after all, it wasn't such a big deal" to the patient and to take the patient's initial reaction only at face value. It takes both skill and knowledge of the patient's typical reaction patterns to separate out possibly excessive defensive denial from a patient's ability to respond adaptively to necessity. In the latter case, it would be pointless and condescending for the therapist to insist that the patient is denying emotions he does not feel. It is a difficult discrimination to make at best when a patient tells the therapist, "I'm just as sick as I ever was but it has nothing to do with ending therapy. Anyway, it doesn't mean anything, so let's just part as friends." A milder form of this reaction is the more dismissive, "The therapy has been useful in its way, Doc, but I won't miss you."

Some patients whose emotional development has been significantly arrested do not seem able to enter a "whole" personal relationship with a therapist. They manage to relate themselves mainly to the healing function of the therapist as a "part-object" rather than to the person of the therapist. When they insist that they do not, and will not, miss the therapist, the therapist will have to consider the degree to which such statements reflect the underlying character formation or a more acute, that is, immediate, but modifiable defensive reaction.

*Projection and Splitting*

The therapist of a patient who favors paranoid defenses will be prepared to see them when he announces his impending departure. The pattern expresses the axiom: if one has been hurt, someone must be held responsible. The person held responsible most often is the therapist, who never should have been trusted in the first place, or it might be the administrator of the clinic, who forces good and well-meaning therapists to abandon their patients. Of course, as when working with any defensive posture, the therapist will keep in mind that the patient is doing the best he can, using the defensive attitudes and tools he has under difficult circumstances. The therapist may find it difficult to help the patient if he, more or less consciously, feels the patient is right either to blame him or to hold "them" responsible.

Some patients have never had the experience of ending a long-standing connection to another person while remaining in a positive relationship. Some can separate only by devaluing the therapist and the therapy.

Some stamp off angrily after denouncing the therapist and the whole field. It takes some measure of skill for a therapist to recognize that perhaps the only condition under which the patient can possibly retain any of the gains he may have made in the therapy is to affectively divorce the now-offending therapist. Milder forms of this reaction include the following.

*Resignation and Apathy*

The patient seems to absorb the hurt of being left and retaliates with a quieter form of devaluation such as, "I knew it wouldn't last. You're like all the rest. This is just one more disappointment for me to live with." Another variety is, "I was just about to trust you and let myself depend on you." Again, the therapist will need to separate his own feelings about "what he is being forced to do" in order to be able to help his patients. A much less common form of retaliatory devaluation is represented by the mixed review contained in this patient's reaction, "Good, I'm glad the treatment is over. Your therapy has helped me, Doctor, but mostly it has let me spend this time with you. Now that we don't have to do this therapy stuff anymore, let's go out so I can show you how good I can be for you too."

## *Endings Without an Explicit Phase of Termination*

The patients for whom endings become problematic depart from the "ideal" in one or more of these respects: they may be attachment-shy or impulsive and action oriented rather than verbally expressive, characterologically given to externalizing or paranoid. Helping them to end therapy usefully, or at least nontraumatically, demands much additional skill and understanding from the therapist. This goal may seem to involve contradictory elements: the therapist will want to involve the patient in as much of a process of termination as the patient can use; at the same time he wants to help the patient end therapy electively within the limitations set by his character structure. The information the therapist needs to decide about these matters has been available to him from the earliest moments of treatment, although he may not have evaluated correctly what the patient's history and behavior more or less clearly foretold.

Consider a borderline patient who, from the outset, tells the therapist in words, as well as in actions, that he is fearful of intimacy in relationships. When the patient improves even slightly, as when the gnawing problem he has been discussing loses its saliency, the therapist must be prepared for the way the patient may express his consternation at suddenly being without his familiar preoccupation; there is nothing to guard him against fearfully intimate contact with the therapist. The sudden diminution of his complaint deprives him of the protective shield of a familiar "conversation piece." Now there is nothing on his mind other than what he cannot bear to face, the unmentionable topic— that he is involved significantly with the therapist.

A therapist who is unprepared for this expectable development, one he could have helped the patient to anticipate, may misunderstand the patient's "acting up" as a new attack of illness or as wanton misbehavior rather than as an idiosyncratic, defensive response to a bit of "progress" that was experienced by the patient as having dangerous implications.

To prepare for the ultimate ending of any patient's treatment, it is essential that the therapist understand the mixture of feelings that typically emerges when a patient accomplishes a piece of therapeutic work, or when a burdensome pain goes away, or when the pressure that brought the patient to treatment suddenly ceases. Of course, how the patient experiences so seemingly beneficent an event varies with the nature of the patient, that is, his character structure, the meaning(s) of (the) accomplishment, the nature of relationship with the therapist, and the state of the treatment (all of which are addressed further in Chapter 6).

The general phenomenon of which that warning is a special case is that, whenever patients complete a bit of work or make some change that implies progress, they generally feel at loose ends. The familiar topic of conversation no longer comes easily to mind, and hence the reason for being in the session at this moment has evaporated. The patient may experience this bit of progress in full measure; he may feel both pleasure and relief, even pride, along with anxiety. Or he may feel only some of the full panoply of feelings and experience even that portion in muted form. The content of the anxiety component is the same as all anxieties, "What will happen next?" "Will the pain come back?" "Will the therapist throw me out now that I don't hurt?" "Can I find something else to talk about?" "Will I get too close to the therapist, or lose myself in the relationship with the therapist?" So muses the patient.

The therapist should be familiar with the patient's repertoire of affective and ideational possibilities and be prepared to anticipate how a given patient will react at such a juncture. So prepared, the therapist might be in a position to anticipate that the patient is likely to experience a recurrence of old symptoms that express his anxiety that the therapist will use this momentary success as a reason to drop him. Another patient may retreat into his former suspiciousness; a paranoid patient may feel lost without the barrier afforded by his "problem," which he could keep between him and the therapist. Other patients might attempt to hide out, hoping the therapist will not notice their improvement, or they might try to interrupt the "dangerous" treatment process in some way.

As I have noted, some patients tend to drop out of treatment at such times. They simply stop coming without announcing their intention, that is, without announcing it verbally. However, the prepared therapist will have noticed premonitory signs that such a reaction is impending. Unless the patient is exceedingly brittle, he usually will give some warning, not usually a verbal and direct one, but the kind of warning an alert therapist gets when he senses a shift in the transference, a drifting away in the session, an effort to create distance between them that seems related somehow to a change in the salience of "the problem."

A brittle patient may end treatment at that point because the therapist did not fully appreciate his discomfort or the danger that the patient was beginning to feel and that the patient believes the therapist somehow is responsible for. The danger is likely to be particularly great, unfortunately, if the therapist has become invested in holding the patient in an extended treatment (for example, "He was to be my long-term case"). The confluence of a patient's anxiety about remaining and the therapist's zeal does not augur well for continuance. If the therapist is aware both that the patient is experiencing a surge of alarm and that he himself feels that his own professional investment in and ambitions for the patient are threatened, he is forearmed. He may be able to relate the patient's new discomfort, flare-up of suspiciousness, belligerency, or lack of interest to the internal change that must have taken place in the patient and then to put into words the patient's latent impulse to get away while he can.

Let me make it clear that, at this point, the therapist should neither want to hold on to the patient nor hope to extend the treatment by preventing the patient from dropping out. Rather, the therapist ought to provide an opportunity for the patient to test out (that is, discuss) the alternatives he faces and to choose whether it would be useful and safe for him to stay on or whether it would be in his best interests to leave. Such a "discussion" generally requires that the therapist put the patient's dilemma, his wordless fears, into words that the patient can accept as truly describing his feelings. To do so, the therapist has to be familiar with the patient's vocabulary for feelings (his affect term hierarchy) and his idiom for danger situations (Schlesinger, 2003) so as to "normalize" the patient's situation rather than to overstate the danger and increase the patient's anxiety and pressure to leave.

To the extent possible, staying or leaving should be elective for the patient, not compelled by anxiety. It may be necessary for the patient to interrupt therapy in order to prove to himself that he *can* leave, that his "will" has not been undermined. Sometimes, if the therapist agrees with the patient that such a move might be necessary for him, the patient can permit himself to stay, but without committing himself to stay; that is, he may explicitly reserve his "right" to leave. Again, it takes more skill than is generally available to beginners, who often are assigned several such patients, to be able to sense the limited resources of these patients and to stay safely within the limits while providing the help the patients need.

It is possible also that a patient at such a juncture has actually accomplished enough for the time being. The test question the therapist should ask himself at this point is, "Would the patient come today for a first appointment?" If the answer is, "No", or "Not likely," the therapist would do well to help the patient end the current episode of treatment without breaking off abruptly. The patient so liberated will feel freer to return if he needs to than if the therapist tries to hold him. The therapist's engaging the patient in such a discussion may also lead to the patient's recognizing that he has indeed accomplished something useful, and further, that he is able to put it into words and by doing so has made it less threatening. The therapist's tactful recognizing that something about that happy event also made the patient anxious may relieve the patient's anxiety sufficiently to make it possible for him to continue in treatment, assuming that he believes it useful to do so.

On the other hand, some more brittle patients can end therapy only as they ended all previous relationships that got to be too much for them— by breaking off suddenly. Only in that drastic way can they retain their fragile self-esteem by maintaining a mythic view of themselves that they owe nothing to anyone and care about no one and about nothing. They may swagger off, perhaps putting the help they received to good use but refusing to acknowledge that they received any.

Again, if the therapist can anticipate this likelihood, he will be in a position to predict with some accuracy when a "sudden" departure might be imminent. By foreseeing that the patient is starting to feel so uncomfortable that he will feel compelled to leave, the therapist might even join the patient in planning the departure. By doing so, the therapist might make it possible for the patient to return to treatment when he feels safer.

For some such patients, continuing in therapy is possible only if they feel that they may break off any time they want to, that is, when they feel they must. Because these patients are as needy as they are defensive, it is essential that a therapist realize that what keeps these patients in possibly episodic treatment is a shaky set of denials and that it is important not to challenge the denials. Indeed, it may even be necessary to support them explicitly (Shectman, 1968; Schlesinger, 1993).

# How to Tell When Treatment May End

*Why Is Ending a Problem?*

Why should ending be such a problem for psychotherapists and their patients?[1] What is there about psychotherapy that makes some patients willing to spend their time and money to visit a therapist regularly when to their friends and family there seems to be no rational basis for doing so? Is psychotherapy unique in this respect? A little thought suggests that it is not unique. The same phenomenon can be seen in emergency rooms and walk-in clinics. One quickly comes to recognize the "regulars"—patients who can be counted on to phone or visit at least weekly. Some of these patients try to legitimate their calls or visits by demanding that something specific be done for them, typically an extra "sleeper" or a refill of a prescription. Others are content to call and, after making some pro forma complaint, chat a bit, and then hang up or leave. We do not usually think of these casual or intermittent contacts as psychotherapy, but these patients use them in much the same way as do some patients in a never-ending psychotherapy.

Every medical practitioner has a small panel of patients (or patients' mothers) who call or come in for any cut, scratch, bump, wheeze, or stomach rumble—in short, whenever they are anxious. All these patients may be bootlegging the fulfillment of one kind of need while ostensibly attending to another. The treatment demanded is not the reason, but rather the excuse for the visit.

This phenomenon was first discovered "officially" by the early psychoanalysts. They were dismayed that their brief and specific therapy, which could be compared in its precision and technique to lancing a boil

---

[1] There are legitimate forms of psychotherapy such as supportive psychotherapy for chronically ill patients that properly ought to be allowed to continue indefinitely, the purpose being to maintain patients in an extrahospital environment as chronic outpatients for whom termination is not a useful goal.

(i.e., the aim was to discharge "strangulated affects"), could drag on as the patient "resisted" the analyst's efforts to interpret the "complex." Although apparently not getting anywhere, these patients did not simply quit, as might reasonably have been expected, but would continue to attend their sessions; they seemed, for obscure reasons, to find this "run-on therapy" worthwhile. In this painful way, resistance, transference, and character were discovered, and various members of the small circle around Freud set themselves to solving the problem that Freud later sadly called "analysis interminable" (Freud, 1937c).

Run-on psychotherapy seems to put the blame on the peculiarities of patients, but let us consider how therapists also may contribute to the problem. The difficulties therapists have in ending psychotherapy have roots in circumstances that existed long before the therapy even began. Most of us have never fully outgrown the beginner's fear that as soon as a new patient sets eyes on us he will laugh and walk out, instantly recognizing us as the neophytes we were (Schlesinger, 2003).

The fear of losing a patient, of being abandoned by the one we desperately need to prove our own worth, leads us to act in certain ways at the outset of treatment that are detrimental both to doing psychotherapy and to ending in a timely fashion. The common stereotype we learn as beginners is that the model of psychotherapy is at minimum a long-term relationship. Our urgent first task, therefore, is to get the patient to become attached to ourselves so that he can stick it out. We were taught, either specifically or by indirection, that nothing much is expected to happen in finite time in psychotherapy or psychoanalysis. Thus we naturally think of our first meeting with a new patient in such terms as, "We are at the beginning of things," "We are warming up," or "We are just getting to know each other," We are "establishing rapport" or setting up a "therapeutic alliance." The idea is that in good time something beneficial to the patient may be accomplished.

I do not mean to imply that the therapeutic relationship is unimportant in psychotherapy. Far from it: research findings (Luborsky, 1976) suggest that it may be the most important element of psychotherapy. But I *do* mean that the relationship, the essential vehicle for the treatment, can also defeat it; the relationship can become the *end* rather than the *means* of treatment. It can become its own reward. The therapist who is too concerned with attaching or even "hooking" the patient may end up with more relationship than the treatment needs, and possibly with a more intensive relationship than the patient can tolerate (see Schlesinger, 2003; also Chapter 6).

Patients differ widely in their need for and tolerance of intimacy and relatedness. A relationship, short or long, may not be at all what a new patient has in mind. Some of the patients we see seem allergic to forming lasting relationships. When driven by despair or fed-up relatives to see a therapist, their implicit question is how to get what they need without entering into a relationship. They are turned off, made anxious, even driven away by therapists whose only concept of how to begin is to exude indiscriminate warmth while expecting the patient to reciprocate.

Rather than evaluating the patient's need for and tolerance for relationship, some therapists assume that all patients have needs for closeness and intimacy very much like their own. Some patients do, but many do not. When evaluating a patient's suitability for psychotherapy, it is equally important to assess his vulnerability to dependency and his tolerance of and need for relationship, and for what kind of relationship. These issues are as important to evaluate as where the patient stands with respect to his presenting problem (Schlesinger, 1969, 2003). This last issue is my main focus in this chapter.

## *Time and Psychotherapy*

It is accepted wisdom that a patient who calls for an appointment and later either calls to cancel or, more frequently, simply does not show up is "fleeing from treatment." I propose that some of these not-quite-patients may have gotten the help they needed through this odd and, to the therapist, annoying and expensive behavior. Before resolving this puzzle, let me deepen it by asserting that effective psychotherapy can occur in as little as one session, or *even less*. I mean by this paradoxical addition that much self-treatment is carried out by patients before they get to a psychotherapist, if indeed they ever see one.

A new patient calls for an appointment. He has been deeply distressed. It took a while for him to realize that his painful state reflected something going awry in his life. When he arrived at that idea, his concern increased to the point of fright, and he tried to deny it. Only then, after finding that he could not shake off or avoid his distress, did he try to solve the problem he had glimpsed. He then took stock, weighed the alternatives his life permitted, and started to lean toward a painful choice that would resolve the distressing conflict. As he wavered, he recalled similar anxious times earlier in his life and sensed why his current situation was so troublesome. At first he was relieved by these efforts, but he soon became anxious again. At this point he called for an appointment.

With the therapist, he reviews this state of affairs. The therapist listens, empathizes with the distress the patient experienced, and helps him to retrace his shifting stance from denial to flight to facing the problem, and his glimmering awareness of its continuity with earlier problems. He then tells the patient that he thinks the patient has solved his current problem and knows what he has to do next. The patient reacts with mild surprise and a mixture of chagrin and pleasure. But, after a moment of reflection, agrees. With the therapist's help, he observes that perhaps he just came in to review the self-treatment he has already accomplished and to make sure that his thinking was sound—to have his therapy made "official."

We could say that the patient came in to this first and only session not to begin his therapy, but to end it, and that he accomplished this act of confirmation in one session.

You can test this idea by inviting your next new patient to describe the course of events that led him to come in. I believe that his account will convince you that these phenomena are universal. Both the patient who comes in to end a successful self-treatment and the patient who comes as a failure in self-treatment (e.g., self-treatment through alcohol or promiscuity) can be viewed as being at the *end of a process of self-treatment*. The patient whose self-treatment has failed feels that he is at the end of his rope, and only when he sees no other choice seeks professional help. Thus, the ending of an episode of self-treatment coincides with the beginning of an "official" psychotherapy.[2] This coincidence of endings and beginnings is a phenomenon to which I refer repeatedly when discussing the construction of an appropriate model for process in psychotherapy.

It is not generally appreciated that a certain proportion of new patients can be viewed as coming in for their first session, not to begin therapy, but to end it. They may substantially have resolved their acute or presenting problem before seeing the therapist and do not need many sessions to review and consolidate what they have already done about it. It is the therapist's essential first task to appreciate that some process must be coming to an end when the patient arrives for a first appointment, to evaluate the nature of that process and its implicit ending, and to treat the patient for it. Only in that context can the therapist establish the purpose and necessity of any additional treatment that may be needed.

Inviting a new patient into a continuing, and perhaps extended, "therapy" without evaluating the success and failure of previous self-

---

[2] Even a patient who presents as a failure in self-treatment can be viewed as succeeding to the extent that he has recognized he cannot do it alone and, perhaps grudgingly, comes for help.

treatment, as well as his need for and tolerance of relationship, would reflect serious mishandling and misdiagnosis. To invite into a continuing attachment someone who may already have accomplished his therapeutic goals, but who has strong relationship needs, is to invite the possibility of an interminable relationship—but probably not a therapy.

Another error, one that usually leads to abortive ending, is to spread warmth, cheer, and welcome over a person who is phobic about intimacy. We may drive away patients who badly need help but can obtain it only in an emotionally cool context in which there are few obvious libidinal or relationship demands. Some patients need to be treated at arm's length (Schlesinger, 1969; Schlesinger and Schuker, 1990; Chapter 6, this volume). Patients may leave therapy prematurely or stay in therapy endlessly, not only because of their own vulnerabilities but also because of therapist behaviors that stem both from wrong assumptions about how to begin therapy and from personal needs and fears that have congealed into an inflexible technical approach.

## Diagnosis for Efficient Psychotherapy

Let us take up the problem of the necessary duration of an efficient[3] psychotherapy. There can be little argument that the amount of time a psychotherapy will require depends on a number of variables, including the nature of the problem, the nature of the patient who has the problem, factors in the patient's life that limit solutions to the problem, as well as the skill and sensitivity of the therapist and the points of view and techniques available to him. Certain processes important in psychotherapy, by their very nature, take time, for instance "working through" or mourning, and restarting stalled development. But if psychotherapy succeeds in restarting a stalled developmental process or if it facilitates mourning, the patient might then be able to carry on alone. Each of these issues requires full consideration as determinants of the duration of psychotherapy and how to end it.[4]

All things considered, however, it is hardly to be argued that a therapy should take no more time than it needs to be effective. Almost from the very beginning of the development of the first systematic psycho-

---

[3] I introduce the term efficient here to stand for the idea that, ideally, any treatment should aspire to accomplish its ends with minimal expenditure of resources, including the time of therapist and patient. As a practical matter, the notion of efficiency is more complicated than that of simple expectation.

[4] For a discussion of many of these issues see Malan (1976).

therapy—psychoanalysis—analysts explored ways to keep the treatment from extending unnecessarily. Ferenczi (1920, 1927; Ferenczi and Rank, 1924) was among the earliest who tried to keep analyses from lengthening unproductively. Ferenczi proposed an "active technique," whereas Rank proposed a nine-month limitation, since, he asserted, the "birth trauma" was at the root of all emotional distress, a period of therapy equivalent to that of gestation should be sufficient (Ferenczi and Rank, 1924). Subsequent writers have refined one or another approach to shorten treatment: more activity on the part of the therapist, or an arbitrary time limit on the enterprise, or both. Proponents of both points of view have provided evidence that their approaches are effective (e.g., Malan, 1963; Sifneos, 1972; Mann, 1976; 1976; Davanloo, 1980).

A review of the literature on brief psychotherapy reveals these same suggestions being made repeatedly. Successive generations have rediscovered that, for many patients, psychotherapy can be kept from dragging on unnecessarily by minimizing certain factors that tend to lengthen treatment and by practicing specific techniques that tend to shorten it. Malan (1963) summarized the factors that tend to lengthen psychotherapy. His list, somewhat augmented, follows:

*Patient Attributes That Tend to Lengthen Psychotherapy*

1. Resistance
2. Overdetermination
3. Necessity for working through
4. Roots of neurosis in early childhood
5. Character rigidity, transference
6. Dependence
7. Negative transference connected with termination
8. The transference neurosis

*Therapist Attributes That Tend to Lengthen Psychotherapy*

9. A tendency toward passivity and the willingness to follow where the patient leads
10. A "sense of timelessness" conveyed to the patient
11. Therapeutic perfectionism
12. Increasing preoccupation with even deeper and earlier experiences
13. A tendency to live life through the patient and to need his company
14. Fear of hurting or offending the patient by ending the relationship
15. The economic value of the patient

We can assemble a list of factors that tend to shorten psychotherapy by inverting the factors that lengthen it. In addition, there are a number of technical maneuvers a therapist may employ to shorten treatment besides setting a definite time limit in advance. These include the following:

1. Therapist activity, for example,
    (a) developing a treatment plan
    (b) interpreting transference early especially around issues related to termination
    (c) refining clear goals with patient
    (d) maintaining focus
    (e) ignoring distractions
    (f) conveying to patient that treatment will not go on indefinitely
2. Being satisfied with limited goals
3. Relatively infrequent visits

Each of these lengthening and shortening factors deserves thorough consideration to clarify, for instance, what we mean by therapist activity (see Schlesinger, 2003). Nor is it clear whose goals are to be met and how they are to be arrived at, or in whose mind the achievements of the therapy, prospective or actual, are to be considered "limited."

The point of view I advocate is that, if the therapist does not set a time limit in advance and yet would like to keep psychotherapy efficient by assuring that it takes no longer than it has to, he will have to know when the patient has accomplished enough so that he can get along without treatment. This obvious idea, intimately linked to the issue of ending of psychotherapy, has received little attention in the literature. Time-limited psychotherapy, of course, begs this question by setting an ending date in advance. The proponents of more open-ended forms of brief psychotherapy do stress the importance of careful work around termination, often in terms of the necessity to interpret a transference reaction, especially the patient's rage and disappointment around termination. They give little guidance however, about how therapist and patient can know when enough has been done so that the patient can carry on without the therapist.

## Landmarks of Progress in Psychotherapy

A therapist has several kinds of diagnostic information available to help him locate himself and the patient within the therapeutic process. Some of the indicators or "landmarks" may be heard in the content of what the patient talks about. If the patient describes new ways for him to solve his problems and reports the effects of applying these new ways, he is also implicitly questioning if perhaps he has had enough therapy, at least for the time being. Since information of this kind is easily recognized, even if its significance for stopping is not always appreciated, let us turn our attention to another source of information, that gleaned from the process itself, and return to consider the various meanings of "progress reports" in Chapter 5.

The landmarks of ending I describe refer to the characteristic ways the patient signals that he has done enough on a formerly pressing issue for the time being. At such moments, the patient is faced once again with what the therapy is all about, "What am I doing here?" much as he did when he began. Whether he speaks of it or not, he has the uneasy feeling that, once again, he is at a new beginning in therapy. These seemingly polar experiences (that is, ending and beginning) have much in common, indeed they are the two faces of the same experience. To continue this discussion, we must first be clear that the terms ending and beginning have several senses that we must consider separately. The common, everyday sense of the terms, as when one is asked, "When does the lecture begin?" refers to chronological time, clock time.[5]

When during his first session, a patient, asks, "How long will this treatment take?" he expects an answer framed in the everyday sense of time, as measured by the calendar. If a literal-minded clinician responds only in that sense, perhaps by offering a plausible range of durations, or more likely with some version of, "It depends . . . ," the patient will give some sign that the clinician has missed the underlying worry.

The patient's reasonable question, framed in reasonable terms about real time, also is driven by anxiety that makes use of the questioning form (Schlesinger, 2003) to express another sense of time, one we might call process time or psychological time, a sense of time that refers to one's location in a process. Consider: the patient is about to begin therapy; we may surmise that he had almost decided firmly to go ahead when he felt a pang of anxiety and had second thoughts, "What am I committing myself to? Do I really want to spend all that money and time? Do I really need it?" He expressed this rush of anxiety-driven,

[5] But not only clock time, as the example indicates. We are not privileged to inquire into other meanings if the question is put casually, in a nonclinical relationship.

second thoughts, perhaps not all of it in awareness, in the worried thought, "When will it end?" The experience of anxiety shrinks time; the feared future event is present right now. We could say that, for a moment, the patient, psychologically, is both at the actual beginning of therapy and stuck somewhere in the undefined middle of things. He is trying to locate a safe sense of "end," a safety that might best be reached in a fantasized "not beginning" at all.

If the therapist is aware of the patient's distress and that his reasonable question contains a subtext and conflates both senses of "time," he can formulate a useful intervention. He might choose to address first the anxiety he presumes the patient is feeling about making a fateful commitment: "I imagine you just had a worried thought about what you are getting yourself into." Assuming the patient confirms his presumption, he could continue helping the patient appreciate that his anxiety is understandable and reasonable. It is likely that the patient will tell him more about how he is feeling and that he feels reassured by being understood. Then, if the patient still desires an answer in literal terms, he could answer in terms of the ordinary sense of time. Frequently, the therapist will find that, if he first addresses the anxiety that he presumes motivated the question, the patient's need for an explicit, that is to say, literal, answer will have disappeared (Schlesinger, 2003).

## *Chronological Time Versus Process Time*

It may be useful to clarify further the distinction between chronological time and process time. Let us return to our understanding that psychotherapy is a process and that the term process implies at least that the matter under discussion takes time, chronological time. Conventionally, we depict time by an arrow, the point indicating its direction of flow, the length of the line perhaps indicating its duration (see Figure 1, next page).

Figure 1 also can depict the simplest possible example of psychotherapy. I do not want to make too much of it, because it does not serve for most practical therapies, but an exchange it could represent might go something like this:

P   "I am afraid there may be something wrong with my head."
T   "It looks OK from here."
P   "Thanks, that makes me feel better. Good-bye."
T   "You're welcome. Good-bye."

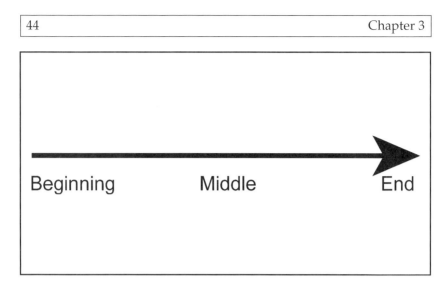

**Figure 1** The process of psychotherapy: A simple model

I have never actually experienced a therapy that brief and simple—or that flippant—but it is not absurd to think that simple reassurance can lead to a profound sense of relief. It is a conceivable, if oversimplified, model for a suggestive treatment for an acute pain of nonspecific origin. The pain that brings the patient occurs at one time and the relief of pain is at another time. The reassuring comment seems to remove the pain and ends the transaction.

The situation would be different if an unconscious conflict had given rise to the pain and worrying about the meaning of the pain was what brought the patient to clinical attention. Then it is likely the worry would be a recurring issue. In this case, rather than saying, "Thank you. I feel better. Good-bye," this brief encounter might end in this way:

P    "Thank you. I feel better now. But I am afraid my pain might return. If it does, may I come back?"

That modified example shows that, as the initial therapeutic transaction winds down, the patient's concern tends *not* to be about the original pain, which for the moment at least has been relieved, but rather about the prospect of ending and what might happen afterward. He has a new problem, a fear of ending, "What will I do if the pain comes back and you (therapist) are not there to take care of it?" and he raises the issue of

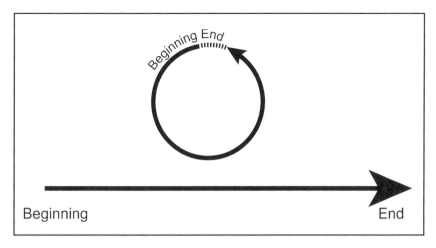

**Figure 2**  The process of psychotherapy: Modified model

beginning again.[6] We might illustrate this circularity of psychological time as in Figure 2.

The modified model in Figure 2 is only a bit more realistic than Figure 1. The patient with a psychological concern (like all of us) also experiences the passage of time in linear fashion. As chronological time passes linearly and inexorably, one has the sense that beginning and ending important life tasks occur at the same point in chronological time (e.g., we speak of the same event as immigration or emigration), but in successive cycles that are relatively independent of clock or calendar. To show the relationship of linear, chronological time and psychological, or curvilinear, time, we need a more sophisticated model. A model that can depict both chronological and psychological time is the helix. The cycles in psychological time progress in corkscrew fashion while chronological time advances linearly along the axis of the helix (see Figure 3, next page).

The most important property of this improved model for our purposes is that the beginning of treatment, or more accurately the first appointment, and the end of treatment, or more accurately the last

---

[6] This example omits much that is essential to understand such interactions, including that the patient does not understand the relationship between what the therapist did and the fading of the pain. This issue is discussed in Chapter 6.

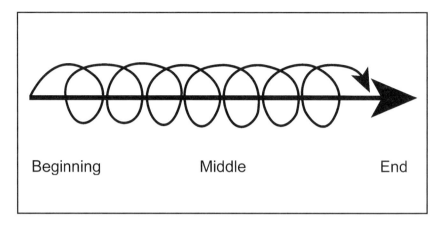

Beginning                    Middle                              End

**Figure 3**  The process of psychotherapy: Improved helical model

appointment, are separated by a gap in real time but may occur at the same point in psychological time. The experiences of ending and beginning commonly run into each other. This model has the capacity to depict that occurrence; the feeling that one is about to begin something may obscure that one has just ended something, an ending that one was reluctant to acknowledge, perhaps for defensive reasons.

> The patient is a woman in her mid-20s, a college graduate, married but as yet with no children. She is employed in her first job, as a secretary in a public interest law firm. She is a good worker and during this first year of employment, she was given increasing responsibility that she has acquitted very well.
> Her supervisor, an older woman, resigned suddenly when offered a better post in another firm. The partners were in a quandary, for they could not replace her easily. After much discussion, they offered the job to our patient who was flattered and bewildered. It meant a nice promotion, a raise, and an opportunity for advancement. She was delighted but felt a strange twinge of unease and said she wanted to think it over. She went home and told her husband, who, of course, was also pleased. That night she had a full-blown anxiety attack, her first ever, and when she finally fell asleep was awakened by a nightmare, also her first. She was still so shaken in the morning that she was afraid to go to work, so her husband suggested that she call his therapist.

The therapist arranged to see her immediately, and, in the course of several visits over about two weeks, the following story emerged. The patient is the younger of two sisters. Her adored and idealized older sister is the designated "successful one" in the family. The sisters had spent much of their time together in childhood and even now are on the phone several times a week. She says she feels quite content with the role of younger sister and looks up to her sister as a substitute mother, as her own mother is characterologically removed and relatively inaccessible to her, the second child. The patient did quite well at college, married, and is thinking of either having children or pursuing her education. But she is holding herself back until her sister has made her own career moves, that is, so that her sister can remain "big sister."

During the second week of sessions, the patient becomes comfortable enough to tell the firm that she will accept the position that they have continued to hold open for her. When she enters the next session after accepting the position, she looks frightened. She did "not exactly have another nightmare" but was sleepless, apprehensive about whether she had made the right decision. During this session, she looks uncertain and finally asks the therapist, "Are you quite sure the anxiety attacks will not come back?" There has been no discussion as yet of something that also was on the therapist's mind—whether the patient needs or wants more treatment in order to consolidate the gains she has made, or whether she has had enough treatment for the time being.

The therapist continues what he presumes was her tacit reference to the possibility of ending this episode of treatment by supposing that she has been considering that she might have solved the problem that brought her and thus can think about stopping. She then tells him what was on her mind when she could not sleep. She had been fantasying becoming a soaring success at her new job but then saw herself ending up like her previous boss, an essentially clerical administrator. Why shouldn't she go to law school and eventually become a member of the firm?

She is both pleased and frightened at allowing herself the fantasized pleasures of outdoing her sister, as well as the real pleasures of allowing her capacities to play themselves out untrammeled. In the midst of these pleasant thoughts, she suddenly has a pang of anxiety and then feels "overwhelmed" and defeated. The therapist is able to link this fear first with the implications of her ambitions for her relationship with her sister and then with the parallel concern that he will no longer be interested in her if she does not continue to have symptoms.

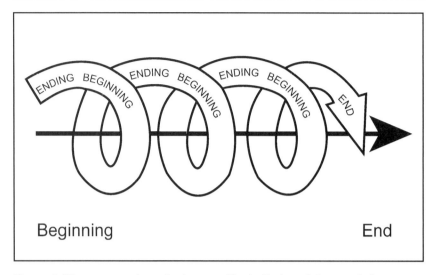

ENDING BEGINNING ENDING BEGINNING ENDING BEGINNING END

Beginning                                                          End

**Figure 4** The process of psychotherapy: The helical model expanded.

He demonstrates to the patient that her fear of another anxiety attack is like a return to the beginning of their time together. She has had a recurrence, in muted form, of the complaint that brought her in the first place. This revival of the complaint as a "marker" of beginning masks her concern about ending, the fear that he will evict her as no longer interesting as a patient. She will be alone, having to face by herself the consequences of her newly unbridled ambition. During this session and the next, they talk about possible further treatment.

She realizes that she has accomplished much more than she thought she would in the few sessions. She also thinks she ought to devote all her energy to her new position, but she probably will want to have more treatment later on; this taste has left her wanting more. The therapist agrees that, for the moment, she might, do better to concentrate on her job, and he discusses with her the advisability of her having psychoanalysis some day. They part with the sense that she has accomplished a piece of work but with no illusions that she is as well as she could be.

The therapist next hears from the patient about a year later when she reports that things are going well. She has not had any anxiety attacks but has noticed that at certain crucial moments she feels herself holding back, refraining from offering a bright idea, fearful lest she be thought "uppity." At the same time, she can see that her job is a dead end and that she really does want to go to law school. In fact, she had already applied to law school and had come to request a referral for psychoanalysis, which he gave her.

Figure 4 may make clearer the patterning of cycles of ending and beginning in relation to the passage of chronological time.

## *Psychotherapy as Organized by "Tasks"*[7]

If we think of psychotherapy from the patient's point of view, as working on a succession of problems, tasks, issues, nagging questions, and the like, we can view the process itself at any moment as organized around the matter or problem that preoccupies the patient. We can think of the patient as having *begun* to work on that task or problem and finally completing or *ending* work on it after achieving a useful degree of resolution. We recognize that, for most problems or conflicts patients bring to us, we can point to no clear beginning. And completing or ending, in this context, merely means that, for the moment, the patient is able to put the matter out of mind. Of course, how the patient manages to do that is of interest to the therapist. By "useful degree of resolution," in this context, I mean that the patient has either acquired sufficient insight, or a change in awareness, or an alternative way of feeling that could lead to new behavior or possibly has raised a defensive barrier to further investigation of the issue.

In any case, the patient interrupts himself, and the phenomena of ending that I am calling attention to will appear. I must emphasize that I am using the terms beginning and ending not with respect to the overall therapy, but with respect to the task or problem that occupies the patient at the moment. For convenient reference, I need a single term for it and use the term task to refer to the whatever the patient is "working" on. My justification for this choice lies in its fit with a usage I deplore, the way patients and clinicians alike refer to "working on a problem," as much of what is called "work" in psychotherapy mainly serves resistance (Schlesinger, 2003). Nevertheless, from this vantage point, we may view the course of psychotherapy as consisting of the patient's working on a

---

[7] "Task" is not a technical term but, rather, a term of convenience. I settled on it for the "thing," issue, worry, problem, or preoccupation that holds the patient's attention until he is able to resolve it enough so that he can put it aside, at least temporarily.

succession of tasks. The patient probably mentioned some of these tasks among the desired goals of treatment from the outset, while others may have been defined only later and are seen as requiring solution so that the patient's overall goals might be achieved.

The therapist who has made a dynamic formulation of his patient, and who has seen the goals of therapy as the accomplishment of one or a series of such tasks, will be alert to the status of the patient's work on each task. He will certainly take seriously any changes and accomplishments that the patient describes, but will also be alert for the appearance of several reliable formal indicators that the patient has accomplished something or has managed to put something out of mind. Each time a patient finishes a task or achieves some subgoal, even a defensive one, the therapist will see that internal change reflected in an observable behavioral change. These observable behaviors can be designated as "markers" that the patient has interrupted himself (to be discussed in next section). If the interruption came about because the patient has resolved the matter to a useful degree, the treatment could, in principle, end.

Thus, therapy may be endable at any number of points—each time some task essential to the therapy has been completed. I do not imply that treatment ought to end at that point. Even in an uncomplicated treatment, more than one therapeutic task may need to be accomplished; after all, every solution brings new problems. The completion of one task, or the ending of one phase, may be only the precursor to beginning another. However, the treatment *may* end at such a point.[8] By recognizing and bringing to the patient's attention the formal indicators, as well as the content indicators, that the patient has interrupted himself—either because he has completed a task or because he has achieved some subgoal or has stopped himself short of pursuing a possibly dangerous thought— the therapist can test out where the patient stands with respect to the matter at hand and where the patient stands with respect to the treatment as a whole, ultimately whether the treatment is optimally endable at this time.

If it is clear to both therapist and patient that the treatment should not stop at that point, the therapist can use the occasion to help the patient point to what he had stopped short of considering and hence what he might want to do next, a process that also prepares for the eventual ending of treatment.

---

[8] And if the treatment is to end, it should be at such a point.

It is not generally recognized that much of the work of termination can be done "in installments" around the occasion of such "mini-endings." The patient can become accustomed to recognizing that he regularly is alarmed by the idea that accomplishment and success are inevitably associated in his mind with separation and loss. By the frequent opportunities treatment affords to experience that connection, he may be enabled to work through some of the implications of that association long in advance of the actual ending.

## Indicators of Accomplishment and Phase Completion

What do the formal indicators, markers, of task completion look like? Patients behave in characteristic ways when they have completed a piece of therapeutic work or have tripped over an unwelcome insight. I use "completed a piece of work" only in a relative sense. It need not be what the therapist would consider a major breakthrough or insight. Indeed, from the "outside" it might seem trivial. It is, however, a change that has dynamic significance to the patient. For instance, the change might signify that the patient has arrived at a slightly new understanding of himself and his situation, might have achieved one of his goals, has changed his attitude toward a formerly held goal, or has taken some tentative step that represents a change for the better in his life. The patient may be accepting or rejecting of the emergence of newness, usually both.

To repeat a truism, every change brings new opportunities and also new dangers. The opportunities as well as the dangers may be intrinsic to the matter of the task; for instance, finding relief from a previous inhibition opens one to a broader life but also exposes one to whatever dangerous possibilities the inhibitions put out of reach. The dangers may also be extrinsic, in the context of our present interest in termination; a prominent danger is the loss of relationship to the therapist in consequence of getting well and no longer deserving therapy. Most of the time, although the patient will have been working toward this intermediate goal for some time, he is not likely to announce that he has gotten to a place from which he finally can, as it were, poke his head through the clouds and admire the view. It thus becomes imperative that the therapist recognizes the various ways in which the patient may betray, that is, both reveal and hide, that accomplishment.[9]

---

[9] I discuss shortly why patients generally do not announce successes.

FORMAL INDICATORS OF ACCOMPLISHMENT AND PHASE COMPLETION

1.  The pace of treatment typically slows. The treatment seems to lose its direction.
2.  The patient's engagement with therapy slackens; his attention turns elsewhere. Although the patient does not necessarily complain, nothing seems to be happening in therapy.
3.  The patient is vague about the last hour and uncertain about why he has come this hour.
4.  The patient may come late or find reasons to cancel an appointment.
5.  The patient's sense of purpose seems gone. A patient demonstrating these signs may not be aware of it, but he is at the point of considering whether to stop or to find a new purpose for beginning again. If the therapist does not intervene, one or more of the following alternatives will occur:
6.  The patient may stop coming, without explanation.
7.  Occasionally the patient may propose that he stop treatment.
8.  The patient may voice fantasies that directly or indirectly refer to stopping, ending, or leaving.
9.  Most frequently, the patient may become so anxious about the frightening thought, perhaps not yet expressed or even conscious, that the therapist wants him to stop therapy. The patient forestalls ending by developing new symptoms or complaints or has a recurrence of old complaints that unquestionably justify his right to continued treatment. Sometimes, an "emergency" supervenes that pushes all thoughts of ending out of everyone's mind.

If he recognizes these characteristic phenomena, the therapist adds to his interpretative possibilities. Rather than considering automatically that the patient in this odd, detached frame of mind is resisting the exploration of some new and deeper conflict, which may indeed be the case, the therapist will also consider that the patient may be reacting to an accomplishment of some kind and, whether consciously or not, is reassessing his relationship to the therapy and therapist. Assessing whether he is viewing progress or resistance, either categorically, or more likely each in degree, is an essential skill for the therapist to develop.

The therapist can settle the differential assessment of the process by first recognizing and empathizing with the patient's uncomfortable sense of being at loose ends; the patient will generally be quite aware that he feels so. The therapist can then follow up, perhaps by noting the suddenness of the patient's change from purposeful engagement to feeling at sea. The patient may be able with just this much help to look inward and identify the change that underlies the shift in the process and thus open its dynamic significance to exploration. By identifying the accomplishment, actual or potential, its relationship to the patient's presenting problem, and its significance, including why the patient was reluctant to acknowledge it, therapist and patient are enabled to take stock of what the treatment has done and what remains to be done. The way can then be cleared either to end or to agree on a new task to work upon.

You might well wonder if this kind of patient behavior invariably indicates a reaction to success and accomplishment. Is the "resistance" always motivated by fear of separation? Could not the problem be that the patient has become frightened by some previously unsuspected implication in what has been coming up and thus is fearful about going on? Indeed, that could very well be so. Resolving this differential assessment of the process is one of a therapist's major tasks. I stress that implications of separation following on success are what trouble the patient because that possibility is the one most likely to be overlooked. The view that the patient must be resisting going ahead and therefore ought to be pressured to get on with it is generally regarded as the only way to understand and deal with such behavior, particularly if it occurs early in therapy.

There are other formal indicators that may signal that an important, but not yet obvious, accomplishment has occurred:

10. Sometimes the first inkling the therapist gets is a shift in the transference, perhaps a hint that the patient does not seem as much at ease with the therapist as he was just the session before.
11. The patient seems reticent, uncertain about disclosing something to the therapist; he may seem to have a "secret." In a not altogether clear way, the therapist with whom he has been so close seems to have become a stranger with whom intimacy might be risky.[10]

Through such phenomena reflecting that he is having an uncomfortable experience of newness and strangeness, the patient may be signaling that, in some important sense, he is wondering about getting further into his therapy, about making a new beginning, one that might have

---

[10] Patients frequently ask suddenly, "Have you always had that picture on your wall?" or in other ways suggest that today feels like a first visit.

unanticipated dangers. Again, if the therapist recognizes that he is not seeing an outbreak of paranoia in his patient but, rather, that the patient is frightened about entering a new phase of treatment, he will have an additional avenue for effective interpretation. He can call to the patient's attention that something must have changed (that is, ended) in the patient's life and therapy so that he can consider the hazards of a new beginning. In this way, the therapist can bring out into the open the accomplishment that surely is there.

These formal indicators that signify when a task has been completed (and that perhaps another task is about to be begun) help the therapist to orient himself within the therapeutic process. Recognizing these landmarks of therapy and sensing the predictable, if not always even, course, the therapist gains important information about the patient and the state of the treatment. In particular, recognizing these landmarks alerts the therapist to an essential diagnostic issue—the necessity to diagnose the process of therapy. Do these signs imply that the patient is "stuck"? That the treatment has stagnated? Is it oscillating without forward movement? (See Chapter 7.) On the other hand, has the patient possibly achieved some resolution of the issue that has been preoccupying him and is now uncertain about the implications of this accomplishment? Perhaps the patient has even accomplished enough of his purposes to consider stopping, or maybe he is fearful that the therapist will jump to that conclusion.

The therapist will have the opportunity to focus on these phenomena a number of times in the course of any treatment, however long or short. The phenomena will develop along the lines I have illustrated only if the therapist is alert to the signs that mark the presence of the underlying conflict when the patient does not specifically talk about achievement. Thus, when, for instance, after a period of quiet and steady progress with decreasing or even no complaining, the patient seems to be at a loss about what to say, comes late, or cancels an appointment, the therapist should consider first the possibility that treatment is no longer necessary rather than that resistance to going deeper must have supervened. These are, of course, not exclusive alternatives; they are linked dynamically. In the context of steady accomplishment, the resistance is likely about fear of recognizing accomplishment lest the therapist react by ending the treatment.

I suggest, however, that we not prejudge the issue. By focusing on the phenomena that reflect slowing down, disengagement, vagueness, a sense of being lost, or being without purpose, and bringing them to the patient's attention, the therapist is able to help the patient understand his current predicament about the therapy. The differential assessment of process that the therapist has to make at that point is to decide whether the resistance has mainly to do with separation following success or is a reaction to anticipated difficulty in going on, or both in some measure. Such phenomena must *never* be ignored.

To summarize, common indicators of task completion that the therapist may observe either in what the patient says (content) or how he says it (formal) are:

1. Direct acknowledgment by the patient that a problem has been solved. *[content]*
2. Indirect acknowledgment by the patient that a problem has been solved (i.e., unconvincing denials about it notwithstanding behavioral evidence that relevant change has occurred). *[content]*
3. Indirect evidence
   a. A formerly prominent issue is no longer mentioned. *[formal]*
   b. The patient's sense of purpose, direction, and engagement has slackened. *[formal]*
   c. Anxiety or other symptoms reflect the patient's fear that continuation of therapy is threatened. *[formal]*
   d. The patient suddenly stops attending to the problem under discussion and begins a new therapeutic task. *[formal]*
   e. The patient shows anxieties typical of the beginning of a phase of therapy without having acknowledged the completion of the previous therapeutic task or identifying a new one. *[formal]*

These indicators can mean either that the therapy has accomplished enough so that the patient and therapist can think of stopping, or that the patient has run into something he ought to get into but that arouses so much anxiety that he would prefer to stall or even to stop rather than go on. How, then, can we tell one from the other?

First, the therapist must, of course, keep in mind that the phenomenon he is observing could mean one or the other. He can then call to the patient's attention that something noteworthy is happening—that the patient is feeling some discomfort that very likely relates to something that has just occurred in the therapy. Does the patient agree that he has been feeling a bit uneasier than usual in the last few minutes (or the last few hours)? Does he feel uncertain about what therapy is all about at the moment? Does he agree that his coming late this time, or the last couple of times, has involved an internal debate about whether to come at all?

Does he agree that he has been feeling better lately for some reason and now feels a bit uneasy about that? Or, on the other hand, is he aware also that he has been approaching but shying away from a topic that he "probably ought to get into"? Does his uneasiness perhaps reflect uncertainty about how the therapist will react to an as-yet-untold piece of potentially embarrassing information?

In short, the technical prescription at this point is the same as at any other point in therapy: to make it possible for the patient to tell the therapist directly what is on his mind that he may have been expressing indirectly; and to enable the therapist to be ready to follow where the patient wants to go. Since going on or stopping in the face of anxiety is a sensitive issue, it obviously takes delicate handling by the therapist if the patient is to explore the meaning of his behavior and face the implication that he is either afraid to go on or is afraid to stop.

As treatment progresses, the therapist will notice that the duration of each cycle of the helix of process (that is, the time the patient spends on any task) tends to shorten. A cycle that took weeks to work through at the beginning of treatment may take only days later on. Several cycles may occur within a session when ending is near, a phenomenon that provides the therapist another, formal, indicator of the patient's readiness to end treatment.

Figure 5 illustrates how the cycles of ending and beginning speed up and recycle faster as the treatment progresses toward finishing.

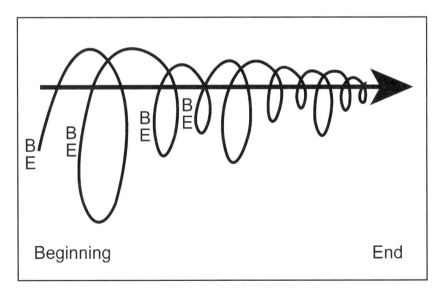

**Figure 5** The process of psychotherapy: Cycles pass more quickly as the treatment advances

## Therapist Resistance to Ending

Particularly at the beginning of their careers, some therapists are unready to accept the idea that patients get well, at least not in finite time. After a few interviews (or perhaps as many as 20) in which the patient has seriously looked at himself and his problems, has discussed various solutions and tried one or more, he may inform the therapist that he is ready to stop. He thinks he has a better understanding of the things that brought him to treatment, has better control of his life, and feels better about himself.

A beginning therapist may feel dismayed. He typically is chagrined when he comes to supervision, certain that he has done something terribly wrong; perhaps he feels mocked and about to be deserted by the patient whom he sees as "acting out" or about to take a "flight into health." How can the patient be better now, when the therapist does not yet understand him and has no idea what he might have done to help? Here is an example:

A therapist reports that he has been working for two months with a 19-year-old female student who came to the clinic distraught because her boyfriend had walked out on her. After several evaluation sessions, the therapist recommended treatment, to which the patient agrees. Shortly thereafter she starts to skip hours, and there was trouble scheduling others.

The patient called to cancel, but when the therapist suggested other times, none of them seemed quite right: the hour would conflict with her karate class or some other important obligation. When the therapist finally noted that she must have some trouble about coming in because no hour seemed good for her, the patient said, "Okay, I'll come in."

Several sessions later the patient says she is feeling better now and did not know if she wanted to continue. The therapist kept addressing her uncertainty about whether she "really wanted to get into her conflicts." She would agree, but after a while she would say, "I am tired of talking about this." She would, however always come back to it. Then she started skipping hours again, just not showing up. She would feel guilty about this behavior, and they would talk about her guilt feelings. The therapist says he is aware that the patient was trying to provoke a negative reaction from him, and he is proud that he was able to avoid it. Instead, interpreting her masochistic pattern; he points out how the patient tried to provoke him to be angry with her.

The therapist turns sadly to the supervisor and says, that despite his efforts, he does not feel that any therapy is going on now. In discussing this case, the therapist quickly comes to see that he has a problem letting go of this patient, a bright and attractive young woman who he expected would be a "natural" for "long-term" psychotherapy. The patient could see how important she had become to the therapist and felt guilty about leaving him, but she was also healthy enough to be unwilling to stay for that reason alone. There was indeed a dependency conflict and enough transference so that the patient could not act firmly on her wish to leave. The therapist has unwittingly been manipulating the transference and misdiagnosing the state of affairs as a masochistic reaction on the part of the patient, with whom he has actually been reenacting some of the patient's adolescent conflicts.

# 4

## Beginning from the Vantage Point of Ending

After doing psychotherapy for a while, a therapist may become jaded and regard first appointments as "routine," just as another patient for the therapeutic mill. It is easy to forget how you felt when you were in the same position, if not as a patient, then as a newly anointed therapist facing your first patient. Recall how fearful you were that you might forget your own name, hopeful that the patient would not notice your nervousness, fearful that the patient would soon unmask you as an imposter, and certain that it would be only a matter of time before you would make a fool of yourself or be fooled by the patient. It is important to stay in touch with those ancient and uncomfortable feelings. One of the worst errors a therapist can make is to lose touch with the excitement and anxiety of beginning with a new patient, to see it as a routine affair that, "as usual," has the patient all stirred up. But, if you wait a while, the dust will settle and the patient will get around to telling you what is "really" troubling him.

It may seem odd to open this topic with the young therapist's anxious fantasies about being abandoned by the patient and ending the paragraph by deploring that he might outgrow that anxiety. I do not mean to fault that therapist for being relieved merely because the patient did not immediately decamp. My plea is that the therapist keep alive the sensitivity to ending that so preoccupied him fearfully at the inception of his career. Now that he has learned that patients seldom decamp immediately after showing up, he will have to keep his sensitivity alive, not by anxiety, but by cultivating concern for how to help the patient get what he needs and leave when ending is safely in hand.

"Safely in hand" begs the question, of course. That issue is at the center of ending and termination and is what this book is all about. In Chapter 3, I spelled out the landmarks that can help a therapist locate a patient within the process of therapy, to locate him with respect to his original reasons for seeking therapy and with respect to the other issues and purposes that emerged in the course of therapy. By attending to the way the patient experiences each of the "miniendings" that occur when he finishes a bit of therapeutic work, and how he experiences the consequent changes, the therapist, in a sense, keeps one eye on events within the therapy and another on events in the patient's larger life.

While it seems more "natural" for the patient to remain concerned about whether the therapy is "doing anything" for him, in most cases, patients become almost totally involved in the process and may even lose track of why they came in the first place. It remains for the therapist, therefore, to share responsibility with the patient for ensuring that the therapy remains practical. This last sentence sums up a major issue of termination; this chapter is concerned with how, from the outset, therapists keep ending in mind.

## *Evaluating a Patient for Psychoanalysis or Psychotherapy*

Over the years, as I conducted seminars about endings and termination, I have invariably found it necessary to review some elementary issues in regard to beginning therapy so as to place the issue of termination in proper context. I cannot assume that you are familiar with the way I discussed these issues earlier (Schlesinger, 2003) and hope not to bore those who are.

I assume that a therapist conducting the evaluation is a skilled interviewer who can be relied on to do a diagnostic examination as thorough as one would expect to obtain in a mental health clinic of the first rank. On this assumption, I am focusing almost exclusively on the additional considerations that a clinician must keep in mind in order to make a recommendation for treatment in psychoanalysis or dynamic psychotherapy. These considerations including especially how the patient is likely to experience the prospect of ending it and how to anticipate whether it will end with a formal phase of termination or with an approximation as close as feasible.

My focus is on the ways in which the eventual problem of ending treatment appropriately can be inferred from the very outset. The issues of particular relevance for ending also are important throughout the treatment. The clinician must take seriously any thoughts the patient voices about stopping, whether because of having gained enough from treatment or because of discouragement about getting anywhere, or for any other reason. As I emphasized in Chapter 3, the messages the patient sends indirectly, metaphorically in words and behavior—what I called "formal" indicators—will give the therapist a good sense of where the patient and he are in the treatment now. If correctly read, the accumulation of this information will eventually help him to bring the treatment to an end in a useful fashion.

## Why Did the Patient Come for Therapy Now?

The first question to occur to any clinician facing a new patient is, why is the patient coming now? Then, what is the patient's "problem," what does he want? While we commonly regard these as different wordings of the same question, they are, indeed, different questions, with different implications. One might assume that, different or not, they are simple questions and should be answerable from the patient's opening remarks; but they are neither simple nor likely to be answerable for some time.

Every clinician discovers soon enough that what a new patient says to justify his arrival is not necessarily the main reason that brings him and certainly is not the whole story. The term problem itself needs clarification. Out of courtesy, we do not argue with a patient who tries to tell us what he regards as his "problem," but usually it is not a problem in the literal sense of the term; that is, it is not an unhappy state of affairs that has a solution. The point of this formal definition is that, if it has no solution, it isn't a problem. Many of the dreary situations we face are not problems in that sense. Some are "existential states"—"That's the way life is." I concede, of course, if the patient is unrealistically troubled about it, that worry could be construed as a "problem" within our purview.

What brings most patients is not a problem but that they are in a "mess," a situation in which the ingredients are both held together and kept apart by internal conflict. Thus, a patient either does not know how to get out of that conflict or is unwilling to do what is necessary, or feels unable to do what is necessary, in order to extricate himself.[1] He is on both sides of the conflict and that mainly is what keeps him in that predicament.

Initial complaints often turn out to serve patients largely as a "ticket of admission," a rationalization that affords an honorable way to ask for help. The initial complaint states a reason, a justification, not necessarily untrue, that the patient thinks the therapist will accept. We can assume that if he had gone to a religious counselor, the problem would have been framed in religious terms, or, if to a physician, in medical terms. For psychotherapists the problem is most often couched as emotional

---

[1] You may be reminded of the joke about the youngster who dug furiously at the pile of manure he found under the Christmas tree certain there would have to be a pony in it somewhere.

difficulties, interpersonal difficulties, and the like. This is to say that the clinician should accept the initial "reason" as true, in some sense, but *not as the whole truth.*

Sometimes the patient's presentation sounds puzzling; the term that often comes first to mind is "inappropriate." Consider the following example merely for its "inappropriateness":

> A man drives up to a filling station and asks for a pound of cabbage. If the filling station attendant is well mannered, he will, without further ado, politely direct him to the greengrocer down the street. But if we suppose that the attendant is a student clinician moonlighting at that filling station, how might he react to that strange request?
>
> We hope that, first of all, as a clinician, he would register its oddness and note that it does not fit with other aspects of the motorist's presentation—he behaves in a generally correct manner. This observation might lead him to want to know more about the motorist's strange-sounding request. And so, rather than shutting off further inquiry by immediately pointing the motorist toward the greengrocer, as did the authentic filling-station attendant, he might respond in a way that would invite the motorist to tell him more.
>
> For instance, he might simply repeat the motorist's request in a matter-of-fact tone of voice: "You want some cabbage." The motorist might then reply, "Yes, I do, and there is no parking space near the greengrocer. Would you mind if I leave my car here for the few minutes it will take me to make my purchase?" The matter might end at that point, the clinician possibly wondering why the motorist didn't ask for the parking privilege in the first place.
>
> Alternatively, the motorist might respond, "I've already been to the greengrocer and all his cabbages have ugly heads and I heard one whispering, 'We don't want to go with him.' You look to have an honest face. Maybe you would know where I could find a mannerly head of cabbage." Perhaps the second response would lead you to think that the student clinician would have done better to have emulated the answer of the know-nothing filling station attendant; being off duty, he hardly would be in a position to deal clinically with the disturbed cabbage seeker.

I invented that fanciful situation to make the point that an analyst, as examining clinician, should take the patient at face value, but *not only* at face value, and respond in a way that permits the patient's story to unfold. After all, we are interested to find out about the psychological reality, the inner world, of the patient, not just "the facts," and the opportunity for that exploration begins with the patient's opening remarks. Two old jokes of opposite sense are apposite:

> One joke puts it, "Anyone who goes to a shrink should have his head examined." While the intent of the joke is dismissive, we can take a useful hint from it. Anyone who presents himself to a clinician should be taken at face value at least long enough for the clinician and patient to discover in sufficient depth why the patient is presenting himself now.
>
> Another joke tells of the two analysts who meet on the street. One says to the other, "Hello, how are you?" The other wonders darkly to himself, "I wonder what he means by that." Clearly common sense must leaven the advice both to accept the patient at face value and to allow the subsequent process to shape the initial understanding. An aphorism is apropos: if tongue and feet disagree, give credence first to the feet. If the patient is here, he probably has good reason, regardless of what he says.

Of course, you will already have come to the conclusion that the behavior that arouses this kind of discussion implies at the very least that the patient is in conflict about coming at all and expresses his mixed feelings by making a confusing presentation in which the wish and the fear about coming are blended in a lumpy way.

What do these observations have to do with keeping in mind the eventual ending of this therapy that has hardly begun. Consider that another way the clinician might think about the reasons the patient offers for coming is to ask himself what it would take for the patient *not* to feel the urge to come to treatment now. The implication of this question is that the therapist would do well also to invert the question that jumps first to his mind when greeting a new patient. In addition to asking himself, "Why is the patient coming?" he could rephrase the question in operational terms as, "What would have to change in the patient's life so that he would not have to come to see a therapist?" or "What would the internal or external circumstances have to be so that the patient would not feel impelled to come?"

Often it is useful to put some form of the inverted question to the patient as part of the initial evaluation. One of its uses is that, by attempting to answer it, the patient likely will inform the therapist about where he locates the source of his difficulties. Are they outside of him, or is he willing to accept some responsibility for the unsatisfactory state of his life? The patient might respond to such a question so as to permit a conversation like this:

P:  "Well, I guess if my wife would stop picking on me and finding fault with every little thing I do, my life would be pretty good."

T:  "That doesn't sound like an unreasonable hope, but I think the wrong person has come. If your wife were here maybe I could work on her so that she would be easier on you."

P:  "Yeah, that would be swell, but I don't think she would come." [Patient lapses into a sullen silence]

T:  "Well, from what you have told me, I guess she might not see things in quite the same way you do. Suppose she did come; I wonder what she would say about this."

P:  "Oh, she would just carry on about how I do this and I do that, and I don't do this and I don't do that. You'd get the whole song and dance."

T:  I see you are pretty fed up with that, hearing it all the time. I guess you feel there is nothing to it, just empty complaining."

P:  "Yes, . . .well, . . . no. Sometimes she's got a point."

This brief exchange illustrates the beginning efforts both to find out what would need to change in the patient's life and also to test out the degree to which the patient is ready to consider making some changes himself. The therapist's first task is to help the patient become involved sufficiently to understand what has brought him to treatment now and to decide if any treatment is necessary now. If it is, a discussion should follow about what needs to be done, and how. But, as discussed in Chapter 2, the task of engaging the patient sufficiently to begin the therapeutic process may be complicated by the fact that patients approach the first interview in very different ways.

However the patient presents himself, the clinician must make his own assessment of the precipitating circumstances, the patient's response to them, and the degree of urgency, as well as whether or not the patient's response represents a "problem" within the expertise of the clinician. At the same time, he must devise an interim "treatment plan," that is, a way of working with the patient that will support the kind of "evaluation situation"[2] he has in mind. In other words, while we intend the evaluation to be diagnostic, we realize that it may also be therapeutic in effect. The patient will have the opportunity to open up the disturbing "mess" and at least begin to sort it out. In doing so, the patient will experience some degree of change, from slight to profound, and will react to the

---

[2] A term of convenience I constructed by analogy to the therapeutic situation, of which it is a near identical twin.

experience of changing. By changing, I mean that, in the course of the evaluation, the patient will come to see something more clearly, or will feel differently about something, or will perhaps learn a name for what he feels, or will look at familiar matters from another point of view. The therapist will be looking for such a change and will use it to judge the use the patient can make of him, or, more precisely, which of the various aspects of a therapeutic relationship the patient will mostly call on.

If we consider the evaluation not as a separate process but as the initial phase of treatment, we will see that the therapist at least can help the patient with a basic problem: has he come to the right place? Indeed, the patient might require a different form of treatment altogether, one more appropriate to his immediate needs, whether or not he can also benefit from psychotherapy. For example, consider the patient I discussed earlier (Schlesinger, 2003, p. 25) who begged for psychotherapy because her husband suddenly demanded a divorce. She just knew it must be she who was at fault. The therapist suggested that her immediate need was for a lawyer and that when her interests were protected, he would be happy to discuss her need for psychotherapy.

The same principles govern other instances when it is appropriate to offer only emergency care or crisis intervention until the patient can become reasonably settled. Only then should one accept the patient into a more committing, attention-absorbing treatment.

If patient and therapist agree that the patient has, indeed, come to the right place at the right time, they can continue the examination of the patient's current state and background. At the same time, the therapist continues to evaluate how the patient's mind works, how he engages with the therapist, and other matters important to consider before responsibly proposing any kind of treatment, including psychotherapy.[3] He will also have the opportunity to study how the patient engages with him, how quickly the patient becomes involved with him, how ready the patient is to substitute the therapist's thinking (as he sees it) for his own, how "adhesive" or dependent the patient is likely to become, how the patient responds to the feeling of being sympathetically understood, and how he reacts to the ending of the sessions. Of course, the therapist will hold all these observations only as first impressions, but many of them will turn out to be stable characteristics of the patient whereas others may change as a function of the therapy.

---

[3] I assume that other forms of treatment, including pharmacotherapy, will be considered as indicated.

*The Capacities Needed for Success in Psychotherapy*

Most discussions of the desiderata enumerate the same set of psychological and emotional capacities of therapists that patients ought to have in sufficient amount. I put the matter relativistically because hardly any patient completely lacks a given capacity: an excess in one capacity may compensate, at least in part, for a relative lack of another. Sufficiency is a matter for judgment by the clinician. It is possible that a similarity in the patterns of enough and not-enough in patient and in therapist may be responsible in part for the "match" between them that research tells us conduces to success in psychotherapy (Luborsky, 1985; Kantrowitz, 1989). These capacities, too, are best evaluated while the interviewer is observing how he and the patient interact during the interview. I list these capacities as antinomies:

ANTINOMIES
1.  Interpersonal sensitivity versus obliviousness,
2.  Engagement versus detachment
3.  Psychological mindedness versus concreteness
4.  Curiosity versus indifference
5.  Preference for externalizing versus internalizing defenses
6.  Tolerance for regression without giving in to it versus intolerance for regression or readiness to wallow in it
7.  Ability to associate freely versus needing to keep thoughts on track
8.  Sense of humor and ability to appreciate absurdity versus literal mindedness
9.  Interest in how his mind works versus wanting quick results only
10. Activity versus passive orientation
11. Liveliness versus stolidity
12. Belief that possibilities for a satisfying life exist if neurotic difficulties can be resolved versus conviction that life circumstances preclude a more satisfying life[4]

A balanced sufficiency of these capacities augurs well for success in psychotherapy. The clinician will also want to see what the patient does with the material that emerges in interviews during the intervals between

---

[4] I include this desideratum with the caution that, like all the other desiderata, it refers particularly to a terminable therapy, one that foresees the patient's continuing to apply his new knowledge and restored capacities without the continued attendance of a therapist. I do not mean to disqualify people who may need life long therapeutic attention, for instance to preclude hospitalization, or people suffering a terminal illness.

sessions: does the therapy continue between sessions? Hence the advice (if the patient is not in psychoanalysis[5]) to space the sessions widely enough to see how capable the patient is at absorbing and applying what he hears in the material. Thus, I add these questions to the list:

1.  Does the patient reflect on what developed during an interview?
2.  Are there reverberations of the therapy in the patient's life?
3.  Is the effect of the interviews cumulative?
4.  What did the patient do with the trial interpretations offered him?
5.  How did the patient change between sessions, and, most important, does the evidence that he is changing trouble the patient either because it opens him to new risks or threatens the continuance of the therapeutic relationship?
6.  How does the patient enter and leave relationships, as judged from the way he behaves when entering and leaving interviews as well as from his history?

The first four of these questions will help the therapist gauge progress in any therapy, whereas the last two are essential to gauge terminability.

The therapist also will want to uncover the conditions under which the patient can love and work, that is, the degree to which the patient's abilities to love and to work are contingent on special, unusual, or risky circumstances.[6]

It is easier to evaluate all these matters if the therapist allows the patient to function in the initial diagnostic interviews much as he would be expected to do during the treatment sessions, the therapist supplying only the amount of leading and explicit support that permits the patient to experience some of the possibilities of the therapeutic or analytic situation.[7] If the therapist is overly concerned about maintaining control of the interview, and especially if he questions the patient relentlessly or coaches excessively, the interview will hardly yield this kind of information. Even if the patient turns out to be a good candidate for medication and support, or for a behavioral treatment, the therapist will

---

[5] That is in a psychotherapy that expects regression and with a therapist who knows how to make use of and how to limit unneeded and perhaps dangerous regression.

[6] I touch on a sensitive area here. Obviously, personal preferences in object choice, taste, and interest differ widely. The essential issue, when estimating the presence of psychopathology, is whether one's choices are compelled, restricted, or relatively free and whether they involve harm to self or others.

[7] The clinician will have to balance the desire to see if the patient can function with only minimal support against the need of most new patients to feel that it is safe to unburden themselves with an as-yet-unknown therapist.

want to discover how ready the patient is to enter a therapeutic situation in which he will be expected to be an active and cooperative participant.

## Evaluation of Current Status

The evaluation typically will extend over several sessions, preferably spaced at least a few days apart, and will have several foci. I mention gathering and organizing historical and demographic data first because they normally are part of the preparatory "psychiatric" or "psychological" examination, but collecting information is not the most important focus when evaluating a patient for psychotherapy. Recording organized information is a useful byproduct of a diagnostic interview, but is not its main point (Schlesinger, 2003). Although the analytic institute may require a candidate to take a history for the chart, it is more important for the eventual proper treatment of the patient that the candidate use the initial contacts to find out about those several factors and qualities of the patient's current life and circumstances that are essential to know in order to prescribe a mode of treatment.[8] I minimize gathering information for third parties not because doing so unimportant, but because beginners, perhaps out of anxiety, tend to regress to what they were taught in earlier clinical training. Weighed down by responsibility for a patient they do not yet know and understand, they hold the patient off as they try to learn as much as they can—beginning with history taking.

This approach has an undesirable side effect. If, as a first order of business, a therapist makes the patient into a respondent to his active inquiry, he also teaches the patient how he would prefer him to be. Training the patient to be a respondent works against the intention to discover if the therapist can engage him as a collaborator in diagnosing (that is, understanding) his situation. It is preferable to engage the patient in a way that simulates to a considerable degree the anticipated treatment situation. It is much easier to predict accurately how a patient will do in psychotherapy or psychoanalysis if the therapist conducts the evaluation in a situation of the same sort.

Going at the evaluation in this way, the therapist will hear about the patient's history and circumstances as the patient organizes them and understands them, a matter as important as the "facts" themselves. In this way, the therapist will learn far more than he would by attempting

---

[8] I have omitted, of course, the usual clinical concerns for the safety of the patient and others that are part of any responsible diagnostic evaluation that I assume any clinician reading this book will not need to be reminded about.

to extract the demographics and historical data in an exercise independent of the patient's need and purpose to tell about them. As the patient tells his story, the therapist will be listening to evaluate the nature and intensity of the patient's distress and its history and to learn what the patient did previously when in pain or when feeling "stuck." He will, of course, be listening to discern the patient's motivation for treatment, his ability to regress safely, and his ability and willingness to fit treatment into his life.

In the reports of evaluations I have read, several essential issues were neglected, including the patient's conditions for, and the limitations he places on, loving and working; his tolerance for intimacy; his ability and interest in collaborating in the process of exploring how his mind works; and his characteristic ways of beginning, being in, and ending relationships. The last issue, of course, is relevant to how the patient will likely experience being in a therapeutic relationship and how he will anticipate and later experience the ending of therapy when his therapeutic goals have been met.

## The First Encounter

Most therapists develop a bit of patter they use to indicate to a new patient that it is now his turn to disclose why he is here and what he wants. There is nothing magical about any "opener," and it is not usually necessary to employ a standard one; an expectant or receptive attitude or an inquiring look will do. Whether invited to or not, the patient, given the least opportunity, will begin to describe his current life circumstances, especially as they account to him, and might also explain to the therapist, why he is presenting himself for treatment at this time. Probably, and also without much assistance, he will also volunteer such historical material as he needs to explain why things have gotten to their current messy state.

If the patient does not take the opportunity to tell the therapist, who is a stranger from whom he wants help, enough about himself and his purposes so that the therapist can understand him, *that omission is in itself a significant communication*. I must emphasize that an important omission should not be viewed as a lack of communication, or an error, and should not be bypassed or overridden or corrected by directly quizzing the patient to fill in the seeming gap. Through his omissions, the patient may be saying that in some sense he is not ready to begin, perhaps not ready to take responsibility for coming to therapy, possibly not ready to trust the therapist, or possibly that he feels so overwhelmed by his plight that he cannot express himself.

Just as likely, the omissions may honestly reflect the patient's view of his situation. That is, if the patient included the material that the therapist dearly would like to hear, it might raise doubts (in the patient's mind or the therapist's) about the validity of his account. These are only a few of the myriad possibilities illustrating that the patient's embarrassed or downcast silence at this point is a communication to the therapist expressed in the language of action; it might be an unconsciously motivated commentary on a story just told (Schlesinger, 2003).

Conflicting messages often are put in a way that is both highly expressive and minimally articulate, and it is well designed to get the therapist to take on the responsibility of "discovering the truth," of winkling it out of the patient by asking questions. Patients often use this technique to encourage the therapist to ask questions, possibly signifying a wish that he take over, to give his opinion, to offer encouragement. Although the therapist may consider any of these possible alternatives appropriate for the occasion, I propose that he first address the patient's silence, unreadiness, embarrassment, or obvious omissions, possibly by offering a conjecture about what he thinks it might mean. That would be a first effort to help the patient to understand his behavior by putting his acting into words, a form of interpretation. For example:

> Haltingly, a patient tells about his recent life, about when his marriage began to go sour, his dissatisfactions with his wife and his job. As he becomes more and more involved in the telling, the story gushes out. Suddenly, his expression changes; he looks oddly at the therapist and slows down, muttering to himself something the therapist cannot make out.
>
> Tempted to ask the patient to repeat what he was saying, the therapist reminds himself instead that the change might be significant and says, "I think something just crossed your mind that you thought better about saying." The patient looks sheepish and says, "I just knew that if I went on you would tell me that it isn't my wife that's the problem, that I am unhappy about everything in my life, nothing about it is right." He looks expectantly at the therapist, who, after a moment says gently, "I think that idea is not a new one but has come to you before whenever you have tried to figure out what is wrong. Perhaps that is why you decided to come in to see me now."

In that instance, the conjecture was partly correct; the patient did have that thought before. But in the moment that he stopped talking, he also had the idea that the therapist would put the blame for his distress solely on him. That additional idea came out in the subsequent moments of the interview.

The point I want to emphasize here is that a therapist does not have to be certain about what is going on to offer a conjecture, but he must recognize that, by stopping himself, the patient is doing something meaningful, acting rather than failing to act. With his conjecture, the therapist begins to put what is going on into words and invites the patient to join him in finding out why it was necessary for him to stop talking. This act is the essence of interpretation (Schlesinger, 2003).

As the patient tells his story, the therapist will observe that he has a theory, or perhaps several not necessarily concordant theories, about what led inevitably to his current situation. Probably, the patient will offer them without realizing he is doing so. If he allows the patient to take the lead in this way, the therapist will have a good opportunity to learn how the patient understands himself, the premises of the script that he enacts in his life. The therapist will be on the way to constructing a formulation of the patient's situation in dynamic terms (McWilliams, 1994).

At the same time, he will be observing the process developing between them, how the patient engages with him at various times, how eager he is to be understood and also how fearful of being understood, whether or not he can empathize with what a stranger who wants to get to know him needs to hear, and how he deals with the several risks attendant on his becoming involved with a stranger. Does he idealize him, hold him off, devalue him, mark him as dangerous, or all of the above at different times? The therapist also will note that the patient offers some information repeatedly, perhaps oblivious to his repeating himself, and also regularly leaves gaps that the therapist yearns to have filled in.

This last underscores once again that there is much important information in what the patient *omits,* perhaps systematically—not the least, of course, the fact that he omits it. But it may not be obvious how to go about uncovering the meaning of the patient's act of omitting, why he omitted the expected information when he omitted it. This last phrase, too, needs clarifying. All telling (of information) takes place at a particular time and place, for a particular listener, and for a particular purpose. A therapist must respect this relativistic point of view, even as he expects that the account he is told ought to be spontaneous, generated at the moment out of a wish to inform him fully. He should expect that the patient wants to "come clean," or at least that the account he hears is as it occurs to the patient right now.

Occasionally, it will become clear to the therapist that he is being told a well-rehearsed story and that he is only the latest of a succession of captive listeners to hear it. It is a story the patient has told any of his friends who will sit still for it, and in the same way, and with the same weary expectation of being given the same advice—"Everyone tells me that I should. . . ." The therapist who recognizes this quality in the telling can sense that, rather than being treated as a possibly helpful stranger, he is being set up to be experienced as no different from the others; he is to be only the next person in line to offer the same useless advice. As he does with a patient who falls silent, the therapist should address first *how* the patient acts, whether with deliberate silence or with scatter-shot verbosity, and only then, if necessary, turn to the content of the story. For example:

> After sensing that the patient is telling him about a problem for which he already knows all the wrong solutions the therapist says:
>
> T: "Your friends all seem to have heard your story in the same way, and they all offer you the same useless advice."
> P: "Yes, and they just don't understand why I can't do it."
> T: "That's so frustrating, isn't it? [patient nods yes] And yet, when you tell me how awful things are for you, I imagine that you expect I will misunderstand, as all the rest do, jump to the same wrong conclusion, and offer you the same advice you can't use."
> P: [looks startled, turns away and starts to cry] "Then you can't help me either?"

Notice that when the therapist took a tack different from that of the patient's friends, who had jumped in to try to make her story come out differently, the patient reacted by stating tearfully that she too believed there was no solution other than the one she kept turning away from, and so there was no help for her. Recognizing the tugs of transference and countertransference, the therapist instead addressed the way the patient told him her story. He put into words her expectation that, like her friends, he would prove useless. He began to appreciate that, in her view, the story of her life could not have a different outcome.

Her story-telling is a performance. Like the Ancient Mariner (Coleridge, 1798), she acts out her plight with the help of listeners she recruits to play the chorus of ineffectual onlookers. They are to witness her impossible situation, not point to a way to change it.[9] Each time she tells one of her friends this story, it invariably ends with triumphant hopelessness as she demonstrates once again that no one understands and no one can help. This time, however, with a therapist as listener, it might turn out differently.

These initial interactions reinforce the general technical recommendation that, when conducting an evaluation, the therapist need

---

[9] Imagine, for instance, that one of the listeners to the Ancient Mariner's tale had suggested, "Why don't you just put the bird down?"

not, indeed ought not, conduct himself much differently than he would while conducting therapy—making the necessary allowances for the fact that he and the patient are still strangers to each other.[10] The therapist's task is not so much to extract information as to organize usefully what the patient offers freely and to see how the patient tries to relate to the therapist and make use of him. The therapist wants to experience the quality of patient's engagement with him in order to evaluate the initial presentation of transference. The question to be answered is, Can the patient use him as a therapist?

To repeat, the therapist can best make that assessment if he behaves much as he would in a therapy session. He will want to arrive at some initial idea about where in the patient's past the current conflicts might have originated, but it is not necessary to come to any firm conclusion about that beforehand; after all, that is what the psychotherapy in part may be about. In the course of the evaluation, he will gather the information he needs to construct a history, but the history he constructs will be different from a chronology; that is, it will not be a story organized mainly by dates, persons, and places, but a story organized by meanings and patterns of meaning (Schlesinger, 2003).

## Transference During the Diagnostic Evaluation

The therapist-as-evaluator will recognize and accept that the patient feels needy and probably is fearful of rejection. Since he wants to be accepted, he likely will be deferential and willing to conform to what he imagines to be the therapist's explicit or implicit wishes.[11] It is essential that the therapist recognize that the way the patient behaves initially involves expectable transference, and it is not usually necessary to comment on it or interpret it unless it seems to be getting in the way. The therapist should also resist the temptation to take advantage of the transference to enhance his own comfort by explicitly or implicitly encouraging a deferential attitude.

The special point in regard to handling transference during the initial diagnostic evaluation is that there isn't a special point—transference is transference at any point in the processes of diagnosis and treatment.

---

[10] I restate this advice, recalling several patients I saw in consultation who returned to me to complain that the therapist I had referred them to had been so off-puttingly silent that they were unnerved and did not feel they could return to him. Sadly, it takes such feedback for a consultant to prune the list of those he refers to.

[11] Or he might be oppositional or prickly to counter such feelings.

When and how the therapist should "deal" with it, that is, other than by recognizing that it is transference and understanding why the patient has resorted to that mode of communication, depends, as at any other time, on technical considerations, chiefly what the therapist expects to achieve by intervening (Schlesinger, 2003). Unlike the hunter in one of Tom Lehrer's (1953) witty songs, the therapist should feel no inner pressure to "shoot at everything that moves."

## Patterns of Engagement

It is important that the therapist be able to identify the way the patient presents himself and to fit it into the patient's repertoire as he is coming to understand it. That is to say, the patient's presentation reflects both the reality of his actual situation—he has come because of a feeling of need and with a realistic expectation of being helped—and his transference, some expectations and anxieties that belong to a story he is more or less unaware of, one that likely is unconscious and that he will communicate through behavior (including nonverbal behavior). The therapist must call upon his ability to disassemble the patient's presentation so as to be able to respond selectively to one or the other aspect of it. The way a patient engages may have important implications for predicting the course of therapy as well as for when and how the patient will end it. Let us consider some patterns of engagement of new patients.

### Examples of the Ways Patients Present Themselves Initially

In later chapters, I discuss the development and ending of their treatments:

*Example: Mr. A*
The patient has been attending this mental health clinic for several years and was treated by a succession of student-clinicians, each for a year. He came originally with a request for "long-term psychotherapy." He feels better when he is in treatment. There is an odd sense of "emptiness" in his life, and he has been able to fill it most easily by "being in therapy." After the departure of his most recent therapist, he asks to speak to the director of the clinic and tells him, "I don't care about anything but having a therapist who won't leave me at the end of the year." The director recognizes that the several episodes of

"treatment" may have succeeded only in confirming to the patient that he can survive only as a client of the system and fears that he now seems interested only in remaining one. The director does not inquire into what the patient might want to accomplish now or what relation it might have to the "depression" he complained of when he first came; the director prefers to leave those issues to the member of his staff to whom he has assigned the patient.

*Example: Mr. B*
A patient comes for a consultation on the urging of his internist. He wants to know if it is all right if he comes just this once so as to satisfy his physician who tells him he can find no disease to account for his vague aches. His several friends who are "in analysis" have been going to analysts "for years." He is envious of them, especially that they have so much to talk about. He feels excluded from their excited conversations about their so much richer lives. But there is nothing interesting about him, "nothing there to analyze." He would like to be like them, maybe even if it takes being "in analysis," but he is much more fearful that he could become "entrapped" like them.

*Example: Mr. C*
A patient comes to a hospital emergency room late one Saturday night complaining of vague aches and pains. The medical resident examines him and finds nothing obviously wrong; the patient seems to accept this reassurance and gets ready to leave. He says he will call back if he does not feel better the next day. It is obvious from the way he is dressed that he can afford private care, but he says he does not have a personal physician and declines a referral to one.

One of the nurses just coming on duty recalls that he comes in every few months in this same way. Armed with this information, and on a hunch, the resident inquires, in a matter-of-fact but friendly way, about this pattern of intermittent visiting. The patient admits that he is worried about a problem that has been bothering him for years, but it flares up only occasionally. He does not know whether he is sick or not, but when he feels "that way," he feels impelled to come in. The resident inquires further, and the patient adds to his original complaints that sometimes, when on the street at night, he feels dizzy and is afraid he will faint and fall down. It calms him to come in, to sit in the waiting room for a while and then to be examined by a doctor. He prefers the emergency room because he will be seen when he feels the need and for its relative impersonality, which includes the near certainty that, when he returns, he will not have to explain himself to the same doctor again.

The medical resident recognizes that the patient has a psychiatric problem and offers to refer him to the psychiatric ER. The patient at first refuses; he is not "crazy." The resident agrees but adds that there are now good medicines for this kind of symptom. Intrigued but reluctant, the patient crosses the hall to enter the psychiatric ER.

*Example: Ms. D*
The patient has been referred by her best friend, who is "in analysis" with the therapist. "She has told me so much about you that I am sure you can help me too." When told that the therapist has no openings in his schedule now, the would-be patient refuses a referral. She says that nobody else will do for her. She would rather wait indefinitely to be treated by this therapist in whom she already has enormous and unshakable confidence. One might say she feels she already is "in treatment" simply by being on the therapist's "waiting list." During the next months she calls occasionally to let the therapist know she is still interested, but she makes no further demand.

*Example: Mr. E*
The patient calls the clinic for an appointment; he tells the admitting clerk that he cannot sleep, is worried, and is not sure what is going on. He wants to talk to a doctor. He is given an appointment for the following week. He arrives a few minutes late, apologizes, and, ill at ease, sits silently. He avoids eye contact as if uncertain about how to begin. After a few uncomfortable seconds, the therapist breaks the silence by recalling that the patient told the admitting clerk on the telephone that he is worried about himself. The patient agrees hesitantly and says that was true last week. But after calling the clinic, he felt better and thought there probably was nothing wrong with him. He meant to call to cancel this appointment but forgot to. Since he had made the appointment and hadn't canceled it, he thought it would be polite to keep the appointment. He apologized for taking the doctor's time as he did not really think he needed to be here.

*Example: Ms. F*
The patient is a young woman, attractive, well groomed, well spoken, and obviously of considerable intelligence. She comes to the outpatient department of the hospital with an unusual request. With some bravado, she unabashedly relates that she is a prostitute, in her words, "a hooker," a good one, she emphasizes. However, she has a heroin habit that costs her $50 a day to maintain so that she can function, and she can no longer afford it—times are hard. She wants help to reduce her habit to one she can afford, say, to $10 a day. She maintains, despite

the therapist's efforts to discover a more elevated need for treatment, that detox is all she wants. When pressed, she sneers at the therapist as having no idea of what life is like on the street; she has long since abandoned any higher ambition for herself.

*Example: Ms. G*
The patient is a graduate student, successful until now, who feels stuck and unable to finish her dissertation. She has the data for her project in hand, and her advisor thinks she is on to something good that could become the basis of a research program. She tells the therapist at the student health center that, despite her wish to graduate and get on with a career, she cannot sit down to work on her dissertation without feeling sick. When she tries to force herself, she cannot make sense of her findings. She had therapy once before, when she left home for college and felt lost and out of place in the big city university. In a few months, coinciding with entering a romantic relationship, she felt better and ended that treatment.

*Example: Mr. H*
The patient, a hard-working and highly competent lawyer who was just made partner in his law firm, awakens one day feeling that he has been wasting his life. He has achieved his career ambition but suddenly realizes that it really was not his idea to become a lawyer; he does not know what impelled him to keep his nose to the grindstone for so many years only to achieve this dubious goal. Now what?

At work, he struggled against the feelings of dejection, futility, anger, and paralysis for several days. Finally, he confided in his wife when he became fearful because the image of a boyhood friend and college roommate who had killed himself kept coming to mind. She got a referral for him from her therapist, and her husband called for an appointment.

Therapists of any experience undoubtedly have encountered patients who presented in some of these ways. There are, of course, many other patterns, all of which have in common that the patient says or demonstrates that he is in conflict about having come for therapy. The examples differ mainly in how the patients experience the conflict and how they present it to the therapist. We could say that the circumstance that brought each of the patients is much the same as all the others: each patient has a "need" and a hope or expectation that the therapist will understand and do something to help.

The differences among the presentations reflect the various ways each patient mythologizes in unconscious fantasy the history of his fearful/

hopeful reaching out for help and now expresses his conflict in transference. To be of maximum help, the therapist has to be able to read the complex of conflicting messages and respond in a way that respects both the actual and the fantastic elements interwoven in the presentation. This task is complicated, but not as complicated as my description of it may seem to make it, for the therapist does not, indeed cannot, respond to all elements of a patient's presentation at once. He can, however, choose the aspect to respond to and generally will respond first to whichever he considers to be more salient, that is, whichever is "on the surface" (Schlesinger, 2003).

How might a therapist respond to Mr. E who apologized for having come in at all. Having in mind the maxim that the therapist should take the patient's presentation at face value (i.e., its actuality) but not only at face value, the therapist responds:

> T: "Clearly, politeness is an important value for you."
>
> P: "Yes, that's the way I was taught. I feel terrible when I catch myself in a breach of manners. That's why, when I forgot to call to cancel this appointment, I knew I would have to keep it even though I don't need it. Of course, that makes me feel terrible also because, by avoiding one breach of manners, I created another, maybe an even more serious one. I am sitting here feeling foolish while wasting your time, and I'm embarrassed about what you must think about it."
>
> T: "I can see that you took very seriously the lessons in manners you were taught. Indeed, you learned them very well. It is ironic, isn't it, that by attempting to be polite, you feel you committed an even more serious breach of manners?"
>
> P: "Yes, of course. But I expect you to charge me for this appointment."
>
> T: "It makes you feel a bit better when you can pay for your errors. [patient nods yes] But perhaps coming in wasn't an error. [patient looks surprised] When you called for this appointment you did feel you had a need you couldn't handle alone [patient nods yes], but as soon as you called, the need no longer seemed so pressing. [patient continues nodding yes, now showing more interest than chagrin] Then I guess you weren't sure if you had only imagined that you had a problem you couldn't deal with or if it is still there and could come back. [Patient nods yes and looks even more expectant.] "Possibly it didn't cross your mind that your problem became less pressing because you decided to do something about it." [Patient looks surprised.] Actually, you did something effective—you recognized that you had a problem you couldn't handle alone so you called for this appointment. And, not being certain it wouldn't return, you quite properly didn't cancel the

appointment. [Patient smiles as he catches on that there might have been method in his unmannerliness, and he shrugs sheepishly, "I guess so."]

The therapist waits a moment and, as the patient did not pick up the lead, adds, "I gather you wouldn't have asked for this appointment today."

"No," answers the patient with a sense of relief at being understood. "I've thought about what bothered me and it doesn't bother me any more."

"Good," says the therapist, "it must have given you some satisfaction to solve the matter yourself."

"Yes," replied the patient, but in a more drawn-out, pensive way that encouraged the therapist to add,

"I guess you are not completely sure about that. As long as you are here, maybe you would like to review what it was all about and how you managed to put things back together." Since the patient does not yet take the lead, the therapist continues, "The problem seemed serious enough for you to call for this appointment and you are afraid that what troubled you might still be there."

The patient nods as the therapist is talking and interrupts him to say, "You mean it is all right to be here even if I don't have a problem today? [not waiting for a response, he hastens to add] Well, as long as I am here, I might as well tell you what was bothering me last week."

Several things are noteworthy in this continuation of the initial interview. First, the therapist respected the patient's embarrassment at "coming without purpose." He empathized with the patient's feelings, even "normalized" (Schlesinger, 2003) his exaggerated concern as justified by his strict code of manners. He did not challenge the conflicting premises under which the patient was operating, and he did not ask for the information the patient obviously was withholding: why he wanted to come in the first place. Instead, he made it possible for the patient to volunteer that information, if only with the thin justification of not wasting time, "As long as I am here, I might as well. . . ." The therapist did not challenge that rationalization either but prepared to listen to what the patient was now ready to relate. He sensed that if the patient turned out to need treatment, which these early exchanges made likely, he would have to be allowed to get into it in his own way, that is, by backing into it.

I have alluded to several principles of technique along the way including, "Start where the patient is," "Don't get ahead of the patient," "Fit the relationship to the patient," "Identify and deal with the patient's expectations and fears," and, most of all, respect that "the patient is always right" (Schlesinger, 2003). I believe all these principles were respected in the foregoing patient–therapist dialogue, but they are not always as easy to apply as in that interaction.

## A Model of Therapeutic Engagement

I have been casting about to find a fresh image to capture the essence of beginning psychotherapy. When originality fails, one is tempted to plagiarize. After all, the wheel is such a useful device. Why not reinvent it? Thus, to remind you of an earlier discussion (Schlesinger, 2003):

Recall that Freud (1913) compared the beginning of psychoanalysis with the opening of a chess game. His main point of comparison was that it is relatively easy to describe the opening game and end game of chess and the beginning and ending of psychoanalysis, while the middle game of chess and the middle phase of psychoanalysis are too complex for systematic description. In that limited sense, the analogy holds. However, consider that the opening of psychotherapy is really very little like the game of chess other than that both involve two persons. There is nothing in psychotherapy that corresponds to the well-defined chessboard that restricts one's moves in two dimensions and in fixed patterns. And there is nothing that corresponds to the fixed number of chessmen, each with prescribed movement capacities. Most of all, there is nothing that corresponds with the essential purpose of chess, to defeat the other player. In fact, in these several regards, psychotherapy is quite the inverse of chess.

Let us, then, invent a game[12] of "inverse chess" as a model for psycho-therapy (Schlesinger, 1973). In inverse chess, two "players" sit across from each other, perhaps across a desk or perhaps facing each other without intervening furniture. They also occupy a relatively undefined space psychologically. Let us assume the players are meeting for the first time. One of the players thinks he wants something that the other player has, but he is not quite sure what that something is. The other player thinks he may, indeed, have what the other person wants, but he too isn't quite sure what it might be. He knows, however, that he has been able to play games like this with others who approached him in this uncertain way.

Each player has many conversation pieces that he has used when playing other two-person games, but neither player is sure what the value of the pieces might be this time. There are no explicit rules in inverse chess, only a kind of working suggestion that each player move at least one piece now and then when he feels like it. The other player may respond by moving one or more of his pieces in a way that makes sense to him and that he thinks might make sense to the other player.

---

[12] I use the metaphor of "game" not as an activity undertaken for pleasure, but in the formal sense, as an activity undertaken for its own sake and in which the point is to behave in accordance with defined rules and to accept the outcome of following the rules.

Last, we need a purpose for this odd game. The purpose, of course, is not to defeat the other player but, rather, to make the game interesting enough for each to want to continue to play the game at least long enough to find out what pieces the other player is holding and how he likes to use them, that is, for each player to discover what implicit rules of engagement the other player (and himself) is following. Then each will be in a position to decide if it would be worthwhile to continue to play this kind of game for other purposes as well.

The inverted chess metaphor highlights the uncertainties and ambiguities that characterize the opening of psychotherapy, particularly the interest of each party in finding out what he wants from the other and if each is able and is willing to provide what the other wants and needs. These ambiguities and uncertainties refer to the circumstances that bring the patient or, better, that force him to come.

The model has the players getting together voluntarily as they would for a game, but, in at least that respect, it may be misleading. People generally seek psychotherapy as a last resort when they feel they must. It would be safe to say that every patient comes to therapy under some form and degree of coercion. The patient may think it is a good idea for him to come now, but the therapist could safely assume that it has been a good idea for some time and that some event or some new appreciation of old events makes it suddenly opportune to seek help. The precipitating event is not necessarily the cause.

Every patient is in conflict about coming and, when he finally presents himself, is at most only 51 percent present. In part, this conflict reflects that the ultimate "reasons" for his seeking therapy usually have their roots in an intrapsychic conflict of whose details he may be only partially aware. Closer to the surface, his conflict reflects that he is properly uncertain that he has done the right thing by coming, and he is properly uncertain also that the therapist can help. In fantasy, he elaborates his uncertainty to a fear that the therapist might laugh at him, look down on him, be disappointed in him, misunderstand him, or, perhaps worst of all, understand him too well.

To summarize this last situation aphoristically, we might say that, whatever the issues were that led the patient to the therapist's office, once he gets there his immediate problem is the therapist. He is alone in a room with a stranger. He is anxious and wonders if he did the right thing by coming. He does not feel free to leave and is fearful that the therapist will either find him crazy, seriously ill, or dismiss him as not worth bothering with. Thus the first thing the therapist has to help the patient with is the problem that he himself represents to the patient. The "surface" our teachers admonished us to begin at is the transference (Schlesinger, 2003).

It may seem a paradoxical reminder that the would-be helper has become the patient's first problem. But consider that, at the beginning of psychotherapy, the patient thinks he needs something but isn't sure he does. He thinks the therapist may have something he wants, but isn't sure he knows what that something is or whether the therapist really has it. He suspects that if the therapist doesn't have it he won't tell him, and if he does have it he might withhold it. Even if the patient got it, he thinks he might be disappointed. He might find out something he would just as soon not know, for instance, that he really is mad. If he trusts the therapist, he may be abandoned, as he feels he was abandoned by other important persons in his life. Or, if he puts a toe in the water, he may be sucked in and never get out. These dilemmas are typical of the fears, fantasies, and expectations of a patient facing his first appointment. It is an act of high courage for a patient to appear in your office for a first appointment. Is it any wonder that so many of them don't make it? And should we be surprised that after having screwed up courage to keep the first appointment, a few don't come back? (I take up in Chapter 7 the problem of the patient who "drops out.")

### Intimations of Ending at the Beginning

Let us return to the earlier examples of initial engagement to discuss what a therapist might have discerned about ultimate ending from these earliest encounters. I take them up in a sequence that fits better with the points I want to make. First, let us address Mr. A and Mr. E.

Recall that Mr. A presented with a wish for "long-term psychotherapy." Briefly, the patient said that he wanted to be "in therapy" to fill a need in his life that he had not been able to fill as most other people do, for instance, with reciprocal relationships of friendship, marriage, or collegiality. This patient baldly presented his need for what amounted to a replacement therapy.

He regarded the relationship aspect of therapy not as a means to obtain a service, but as an end in itself to repair a deficiency in his personality. The relationship would not be personal but, rather, a kind of commodity that anyone who would stay put could provide.

I put my deconstruction harshly not to set up grounds to reject the patient but, rather, to remind us that something like this demand for relationship for its own sake occurs in most therapies, especially those that go on for some length of time. Usually, however, there is not such an identifiable inflection point at which the therapeutic relationship switches from being instrumental to becoming an end in itself. The several "phases" through which therapy normally passes may be punctuated by alternation between periods of focus on "problems" and focus on how to hold on to the relationship with the therapist in spite of the seeming lack of current need for therapeutic attention.

*Example: Mr. A*

Mr. A came with a request similar to Mr. E's. In this instance, however, the director of the clinic heard in the patient's presentation that the way the clinic had treated him might have been responsible for fostering his tendency to regressive dependency. What might he expect the more skilled staff member to do that a succession of student therapists had not done? Clearly, he hoped that the more experienced clinician would offer the patient a new beginning rather than the "permanent assignment" the patient had requested. Ideally, the therapist would squarely face the problem of induced or fostered dependency and help the patient evaluate not only why he came to the clinic in the first place but also his current life circumstances and what the goal of additional therapy might be. In short, he would attempt, with the patient, to build a potentially terminable therapy.

The staff therapist to whom Mr. A was assigned evaluated the patient's needs, strengths, and circumstances. Seeing no indication for a supportive treatment of indefinite duration, which was the patient's prescription, he tried to focus his attention on a particular difficulty the patient had mentioned, a behavioral trait that kept the patient isolated. With the patient's agreement, they agreed to work on this trait, the implication being that this episode of treatment might accomplish enough so that the patient could go on for a time without therapy.

*Example: Mr. E*

After Mr. E's therapist had helped him feel that, despite his reservations, he had done the right thing by coming in for this appointment, the patient unburdened himself about his "crisis." Once again, he had found himself in a social situation in which everyone had somebody and he had no one. He forced himself to accept the realization that he was a "hollow man" who must purchase relationship in order to feel complete. To him, that was the way it was and there was nothing to be done about it; it would be foolish and frustrating to want more. He then revealed that he had been hospitalized several times but was, when properly medicated, able to support himself and function marginally in society. However, sometimes he "forgets" to take his medicine.

As the therapist hears the patient's story emerge, he begins to consider that an appropriate treatment regimen to keep him functioning at his best might be to offer him a continuing treatment relationship that makes few demands on him and that he can keep alive with relatively infrequent visits for medication checks—a chronic treatment relationship, so to speak, for a chronic condition.

A caveat: I have described a therapist designing a practical solution that could serve the patient and society well; it might avoid repeated unnecessary hospitalizations and also permit the patient to function at his best. But we must not foreclose the possibility, however remote it might seem at present, that in time and with support in a relationship with low demands, the patient will grow and change enough either to reduce his need for support or to become eligible for a more ambitious therapy. In short, although one possible outcome of this treatment is that it might be endless; another possibility is that the patient might outgrow his need for it.

*Example: Mr. B*

Mr. B came with a more obvious conflict about beginning. While fearful of entrapment, he chafed under the severe restrictions with which he felt forced to live and was unaware of the degree to which they were self-imposed. The evaluating therapist helped him to explore these matters in his past and in his current life. He discovered that, while the patient was now shying away from intimate relationships out of a fear of being found wanting, he has not always done so; his reluctance to form relationships began during early adolescence, when his father fell ill and died unexpectedly. The patient also seems to have had a much richer intellectual life than he himself appreciated or credited.

As the patient caught a glimpse of how little he was allowing himself of life, his interest in doing something about it increased. He accepted the recommendation for psychotherapy. As the therapist, who also was trained as a psychoanalyst, came to know him, he inferred that one of the themes guiding the patient's life was that he lived in fear that the little he had would be taken from him and that the more he gathered, the sooner it would be gone. He felt that, like his father, he would sicken and die if he allowed anyone to depend on him. The patient lived on the edge of life and felt able to ward off loss, ultimately death, only by assiduous self-denial. The therapist became concerned, as he gained understanding of this dynamic, that the treatment might not be ended successfully, "successful treatment" being so burdened with dire implications.

*Example: Ms. F*

At the staff meeting to which the therapist presented his findings about Ms. F the immediate consensus was to reject the patient as an antisocial character unworthy of any psychological treatment at public expense. After much discussion to air the unacknowledged value systems of several influential staff members, the staff agreed, though with much muttering, to accept the patient and provided her the period of inpatient treatment she asked for.[13] On admission, most of the nursing staff members were impressed with her serious, business-like adherence to the treatment regimen, which at that time was not pleasant.

The patient was aware of the dissension about her among the staff members. She maintained her dignity and did not try to ingratiate herself with those who disapproved. She clearly wanted to be seen as a model patient who asked for no consideration other than the treatment she requested. She attended and participated in all activities on the ward and, in her individual appointments with her attending psychiatrist, asked searching questions about the possibility of more ambitious treatment.

After about 10 days in the hospital, the patient felt she could manage a $10 per day habit and was discharged. Good riddance, thought the few unreconciled staff members, what a waste of public money. Others were sorry to see her go; she could have done much more for herself.

*Example: Mr. C*

This patient hardly invited concern about ending a treatment relationship; his immediate goal was how to get relief from what bothered him without entering a relationship. He had gone to some lengths to avoid engagement. Nevertheless, and with only a little protest, the patient did accept the referral to the psychiatric emergency room. The medical resident who referred the patient called ahead to alert the psychiatric resident so that the latter greeted the patient in the casually welcoming way the medical resident described and waited for the patient to begin.

The patient preceded telling about himself by repeating the medical resident's "promise" that there are new medicines for his kind of symptom. The psychiatric resident agreed and said that he would like to complete the examination to find out which of the new medicines would be best for him. The resident also wanted to find out the basis

---

[13] Readers familiar with current hospital practice will realize that this example dates from an earlier epoch.

of the patient's skittishness about doctors. Might it imply a condition on the schizoid spectrum or a more isolated fear? The resident also wanted to give the patient enough time to test out his capacity for relationship, so after a brief interview in which he felt he had made a useful contact, he suggested the patient return to see him in a few days when he would be in the outpatient clinic.

In what amounted to an extended evaluation over several sessions, the patient warmed up and began to use the resident as a therapist, revealing for the first time to anyone the experience of abuse he had suffered as a child at the hands of a boarding-school teacher. He also told of his lifelong fear of authorities. He did not mention his initial wish for medicine, and the resident, for the time being, did not raise the subject either.

After a few sessions he had set up on an ad hoc basis, the resident observed that the patient seemed to be using the meetings to understand himself better. The patient agreed, and they formalized the psychotherapy that had already begun, though not yet named as such. Though alert to the possible diagnostic implications of the patient's avoidance of relationships, the resident did not find the stigmata of a borderline personality disorder and, at this early point, did not hear anything that presaged specific problems about eventually ending therapy. He found himself looking forward to meetings with a person who now appeared to be a promising therapy patient.

*Example: Mr. D*
The therapist registered as worrisome the patient's willingness to put off her therapy until he, and only he, would see her. He speculated about the possible dynamic meanings her adamance might have, but all that seemed certain was that, at very least, she valued getting help now less than being his patient some day. At the time, he had no idea why she wanted treatment or what her needs might be. He knew only that what had led her to call him was the example and perhaps envy of her friend. Her extreme, preformed idealizing transference led him to conclude that if he took her into treatment, she likely would have trouble ending it. He reserved judgment until such time as the patient would call again in a few months, as he had suggested to her.

*Example: Ms. G*
The therapist heard the graduate student's story and reviewed the notes of her earlier contact with the clinic. He noted the consistency between the way she had once dealt with coming to the university and her problem now in leaving it. He agreed that she probably could use therapy. He did not anticipate a problem in ending treatment, for

he noted she had quit her first episode as soon as she was feeling better. He thought it more likely she would want to stop again when she had overcome her work inhibition; but, as that was her focal complaint, getting her over it might make for a satisfactory episode of treatment.

*Example: Mr. H*
As the therapist listened to the patient tell about his "midlife crisis," the patient went on without prompting to review his indecisiveness about going to law school. The law was neither his first choice for a career nor even a major interest. Rather, his family had assumed from early on that he would become a lawyer, like his father and grandfather, and thus would continue an illustrious tradition. The issue of compelled choice and buried ambition recurred repeatedly as the patient filled in his history during weekly sessions.

The therapist, who was analytically trained, began to think that the patient was a "natural"; he had begun to associate freely and could listen to himself and use the therapist's mild, as yet nonspecific, interventions as encouragement to continue. The therapist debated with himself whether to continue with the patient on this weekly schedule, which the patient obviously could use profitably, or propose that they set up a formal psychoanalysis.

When after several weeks the patient seemed to slow down and looked inquiringly at the therapist, the therapist observed that the patient seemed to have understood intuitively what would be helpful to him and had gone about it without coaching. The patient laughed and said he had just noticed that he had been "carrying on" as if he knew what he was doing, but, oddly, he was feeling better about himself. He did not feel cornered, as he had when he first called, and could see that some things in his life did make sense. The therapist reviewed what had taken place between them and outlined the choices that were open.

Before the therapist could comment, though, the patient quickly said that he did want to have analysis, indeed had thought about it several times early in his career but had put it off for lack of time. He knew that was partly an excuse; he was afraid that he would want to get off the track he was on and could not face his family as a "drop out" from the career they had picked for him. The therapist agreed that analysis seemed indicated and thought to himself that everything he had seen until now presaged an eventual "ordinary" termination.

# 5

# Endings for "Beginners"

It is a sad commentary on their education and training that many psychotherapists and analysts, even those of some experience, tend to remain neophytes with respect to understanding the natural history of therapy as it winds down and how to evaluate the possibility of ending treatment electively with a phase of termination. The reasons are not entirely, or even mostly, the fault of the individual therapists; rather, they lie in the training system, mostly the public clinics affiliated with the programs in which therapists receive their basic clinical training.

Let us consider the background of this situation. For many years, public hospitals and clinics served mainly medically indigent patients. The better clinics usually were affiliated with the medical schools of universities and served as centers for teaching physicians and members of the other helping professions the skills they need for practice. With or without their consent, the patients were also "teaching material"; they paid for their care, as it were, by submitting to much more poking and prying into their bodies and minds than would be necessary for their care. In that way they provided opportunities for incipient clinicians to learn their skills. With the advent of Medicaid and Medicare, there are few truly indigent patients with no claim on public programs.

Nevertheless, the tradition continues that patients in public hospitals and clinics, and many private and university-affiliated hospitals, are also teaching material. For general health, the system, by and large, serves both patient care and clinician education reasonably well, even though funding mechanisms limit length of stay and restrict the nature of treatment for economic reasons.

In the mental health area, however, particularly in outpatient clinics, the needs of clinician education fit less well with the needs of patients for care. While psychopharmacology has made rapid advances in recent years, it is increasingly recognized that, for many patients, the combination of medication and psychotherapy is more effective than either alone. Also, although all care is delivered in the context of a helping relationship, a patient's acceptance of care and his degree of collaboration with the treatment regimen depends on his and his family's perception of the quality of that relationship.

This dependency is doubly, if not infinitely, truer for psychotherapy. The quality of the treating relationship, and especially the degree of confidence and trust the patient develops within it, are key to achieving positive results (Luborsky et al., 1985; Safran et al., 1990). Confidence and trust in a relationship rest on the expectation that one's interests will be respected and one will not be taken advantage of. In private practice, the expectations that the patient's interests will govern and that the therapist will see the treatment through usually are easily met.

But in the training clinic, despite the good intentions of therapist and staff members (see Pumpian-Mindlin, 1958; Keith, 1966; Glenn, 1971; Martinez, 1989), patients' treatment needs are regularly overruled by the design of the training program. As a result, the patients' expectations of continuity of care are routinely violated, and the clinic accepts these violations as unfortunate but "normal"—just the way things are done. To be specific, clinical training programs assign students to a clinic for a limited time. Psychiatric residents generally are assigned for a year. Clinical psychology students and social work students are generally assigned for a semester, approximately 15 weeks, and these students may be allowed to take off for the spring and fall breaks of their universities. A skilled therapist might be able to complete an episode of psychotherapy within a year, or even within a semester or less. But some training programs influenced by psychodynamic thinking generally do not cultivate that skill; they consider proper psychotherapy to be necessarily open ended, in that way to earn honestly, as it were, its soubriquet "long-term psychotherapy."

Burdened with the wrong expectations that good psychotherapy in principle must be a lengthy affair and that nothing useful can be expected to happen in finite time, an incoming beginning therapist finds that most of the patients assigned to him for psychotherapy are those left behind by members of the previous class. Having had little or no teaching about endings and termination and no clinical experience in ending psychotherapy constructively, like generations of would-be therapists before them, these young therapists are instructed to announce to their patients, as the date for their rotation draws near, that the patients will be "transferred" to someone in the next class. Thus, whatever brought these patients to the clinic in the first place, now they suffer, first of all, from the anticipated loss of the therapist to whom they have become attached.

It is a daunting prospect for the incoming therapist to be faced by an angry patient grieving the loss of his former therapist, who also is a colleague of the new therapist. The new therapist is also burdened by the guilty realization that shortly he too will abandon the patient, if the patient does not leave him first. It is not an auspicious beginning for either therapist or for patient.

It does not take more than a rudimentary social conscience for a beginning therapist to feel guilty about the perceived "necessity" to abandon patients when it is time to go on to the next rotation. Therapists are not encouraged to talk about these painful feelings, and they believe it is wimpish to do so. It has become part of clinics' tradition that rotation is one more tough time in training, and trainees are expected to suppress their feelings and push through it. They are not taught about the principles of ending but only about the administrative measure of "transfer." As their tenure in the clinic winds down, conscientious therapists find it increasingly difficult to face the patients they were once so eager to keep in treatment and then became attached to.

Supervisors have to insist that the therapists tell the patients about their imminent departure while there is still "time to talk about it." But what is there for them to say other than, "I too am going to abandon you, and I feel terrible about it." Hoping that the patients will leave of their own accord, the therapists tend to put off telling them about the impending end. Whether burdened by conscience or not, under these daunting circumstances, the therapist may become so ineffectual that some healthier patients do quit. The more vulnerable ones may regress. Some patients rise to the occasion and reassure the therapist that they know he would never do this of his own accord but is forced by the clinic or by the training program to leave them.

It is part of clinic folklore that around rotation time everything in the clinic is expected to come loose; patients fall apart and some overworked staff members quit. Those who remain grieve the loss of the trainees of whom they have become fond. Administrators who may have come to take this system for granted may think it kinder both to the guilty departing therapist and the grieving patient to support the convenient fiction that the treatment merely is being interrupted; perhaps there will be a few bumps, but then the treatment will continue much as before with the new therapist. This probably is not the first convenient untruth the would-be therapist will have to swallow in the course of training.

And so, the incoming therapist has the unenviable first task to treat the patient for the experience of having been abandoned by his colleague. As a decent and humane would-be helper, he is drawn to identify himself with the abandoned patient and feels angry with the abandoner. He also realizes guiltily, however, that in time he too will repeat the same offense. If he asks for supervisory advice and support, he is likely to be given the implicit suggestion to rely on denial, that is, "That is the way the clinic functions and we have found it doesn't make any difference." How can we expect a young therapist to help the patient with his sense of loss when, even while recognizing that he too will soon be a perpetrator, the therapist appropriately is furious with his departed colleague for putting him in this position? This practice seems designed to breed cynicism.

If the administrators of the clinic wanted to do something about this situation, how might they go about it? Where would they find the supervisors competent to teach about endings and termination? The supervisors likely were trained in the same clinic and in the same tradition, so that they too may never have ended a treatment electively. It is also important, if disheartening, to mention that clinics may have other reasons to encourage this pattern of never-ending treatments. First, just as in private practice, empty slots represent lost income to the clinic, and, second, by encouraging "transfers" they are guaranteed a pool of "clinical referrals" instantly available for the next class.

Further, clinic administrators may think it more humane to "transfer" a patient than to help the newly minted therapist with the difficult task of ending a treatment optimally, by terminating. Of course, it would be ideal if, given the desire to do it and the presence of knowledgeable supervisors, the clinics attempted to teach trainees how to end the treatment of those patients who have gotten enough help and how to interrupt the treatment of patients who cannot yet make it on their own so as to ease their reassignment to an incoming therapist.

At this point when lecturing, I often ask the audience if any of them ever ended a treatment electively in the course of training. I do not recall ever seeing a hand raised.

Although analytic institutes do not have the problem of therapists with brief tenure, they also have difficulty teaching about endings and termination. Analytic candidates typically are taught these subjects in the last year of the curriculum. By that time few, if any, have a case nearing completion, and they generally are still in training analysis. Thus, they have no clinical material to support or test the theory they are taught in class. In my own teaching, I have had to rely on the good will of graduates willing to return to present a terminated case in some detail. A simple solution, which to my knowledge is nowhere adopted, is to delay teaching about termination until the candidate or graduate has completed a case under supervision—preferably after he has terminated his own analysis—and offer the subject as a postgraduate course.

*Teaching About the Ending of Psychotherapy*

When there is an institutional limit to the duration of treatment with any one therapist, the therapist (and patient) should be helped to deal honestly with that fact and to deal with the feelings about it that inevitably are aroused. If you were trained in one of the better clinics, you might immediately protest that you did just that with all your patients: you carefully explained to them, as your supervisor recommended, that you were a trainee and would be on this service and available to them for only a limited period, until say, June 15 of the following year. Searching your memory, you may also recall that most patients, especially the new ones, let that information pass without comment. Perhaps they wondered silently why you thought it necessary to tell them your plans for next year. After all, they just came in to get a little treatment and had no intention of being here that long. On the other hand, the "transfers" hardly needed to be told that you were a "temp," and perhaps they looked away from you, thinking, "He's another one."

It is necessary for incoming student therapists to make such an announcement to fulfill the requirement to obtain patients' informed consent, but a simple announcement does not serve the purpose I have in mind. Consider that the patient newly entering treatment has no idea how he may feel after a while; he has no idea at the outset that he may become so attached to the therapist that this relationship may turn out to be one of the most important of his life. The therapist cannot rely on having made such an announcement to absolve him from guilt when the training program requires that he leave his patients somewhere in the undefined middle of their treatment. Furthermore, is it not presumptuous to announce to a patient one barely knows, at the very beginning of his treatment, that he likely will be unable to obtain the help he needs from the treatment he is about to begin with you and that he may have to go on much longer and with another unknown therapist?

Two incorrect assumptions are built into the scenario that leads to that announcement: First, the dynamic psychotherapy that I presume is being taught imitates psychoanalysis mainly in several of its external characteristics, primarily that it is open ended and generally takes considerable time. A corollary is that the therapist should not expect anything useful to happen in near time. The mode of treatment is likely to be the same for all patients, that is, nonspecific and without any particular focus. The second assumption is there is nothing specific and immediately useful that the therapist can do to help the patient at this juncture, just as there was nothing the departing therapist could have done earlier to preclude arrival at this juncture. Let us test these assumptions.

## Principles of Ending

First, let us agree, for the moment, that we are discussing treatment that can end, that is, therapy that can come to a "natural" end when the patient has resolved enough of the difficulties that brought him into treatment in the first place so that he would not apply for treatment now. I put this definition in the most general form so as to apply to all endable therapies. I want to exclude from consideration at this time treatments that are intended to become continuous, typically treatments for severely and chronically ill patients who may require lifelong medication and supportive care to function out of hospital. Patients Mr. A and Mr. E may be of this kind. In Chapter 6, I return to consider how these ideas may apply to them.

I discussed in Chapter 3 how a therapist can tell where a patient stands in the process of therapy, that is, where he stands with respect to the circumstances that brought him in the first place and where he stands with respect to the possibly different issue with which he is immediately concerned. It is necessary to put matters in this roundabout way because, unlike matters in medical treatment, when the patient has resolved the issue that brought him, he may not feel ready to stop. As I noted, the initial complaint may have been formulated so as to justify consulting a therapist and, like a ticket of admission, once punched is of no further use. Even if the initial complaint was a most troublesome issue, once having resolved it, the patient might say to himself, "If I can solve that one, there are several more I would like to tackle."

It is fair to say that psychotherapy may bring latent issues to attention as well as solve them; one of the effects of a good psychotherapy is that it raises the expectations of the patient. Some patients are content to go on with their lives as before once they come to terms with the issues in the initial problem. Many others, once they have been helped to see how they have misconstructed and misconstrued their lives, are no longer content simply to be free of pain. Recall too that episodes of psychotherapy, organized around troublesome issues or "tasks" that preoccupy the patient, are of variable duration; most therapies will include several. It is essential, as discussed in Chapter 3, that the therapist learn to read the "markers" of task completion that patients present so that they may weigh the possibility that the patient may be ready to stop.[1]

---

[1] Several lists of criteria for terminating analysis have been offered; the one by Rickman (1950) is typical, though it reflects the political sensibilities of that era in regard to heterosexuality and the Oedipus complex. Despite such efforts at systemization, several studies (for example, Glover, 1971) found that most analysts rely on intuition when deciding on termination.

As a supervisor of psychoanalysis, I have noticed a general tendency for candidates to ignore, or at least be reluctant to comment on, indications that a patient is improving. Of course, I do not advise that the analyst congratulate the patient or even comment approvingly on his progress. More usefully, the analyst should be alert to the patient's not mentioning his improvment in some respect, and perhaps comment on that omission.

The usual explanation candidates offer for withholding comment is the wish to "avoid suggestion" or a fear of "gratifying the transference." As a result, and as B. F. Skinner (1938) might have predicted, patients tend to say less about improvement and more about discomfort or pathology; the latter statements nearly always get a rise out of the analyst. However, it is important that the analyst observe, and when indicated, comment on ways in which the analytic patient is changing. He must also listen for the mixed feelings that surely will be present about the positive and negative implications of changing, and he should expect that the patient will always meet the experience of changing with reluctance as well as pleasure (Caselnuovo-Tedesco, 1989).

## Ending Psychotherapy and Psychoanalysis with a Phase of Termination

To illustrate the application of the principles discussed in the previous chapters, what follows presents in some detail the ending of the treatment of one patient of the kind who might present to a student health clinic (Example Ms. G in Chapter 4). She has a problem that is suitable to address with a dynamic psychotherapy and has the capacities needed to use one. This more fully developed illustration and the one after it, about the ending of a psychoanalysis, help to clarify the briefer discussions of how these principles apply to the ending of treatment of patients who require less in the way of work on termination.

*Example: Ms. G*
*Ending the Psychotherapy of Ms. G, a Patient in a Training Clinic*
Recall, this patient came to the student health clinic when she was unable to finish her dissertation. In about two months, with the help of the therapist, she connected her inability to finish her dissertation with her previous funk on entering college. She then was able to recognize that on many other occasions she had experienced minor episodes of the same sort that caused her to put off a developmentally significant step, including the first time her parents offered her a stay

at a sleep-away camp. She came to realize that the prospect of graduating and going on the job market was only the latest developmental step to frighten her. The opportunity to review her history in these terms helped her to put her present difficulty in perspective, and she said she no longer felt anxious about the prospect of working on her dissertation. She did not say, however, that she had actually resumed work on it, nor did she mention feeling the pressure of time that she would likely feel if she were actively preparing to graduate on time.

The therapist reported to his supervisor that he thought she now seemed to keep her appointments regularly more out of politeness than need. She made small talk, picked up topics and dropped them, and commented from time to time that things were fine at home and school. Then she would look at him expectantly. He guessed that she might be waiting for him to dismiss her.

She was fast approaching the number of sessions the clinic allowed students, and he was worried that he had not heard about any progress on her dissertation. But the therapist did not mention that observation to the patient. The supervisor, inferring that the therapist thought he ought to have responded to the patient's expectancy of "dismissal," guessed that the therapist felt reluctant to pick up that cue. The therapist nodded agreement and mentioned, diffidently, that the patient seemed interested in him; she commented on a new tie he had worn one day and asked about one of the prints decorating his otherwise spare office.

He was a bit chagrinned to realize that, although he "sort of knew" that the treatment had lost its focus and was no longer centered on solving any problem, he rather enjoyed the relaxed atmosphere and her friendly attention. He was pleased by "his" therapeutic accomplishment and so was in no hurry to discharge this patient, who was much more pleasant to work with than his other much sicker patients.

He mentally justified his reluctance to pick upon the hints that the patient was ready to end this episode of treatment by thinking that she probably had other problems that shortly would come to the fore. It would be more expensive for her to get treatment for them if she were no longer eligible for treatment at the student health clinic. Without any help from the supervisor, he winced as he saw through his own rationalization. He added that he was confident that, if she thought she needed more treatment, she knew how to obtain it. Nevertheless, he was not certain how to make use of this new view of the process.

With the supervisor's help, he arrived at a plan. When he next met with the patient, he found an opportunity to remark on her satisfaction with her restored ability to work on her dissertation. She responded that she indeed was pleased and, for the first time, reported that she had resumed work on it and detailed how well the project was getting on. She expressed her thanks, fervently, almost tearfully, the therapist thought, for the help she had gotten from him. For a moment, her thanks disconcerted him and almost diverted him from his plan to bring up the possibility that she might be ready to end. He felt it would be ungracious to disturb the warm atmosphere in the session by saying anything that would imply that he wanted to be rid of her. Then, too, he had a thought in the back of his mind that if he were to suggest ending, she might relapse.

Pulling himself up mentally, he reached for a suggestion the supervisor had made and joined her in appreciating that she had made good use of therapy. He added that he guessed that she must think that she had accomplished what she had come in for. The patient's face darkened as she agreed, haltingly, that she certainly had thought about it and wondered how much more therapy she might need. Yet she had been afraid to raise the question because her work inhibition might come back. What then? Would she have to come back? Would the therapist even want to see her again if she failed to live up to his expectations?

Both therapist and patient seem to have similar problems about ending the treatment. First, because of their attraction to each other, they are reluctant to face that what they came together to do has been done. Second, each worries that the good result they have obtained will be ephemeral, and they will disappoint each other. Finally, for the patient there is the possibility—the dark underside of that fear—of a wish to hurt the therapist for being willing to let her go. It is through this array of fears that patients and therapists alike usually express their anxiety about ending a therapeutic relationship.

As the supervisor had predicted about the patient (and similarly for the therapist as well), once she recognized and named her fear openly, its intensity diminished. She then could link it to the "willies" she had experienced when getting ready to leave home for college, when she worried about who would take care of her if she got sick among strangers. In the course of discussing her past and present concerns, she also admitted, by the way, that she enjoyed the relationship that had developed with the therapist; he was not that much older than she, and she had fantasized that he also felt attracted to her. She added that her boyfriend, too, wondered why she was still in treatment.

The patient then supposed, as the therapist had hinted, that it probably would be appropriate for her to stop. With visible relief, she agreed with the therapist's suggestion that they meet two more times "to see how things go." As the therapist discussed with his supervisor, that suggestion expressed his reluctance to stop, rationalized by a concern that, if they stopped at once, the patient might "regress."

In the next meeting, the patient reported that things were OK but that she had had a restless night or two and a dream she could not quite remember; she thought it might have involved her mother's taking ill and the patient's having to return home. With the therapist's help, she could relate it to the fear that something might come up so that she would not be able to graduate. With a little laugh, she said that sometimes she thought she would rather be young again and at home instead of about to graduate from college and having to find a job and also having to decide whether to build a life with her boyfriend. Patient and therapist agreed that, while the treatment had helped her with the acute problem of her inability to finish her dissertation, it had also linked that acute problem to larger developmental issues that remained troublesome. She felt more ready now to finish school and agreed that some day she probably would want to resume treatment. She now realized that therapy was the way to work on problems that she could not handle alone. For the time being, however, she would do better to concentrate on finishing her schooling.

In the second of the two additional meetings they had scheduled, she went over much the same ground. About halfway through the session she seemed to run out of things to say. With a laugh, she guessed she had just come to the end. The therapist, having regained his courage, joined her in that impression, and they shook hands to say good bye then without waiting until the scheduled end of the session.

There is much to comment on in this example, not the least that the therapist's disinclination to stop meeting with the patient mirrored the patient's own fears. Each was afraid to bring up the obvious fact that the patient had already accomplished what she had come to do and that their meetings had drifted from the original therapeutic intent. In this instance, it was enough for the therapist merely to raise the issue to help the patient face her fears that if she were to acknowledge she was no longer "sick," she would have to stop immediately, and that if she stopped coming she might fall ill again.

*The Ending of the Psychoanalysis of Mr. H*
The issues that marked the ending of the dynamic psychotherapy of Ms. G also permeated the ending of the psychoanalysis of Mr. H. By current expectations of duration, this patient's treatment was relatively

brief; the analysis lasted a bit less than three years and ended when he felt satisfied by the changes he had made in himself and his life.

Looking back on his life, he recognized that he had entered the "family business" of law out of resentful obligation, that he felt he had no choice in the matter. This personal myth made it impossible for him to consider that he might have chosen the law for himself if he had had the opportunity, that is, the inner freedom, to do so. Indeed, although the family's hopes for him rationalized his feeling that he had been coerced into the field, he could not call on coercion to account for the way he had applied himself so assiduously to his studies that he made *Law Review;* or that he had graduated at the top of his class; or that he had been offered a place in a prestigious firm, although the family firm also wanted him to join it.

The crisis that brought him to analysis turned out to be a spasm of conflict derived from the myth based in unconscious fantasy that, because his family had forced him into it, he had to experience working at the law as an onerous duty. It had become a matter of pride and personal definition that he was only doing his duty and did not enjoy his work. Additionally, if he permitted himself to enjoy working, it would mean that he had sold out his sense of social justice and that his lifelong, principled objection to coercion was not a serious one. Enjoying his work would also puncture the fantasy that he could take revenge against his father by being miserable in his career while secretly indulging a masochistic fantasy of submission.

Yet it became increasingly difficult for him to deny the growing realization that, in fact, he did enjoy aspects of the job and looked forward to getting on with the projects assigned to him. He rewrote his job description to take on the firm's obligation for pro bono work, work he fully enjoyed and that gratified his wish to be for the underdog. He found that he could perform public service in addition to taking on enough remunerative work to rise in the firm, to become one of its "rainmakers." When he stopped fighting himself, he found he could do both jobs and still have time for his family. Under his leadership, the firm won national recognition for its socially relevant contributions. His family life had always been reasonably good; at least it was peaceful if not altogether fulfilling, and it became better.

His wife, who was not a complaining sort, had sought psychotherapy for a sense of failure as a wife. She felt she had become an appendage to a career her husband despised, harmful to him if she tried to help him, and useless if she did not try. As he changed, so did she. She began to expect more of him and was pleased that he willingly provided it. They spent more time as a family; her husband and she were gratified to discover that he enjoyed being a parent. As the children spent more of their time at school, his wife decided to resume her own interrupted career and applied to law school.

Meanwhile, back on the couch, the patient continued to associate unabated, coasting along.[2] The analyst noticed that the patient's associations followed their familiar path, but there was little "bite" to them; there was a relative lack of tension or urgency in the way the patient spoke and the minimal tension of expectancy evoked in the analyst. The analysis had settled into predictable patterns and seemed no longer to be serving an external purpose; apparently, it moved along on its own momentum. While the patient's life was now full, with little time for the golf he once had liked to play, he gave no direct indication of impatience or resentment about the amount of time the analysis took out of his week. For his part, the analyst had long hoped that someday he would have a patient who would arrive at the ideal state of analyzing for analysis' sake. Sadly, he feared that, in this instance of his hoped-for ideal case, the analytic process was not "deepening" on its own; the material was familiar and the patient could do the little analyzing that might be necessary. He seemed to have little need for help from the analyst.

For the last few months, the analyst had had a nagging sense that he was overlooking something. He reviewed his notes and searched his memory until he realized that he was looking for reasons to continue the analysis, that he was loathe to give up this patient. He tried to recall if any of the issues that had come up earlier in the analysis had been dropped short of being worked through sufficiently, and he tried to recall if any potential issues he had noticed had been bypassed. His review yielded the impression, one he reached with some regret, that probably they had done enough analyzing for the time being. He decided to test his hunch.

At the beginning of the next analytic week, to allow time for the patient to react, he looked for an occasion to bring up the idea of ending. In this new frame of mind, he listened to the patient's associations in a new way. He realized, to his chagrin, that the patient, by the very predictability of his associations and the lack of tension that had caught the analyst's attention, might have been conveying his own sense that he had done enough. So there was nothing new for the analyst to listen for; it was all there and had been there for some weeks, maybe longer. The patient had been telling him, and also hiding from him and from

---

[2] I present the following material as if in a single session although the actual time span was several months.

himself, that he, too, was aware that he had done what he had come to do but nevertheless was reluctant to give up all that the analysis had come to mean to him.

The analyst noted that the patient had opened by associating to the latest events at the office. The patient now understood what was going on as the law partners agonized in their familiar way about whether or not they should do what everyone knew had to be done about some arrangements at the firm. He found himself in the comfortable position of "going with the flow"; he let them deal with their anxieties about change. He was proud that he felt no need to intrude on their dithering or to belabor that they were ignoring obvious matters. If they wanted to deal with their problems in that way, why should he care?

With some discomfort as he realized that he, too, had been slow to catch on to the obvious, the analyst contrasted the metaphoric reference to the analytic situation with the odd way the story ended, as if the partners sparring over irrelevancies while ignoring the obvious would not affect the patient and the rest of the firm. The analyst commented on the patient's contentment about seeing what obviously was going on but not feeling it necessary to "rub anyone's nose in it" (using the patient's idiom); the patient could wait until the powers that be figured it out for themselves. The patient agreed, seemed a bit flustered by the implied compliment, and guessed that he had become more sensitive to interpersonal matters.

His associations led away from the office to matters at home. Their oldest daughter was struggling over whether to attend a college here in the city that had accepted her, a choice that would allow her to live at home, or to take up acceptance at a research university some distance away. Recalling his own resentment at believing that his family had compromised his right to choose a college for himself, he tiptoed around that issue and took it up only when she brought her worrying about it to him. He and his wife agreed not to advise her but to let her make up her own mind. Still, he was aware that his daughter knew full well what he and his wife preferred her to do.

As he listened, the analyst now heard how the patient's associations were organized by the same "ending theme" as they dipped into in each venue of his life: things are coming to a head, an obvious decision has to be made but one should not force anyone to do what sooner or later she would come to realize she had to do (Loewald, 1988; Greenson, 1992). The analyst commented that there seemed to be consistency in the patient's outlook as he reviewed matters in the various areas of his life. He mentioned the unifying theme. The patient remained silent for a minute or so, clearly reflecting on the analyst's words. When he resumed, his tone was reflective and a bit sad as he said he had just gone over things and agreed that, everywhere he looked, someone was putting off doing something that had to be done. There was something sad about it, but only sad; there was no tragedy involved.

He added that he guessed he had been thinking off and on that it was getting to be close to the time to begin to think about ending his analysis. He had had that thought from time to time in recent months but always had put it out of mind as premature. He reminded the analyst that he had always had a tendency to get ahead of himself and he did not want to rush this decision. The analysis was too important to tamper with, and he did not want to do anything to spoil it. The analyst remarked on the contrast between his current attitude and his attitude when he began the analysis, when he went at it as if he knew exactly what he was doing. Now that he had been at it for some years, he was afraid he would make some big mistake and spoil it.

The patient caught the absurdity in this comparison but confessed that it was, indeed, the way he felt—with one misstep now, he might ruin it. The analyst kept silent to allow the patient to associate further to this puzzling state of affairs. Finally, the patient said, "I guess I am anxious lest I mess up. Things certainly are better in my life and I have gotten much more out of the analysis than I had hoped for. In fact, when we began I felt hopeless that you could do anything for me; I was in a cul-de-sac and there was no way to turn. It just occurs to me now that I have no idea why things are better; they just are, and if I stop coming, it all might collapse."

Now that they had faced the previously avoided idea of ending, the analyst relaxed and let the patient take the lead again. His associations went through their familiar paths but now were informed and organized by the patient's awareness that he both wanted to leave and get on with his life and was fearfully reluctant to give up coming to his sessions. He then mentioned for the first time how much time attending his sessions took out of his day, and yet he felt that he would like to stay on forever.

He arrived by himself at the awareness that his way of referring to "the analysis" both fit with the magical idea that it was a disembodied procedure that protected him from harm and also made it less necessary to face the fact that he felt love for his analyst. He mentioned that this admission was embarrassing not only because of its homoerotic implications but also because only recently had he come to see his father as a broader and more complicated figure than he formerly believed and that he had discovered he also felt love for him. Mostly, he viewed the analyst with respect but also had draped him with transference from the deeply resented father, whom he viewed as having imposed his will on him.

As the patient continued to analyze, the sessions no longer seemed predictable. Much of the content of the material was familiar, but infused with tension derived from the patient's wish/fear about ending. Although the material wound through familiar sequences, the analysis itself seemed to have taken off again with new vigor. New interactions appeared among the old themes and, as the patient looked at familiar ideas from this new vantage point, they acquired new significance. It was as if the story of his life, which he had been over so many times and so wearily, now became fresh. It was a great discovery; the new recollections he added to old memories convinced him that he had once felt he had the exclusive love of his father and that he also had loved him. How could he have retained only the memories of resentment?

He also discovered that, as he had felt with respect to his father, he was concerned that he would disappoint the analyst if he found a gratifying career outside the analysis. In addition, he was surprised to discover that he was concerned that if he left the analyst, the analyst might feel abandoned—a fine way to treat the one who had done so much to free him from the shackles of neurotic subservience and rebellion against his father. He certainly owed his analyst a debt of gratitude, one that could be repaid only by his remaining with his analyst/rescuer, he believed.

Once impelled by the analyst's few comments about the patient's metaphoric references to things being ignored that had to be done, the patient seemed able, with little help, to continue the working through of offshoots of his unconscious fantasy. As the analyst observed the patient analyzing, he felt tempted to intrude, to tie up things just a bit more, to make matters even more clear to the patient, to lecture about some of the "textbook" aspects of the process. Taking hold of himself, he checked his impulse to meddle. He recognized in it a transference toward the patient, a wish to preserve his former importance in the patient's life and saw also a bit of envy about how well the patient was doing.

Looking back on the course of the analysis during the most recent months, he realized that he had perhaps awarded himself too much credit for beginning the termination phase with his several subtle but effective comments. He felt chastened to realize that the patient had been moving toward terminating in his own way for some months, though not voicing all his associations, and that he had not picked up on what the patient was doing until the patient made it obvious. While he felt a bit deflated by these self-observations, he found that accompanying the patient on this last phase of their work together strengthened his confidence in the power of analysis, especially when the analyst is careful not to get in the way of the patient.

The analyst noted to himself that, while the patient clearly was involved in working through in the manner of a "classical" termination, neither of them had brought up the matter of the date when they might stop meeting. He felt a twinge of alarm as if he had been overlooking that all this work of termination might have been only a theoretical exercise. He had planned, as he had been taught, to allow sufficient time for termination. But how long would that be? And when should that time start? Should he set a date at all, or just let matters proceed "naturally" (Goldberg and Marcus, 1985)? Just as he was about to raise this issue with the patient, the analyst stopped himself with the familiar mantra, "Why now?" Why did he suddenly feel it urgent to raise the practical matter of setting an ending date? He recalled then that the patient, on several occasions, had referred in passing to his wife's wish to take an extended vacation next summer before beginning her law studies.

Recognizing the source of his impulse to intrude, the analyst decided to wait until the patient again alluded to his wife's wish. He commented that the patient had mentioned his wife's vacation hope several times recently and had given the analyst several opportunities to consider its implications and the impediments to fulfilling it. The patient laughed as he caught the import of the dry way the analyst had put his comment and admitted that he would prefer to put the whole matter of ending on his wife—or on the analyst. However, he, too, had been thinking about ending. As the vacation would mean a long interruption, it would be a logical and convenient time to stop. There would be at least six months to work toward ending before he left on vacation.

The analyst first noted that the complicated way the patient had put matters seemed to express his reluctance to raise the question of when to end the analysis. The patient spoke next of his mixed feelings about stopping and the way he had initially withheld encouragement of his wife's wish for a "last vacation" before beginning law school. He felt that his withholding attitude was niggardly, for he was all for her ambition. Indeed, the process reminded the analyst of how the patient had sounded when he first agreed that he too had some thoughts about ending. He realized that the patient needed to work through this decision once again in the context of setting a date.

Several sessions later, the issue of his wife's wish for a vacation came up again and the patient asked the analyst directly for the first time what he thought about the plan to end when they went on vacation. The analyst then reminded the patient how weighty a matter it had been even to consider ending the analysis, how ending had remobilized all the major themes of his analysis to be worked through once again. He thought it was, indeed, time to consider when to stop but suggested that the ending and the vacation were separate matters. To tie them together for convenience would minimize the importance of ending, making it a "might as well" kind of decision. The patient agreed that it would be ideal to decouple the two events but that coming back from a long vacation to resume analysis only to end it shortly thereafter did not seem to make much sense to him. The analyst agreed that it would not make much sense to interrupt the analysis for a vacation and then resume for an expectably short time.

The patient was silent, and, from his movements on the couch, the analyst sensed he was uneasy. The patient broke the silence, "You mean I could stop before going on vacation?" Now the analyst was silent. The patient seemed to brood silently for about a minute, an unusually long silence for him. He then broke the silence by asking querulously, "You want me to leave right away?" The analyst commented on the patient's change of mood, and the patient snapped at him, "Damn right, I feel you blindsided me. I thought it would be my decision when to stop and now you took it over. It's the last thing I would have expected from you."

Momentarily disconcerted by the vehemence of this usually reserved and polite patient, the analyst thought to himself, "This is what has been missing: the termination has been all too smooth and reasonable." He waited a few minutes for the patient to continue his angry reproach. When it was clear that the patient had lapsed into sullen silence, the analyst hoped to help him resume by commenting, in a matter-of-fact tone, "I blindsided you."

"Yes," the patient snapped, "I thought I was following the plan and arranged for a decent ending since we wanted, that is, *she* wanted, a long vacation, why not combine them?

"Indeed, why not combine them," echoed the analyst.

The patient went on in a resentful tone, essentially repeating himself about having been taken over.

The analyst agreed, "You certainly seem to have been taken over. I want you to stop your analysis, and your wife wants a long vacation. Why not combine both demands and get them over with at once?"

The patient was silent, but now seemed to the analyst to be more reflective than sullen. He started to speak several times but stopped himself before uttering any words. The analyst commented, "You are having a hard time saying what you think."

The patient replied in a bemused tone, "It's more that I don't know what I think. The way you just put it sort of repeated what I had just complained about, but when you said it, it sounded altogether different. All of a sudden, I realized that I felt that I was following your plan and my wife's plan; none of it was my plan. And yet, that's nonsense. I have been thinking for months that I could get along quite well without analysis; I've really gotten from it everything I need and still it takes up so much of my life. But when you said that about not coming back to finish here, it felt like a flashback of having my wishes vetoed. Of course, it wouldn't make any sense to come back from a long vacation for sort of a ceremonial windup of the analysis.

"But when it occurred to me that I could stop sooner, my heart sank. I just knew you were telling me without saying so that you want to be rid of me. In that moment, I felt just as I did when I took the train to law school. They all came down to the station to see me off. The train was late, of course, and my father kept looking at his watch impatiently as if he were restraining himself from shaking it to make the train come sooner so that he could get to his golf game. It flashed through my mind at that instant, 'He doesn't want me to be just like him; he just wants me out of the house.'"

The analyst commented, "That is the thought that brought you into analysis."

"Yeah, that's crazy. Haven't I gotten rid of all that? Has nothing really changed?"

With that exchange, the analysis resumed. Setting a date to end could be viewed as a simple but necessary arrangement, but, rather than being a final or semifinal step, it actually ushered in another episode of analyzing. All the familiar themes of the patient's development were touched on again, this time in the context of ending; and the conflict of choice versus coercion once again appeared as the central dilemma, no longer controlling, but not yet expunged either (Ekstein, 1965; Miller, 1965).

As the planned vacation was still five months away and considering all his other obligations and the changes in his schedule that a long vacation would require, the patient proposed a date about three months off, a Wednesday, midway through the analytic week so as not to have the end coincide with the weekend break. He figured it might take that much time to see how a definite plan to stop would go down, and there would be enough time afterward to see how not coming any more might feel. The analyst agreed that it seemed to be a reasonable plan.

As the analyst expected, the patient was able to analyze in this penultimate phase; the anger and resentment that accompanied his willingness to accommodate to the wishes of others appeared in his dreams and in an occasional daydream. Also, after a while, as the analyst expected, the ending date the patient had chosen, which he had put as far in the future as he could without impinging on packing for the vacation, now seemed to be too distant, so far off that the patient wondered how he would fill the time. He felt he had covered all the bases; his mind was on things at work and at home. He no longer was eager to understand; he was more in a doing mode.

The analyst said, "It sounds as if you would like to revisit the date-setting."

The patient lay motionless for a few moments and then said with a laugh, "Of course, that was what was on my mind. Why did I put it off so far? But now, when you sort of hinted that we could actually move it, as if the date weren't carved in stone, it scared me. I don't think I want to give up any of my time."

The patient was struck by how easily his anxiety about ending could be revived, and again this realization fed another episode of analyzing, this one lasting only a couple of sessions. He expressed appreciation that the analyst had not taken him up on his desire to stop earlier than the date he had first chosen. He knew he could stop sooner if he wanted to, but he would rather stick to his original decision and see what came up in the remaining weeks if he felt no pressure either to act or to refrain from acting.

And so it went. With little help from the analyst, who still had to restrain himself from intruding, the patient continued to analyze but with a degree of detachment that the analyst understood as identification with the role of the analyst even as he experienced fully what he was describing. When he was sure of his impression, the analyst commented on his observation. The patient confirmed that he had noticed it, too, and that his ability to observe himself now lacked the self-criticism that he formerly felt was an inevitable part of self-observation. He was now looking at himself with friendly interest rather than looking for flaws.

The patient then confessed that for some months he had been nurturing a plan to find some way of thanking the analyst for the years he had invested in him and for giving him so much more than he could have thought to ask for. He really had had no conception of what analysis could do for him, and even now could hardly recapture the hopeless frame of mind he was in when he began. He realized that while the impulse to give something to the analyst was real, no material gift could express what he had to say, and so he stopped thinking of how to find an adequate one. He would just have to live his life in a way that reflected what he had obtained from his analysis.

He added, in that same spirit of confession, that had some twinges of anxiety as he tried to rehearse how it would go on that last day. He had to stop himself from asking the analyst for reassurance that if he were to discover, somehow, that stopping so soon was an error, he could call for another appointment. He wondered how soon the analyst would fill the hours he would leave open. Would it even be possible for him to return? Wasn't he just slamming the door on himself? What if he did need more? He didn't wait for the analyst to answer, although the analyst had no intention of interrupting this process. The patient added that he recognized that old anxiety for what it was; he realized that there was no way to leave without feeling some anxiety and that once again he was vulnerable to feeling that he could own what he had obtained only if he stayed under the protection of the analyst.

In this spirit, when the end of the last session on the stated day arrived, he stood up, reached for the analyst's hand and shook it firmly and left, but not without first wiping his eye. The analyst too had some moisture to deal with and he was glad that he had an empty hour to follow. He did not feel ready to see another patient immediately.

What can we learn from this example? Note first that the analyst was able to recognize when the patient had done enough analyzing for the time being. He did not have in mind any ideal of a "thorough analysis" to which he and his patient would have to subscribe as a matter of principle. Ending is a practical matter; a point of diminishing returns had been reached (Menninger and Holzman, 1973). The indications for ending came both from within and from outside the analytic setting; psychoanalytic values and practical concerns converged to suggest that it was time to think of ending. The analyst's governing concern was to assure that the style of ending would be an analytic termination.

Once he understood that the patient had been signaling that he had done enough, the analyst helped the patient analyze his conflicting feelings about ending and, in doing so, came to realize that he also had to work on his own conflicting feelings. Note that the analyst dealt with the matter of setting a date for ending, sometimes thought to usher in the ending phase, as properly a late concern, almost anticlimactic in nature. As the patient considered the possibilities and dithered about the date, the analyst saw that the patient was expressing anxiety about ending itself. Thus, the analyst did not attempt to firm up the date but left the initiative in date-setting to the patient, allowing him to use this "mechanical" or "structural" matter to serve as a metaphor for the process of ending itself.

As the analyst expected, each time the patient came to some understanding of his mixed feelings about ending, he found the impetus to resume analyzing with a new purpose. In each of these increasingly brief recyclings, the "material" circled through its familiar course as the patient worked through the same underlying issues. Each time, some new idea, or alteration of an old idea, emerged to enrich the patient's understanding of his history of events, relationships, and states of mind and to reward him for persisting.

When the analyst became aware that the patient was attempting to mitigate the pain of separating from the analyst by proposing to end when he and his wife, mainly his wife, wanted to take a vacation, the analyst did not immediately interpret, in the sense of naming, the motive he suspected had inspired this plan. Instead, he opened a process of inquiry that eventuated in interpretation merely by his speaking of the desirability of keeping the ending of the analysis as a unique event. The patient confirmed that, for him, keeping the vacation and the ending together had become overridingly important, although presumably merely for reasons of convenience. To deconstruct his stance, one might put it as, "The analysis is actually over. There is nothing more for us to do than to go through the little exercise of ending it formally. After all, it wouldn't be practicable to return after an extended vacation for the few sessions it might take for the relatively trivial matter of ending it."

That practicality hardly was the issue became abundantly clear when the analyst hinted that they could decouple the ending and the vacation by stopping sooner. Then the hurt and anger the patient felt because he believed he was being forced to separate from the analyst, who, the patient thought, wanted to be rid of him, emerged full blown and opened another brief episode of analyzing. He had previously managed to ward off this more or less unconscious conviction with the "might as well" solution. The analyst allowed the patient to experience fully both his pain and his doubt about ending and his dire suspicions about the analyst's motives. The analyst did not interfere with the way the patient now experienced him in a paranoid way, nor did he offer explanations to "clarify matters." Rather, his guiding purpose was to intensify what the patient was feeling, or at least not to diminish the intensity of his feelings. In that way, the analyst maintained the same position during the ending phase as he had during the rest of the analysis.

Once again, the patient worked through the depth of his attachment to the analyst and its resonance with his attachment to the image of his controlling father. He took this opportunity to reanalyze the fantasy that he owed his status in life and his gains in the analysis to his father and now to the analyst. This reexamination was the central issue in terminating.

Even in this extended narrative of the ending and termination of an analysis, I have omitted much. I have focused on the experience of the patient and only alluded to what transpired in the analyst's mind other than his technical decisions. In Chapters 7 and 8, I discuss what has been called the "involuntary participation," the transference and counter-transference of the analyst, and how they impinge on termination of analysis (Menninger and Holzman, 1973).

## The Ending of Treatment for Patients A–F

These are patients who mostly did not become so intensely involved in a relationship with the therapist as to require extensive efforts to work through the meaning of separation and its implications for maintaining the gains of therapy. It is not clear whether the lesser degree of involvement reflected their personality organization or the format of the therapy. Note, however, that the therapist of one patient (Ms. D) feared she might become excessively involved, and so adopted a treatment format he thought would minimize that likelihood.

### The Ending of the Psychotherapy of Mr. A

The staff member who accepted this referral agreed with the director of the clinic that the clinic had exploited the patient's acceptance of the role of "practice patient," one who submits, however resentfully, to repeated "transfer" to a new and inexperienced therapist. He realized that by socializing the patient in this way to remain a client of the system, they had laid a poor ground for a psychotherapy aimed at change. The staff member took some encouragement from the fact that the patient finally had rebelled effectively against the latest transfer. The staff member guessed that the patient must have gained some sense of personal agency from the several episodes of treatment. He hoped that, with the offer of a therapy that would not be under training auspices, the patient could join in building a focused therapy that, in time, might arrive at a planned ending.

The new therapist also believed that the outcome would depend further on the patient's ability and willingness to envision the potential rewards for changing his outlook on life versus the actual costs of settling for a dependent and victimized position. He explored with the patient several possible intermediate goals for such a treatment and settled with him on one that seemed to the therapist to be easiest to achieve.

A therapist of any experience will be skeptical about whether this patient's seeming acquiescence to the proposal of a presumably goal-limited, if not time-limited, treatment would "stick." Indeed, as it turned out, the patient agreed simply because he felt it would be the only way to remain at the clinic. However, the staff member was a skilled therapist and directly challenged the patient's fear that making progress would threaten his tenure at the clinic.

After making this new beginning, the therapist was then able to interest this reluctant patient in looking at one of the issues that they had identified, the self-defeating behavior patterns that had been impairing his social life. When the patient grasped how his odd behavior repelled prospective friends, he found that he was able to modify his approach slightly and met with some success. Feeling newly armed with improved social skills, he accepted the therapist's suggestion that, in addition to his psychotherapy, he consult the clinic's social worker for help in accessing other community services that specialize in adult activities. Before long, he expanded his social life so that he no longer felt confined to spending his after-work hours alone in his apartment. He also developed a grudging respect for the therapist, who had refused to write him off, as he himself had done, as unable to change.

His initial success at negotiating encouraged the patient to raise his expectations of psychotherapy and immediately afforded the therapist an opportunity to address Mr. A's fear that he was only being "jollied out of his right to treatment."

During the next several weeks of these negotiations, the therapist tested out his earlier impression that, despite their initial success, the patient's sense of connection was less with him than with the clinic as a place of refuge (Reider, 1953). After several more such "minor" successes, the patient agreed with the therapist that it might be useful to "take a break" to see how things might go without therapy for a while to test his ability for independent living. With the therapist's agreement to remain available, he hesitantly agreed to interrupt his psychotherapy with the proviso that he could return if he felt he needed to. With the promise that he could return if necessary, the patient showed little distress about a leaving and seemed almost eager to try his wings in the community. He needed little of the working through we associate with termination.

> The patient's "break" from treatment lasted about two weeks; he called, not presenting himself as an emergency, but rather wondering if the therapist would have some time to see him. The therapist arranged to see him immediately. When the patient arrived, it was obvious that he had not expected to be seen so quickly; he was flustered and had trouble finding enough to talk about for an entire session. The therapist guessed that he had been surprised that he was not more anxious when he found he had gone a week without an appointment and had called mainly to see if he really could come back if he needed

to. The patient agreed, a bit sheepishly, and added (as the therapist expected to hear) that he had felt OK as soon as he hung up the phone after speaking with the therapist. He felt reassured that the therapist would be there if he needed him.

This unconventional plan aimed explicitly at providing the patient a new beginning of a form of psychotherapy that might prove endable, or at least episodic. The clinic director designed it jointly with the new therapist partly in response to feeling responsible for the previous exploitation of the patient, but also because he thought it would be the right treatment for this patient. He believed that, even if the patient had not been mistreated by being subjected to repeated transfers, he still would require considerable support to prepare him for independent living. While the planned treatment would be continuous in principle, in practice it would be episodic. The director suggested that each episode in the planned "therapy interruptus" would end with something like a process of termination intended, like all terminations, to help the patient own the gains he had made.

In fact, a terminable therapy did not develop. At the end of his first return visit, the patient asked if he could call "once in a while" and, when reassured, left looking pleased. He did call about monthly at first. He wanted only to talk with the therapist, not to ask for an appointment. After they exchanged pleasantries, he would end the conversation not exactly with a complaint, but hinting that things were "all right, so far." He showed no desire to work on any of the other problems that he and the therapist had identified at the outset. The therapist and director of the clinic agreed that they had hit on a format that worked for this patient, who could keep his life together with only the minimal contact with the therapist that signified the support he felt he needed and did not pressure him to change (Shectman, 1968).

## The Ending of the Psychotherapy of Mr. B

This example affords the opportunity to discuss the problems of ending and terminating when the therapist anticipates the possibility of a "negative therapeutic reaction." We tend to use this term of dire significance when we fear that the patient, perhaps even out of sheer perversity, will manage, through a kind of inverted alchemy, to convert the gold of therapeutic progress into the lead of stagnancy and perhaps settle for the smug despair of defeating the therapist. Obviously, I do not approve of the term; it is a way to blame the patient for failing to benefit from what the therapist believes to be proper treatment. At best, it merely assigns a bad name to a phenomenon that occurs in milder and temporary form in every psychotherapy. Every patient, for reasons of his own, at times may fear more what might happen if he changes his ways, that is, changes his personality, than if he remains safely if painfully as he is. From the systems point of view, the phenomenon reflects that all systems, personality included, resist efforts to change them (Schlesinger, 2003).

> The theme that gains lead inevitably to loss recurred throughout this treatment. Like the theme in a musical rondo, it appeared each time the patient took the currently salient topic as far as he could for the moment. The therapist understood that the theme was a "marker" and that each recurrence marked that the patient was winding down work on the task of the moment and was about to begin another. The therapist used the opportunities afforded by these "mini-endings" to take up and help the patient work through the fantasy that he could only lose by gaining and that he could not afford to be dependent on others or for others to depend on him. In this way, in distributed fashion, at each mini-ending, they rehearsed some of the work of termination. The therapist found encouragement in this repeated process and renewed his confidence that ultimately the treatment would end with the patient's being able to retain his gains.

The principle to which I recur, that some of the work of termination can be accomplished in distributed fashion at multiple mini-endings, applies to all psychotherapies. It is particularly important that a therapist keep ending in mind from the beginning and work on mini-endings if he doubts that a terminable treatment will be possible.

## The Ending of the Psychotherapy of Mr. C

This patient began therapy in an unusual way. The emergency room nurse who recognized him as a repeater was also sensitive enough to notice that there was something odd about his presentation. Rather than dismissing him as a GOMER,[3] she reported her observations to the medical resident. He agreed that the patient's behavior was strange but possibly understandable, showed interest in the patient, and allowed him to discuss his situation long enough for the resident to make a referral that could stick. Recognizing the skittishness of this patient, the medical resident alerted the psychiatric resident to the nature of the case and thus facilitated the patient's entry into a useful treatment. We may infer that the patient was more ready now to accept a psychiatric referral than

---

[3] Acronym for "Get out of my emergency room."

during earlier crises, but the sensitivity with which the nurse and the two residents dealt with him probably was key to his successful entry into psychotherapy.

> The content of this psychotherapy continued to develop as the psychiatric resident who became the patient's therapist anticipated. The therapist informed us that the patient's skittishness about authorities extended to doctors and other "helpers" who were supposed to look after children but instead exploited them. The patient was embarrassed at having been abused and fearful that, if he told about it, no one would believe him. The mild paniclike attacks that he sought help for in his visits to emergency rooms seemed to be related to memories of these early experiences. Mainly, it turned out, the attacks would occur when the patient suddenly noticed that he was walking near a church. When he associated his symptom with this stimulus and with the memories of childhood abuse, his symptoms diminished sharply.
>
> In the weeks following, the therapist noted that the patient's interest in therapy seemed to diminish as his symptoms resolved. His associations shifted to his increasing activity. His life expanded because he was no longer afraid of fainting. Now there were many more events to talk about. He began to come a little late to sessions; on more than one occasion he reported that he had almost forgotten to come, and he cancelled one session because he had become so "busy." When the therapist commented that this pattern suggested that therapy was no longer as important to him as it once had been, the patient agreed a bit shamefacedly that he had not been thinking so much about his therapy recently, now that things were going so well for him, and he feared that the therapist might mistake his loss of interest for ingratitude.
>
> Throughout the therapy, the therapist had kept an eye on the way the patient related to him. He was not sure what to make of the fact that, while the patient seemed increasingly comfortable in sessions after he disclosed his fear of doctors, among other authorities with priestlike functions, the relationship did not seem to deepen, as he had been taught to expect. He enjoyed working with the patient, who gave him no trouble, unlike some others. The patient came on time, never missed a session, and made no effort to overstay. He was friendly enough and polite and did not argue with the therapist even when he did not fully agree with a suggestion. He seldom addressed the therapist directly, never referred to their relationship, and never reported a dream.
>
> The therapist was troubled that he could not detect any of the usual signs of transference involvement, and he was not sure if he was seeing

defense against transference (Gill, 1982) or actual absence of transference. The patient's concern that the therapist might take his shift of interest to his life outside sessions as ingratitude was possibly the first indication, the therapist thought, of transference.

Some weeks after the patient had first put together his symptoms and his history and saw the reasonableness of his fearful reactions in terms of his earlier experiences, he said he felt ready to leave therapy. He was highly satisfied with the results and thought he could manage now.

Even though there had been hints that the patient was disengaging, the therapist was surprised by this quiet announcement. He was ambitious for the patient and proposed to him that he could do even more for himself if he continued, but he could not convincingly point to areas in the patient's life that obviously needed more attention. In the face of the patient's clear but polite indications that he had no interest in continuing, the therapist desisted from further persuasion. In the course of this discussion, they reviewed what had happened, and the therapist took some satisfaction in hearing that the patient had accomplished more than symptom relief in his nine months of psychotherapy. His relationships with friends had deepened and for the first time in his life, he looked forward to the possibility of dating; the fear that he might faint had previously kept him from taking that chance.

Even though the therapist would have preferred to continue, he accepted the patient's desire to stop and suggested they continue for a short time while keeping ending in mind. The patient agreed. The therapist had been hoping that the case would end with a "classic" termination, but thus far the patient had shown none of the signs that he was troubled by the prospect of losing his relationship with the therapist, which as usual, he seemed just to take for granted. He thought that perhaps he should be doing more to bring the therapeutic relationship "into the process." When consulted, his supervisor discouraged that move and suggested he just stay with the patient's plan and await developments along the line of a probable transference that the patient had opened when he expressed concern that he might be thought ungrateful.

Keeping this suggestion in mind, the therapist could hear that a new theme with implications of transference had emerged. He sensed from the patient's other associations that the patient now felt bound to him by ties of obligation and that the patient's acquiescence with the therapist's suggestion to stay for a short time longer expressed that feeling of obligation; he was willing to extend the treatment for the benefit of the therapist.

He gently raised that possibility and the patient agreed; it was the least he could do to repay the therapist for the help he had given him. The therapist could then link this attitude to another theme that played into the patient's feeling that he was unable to object to the abuse he had experienced as a child. He believed he never would be good enough to meet his parents' expectations. Therefore, to be worthy of even the little attention he received, he had to exceed himself as a "giver" and be certain to repay any favors, even by tolerating the abuse.

The therapist believed that in the course of the next few weeks he and the patient had worked through the implications of this transference pattern as much as they were likely to. He observed that the patient's relief from symptoms seemed enduring, and there was no flare-up in the context of impending separation. The patient was happy to stop, was appropriately thankful, and volunteered that he knew he could call if he thought he needed further help.

### The Ending of the Psychotherapy of Ms. D

The therapist half-hoped this patient would not call back. Her eagerness to see him and only him was off-putting and, knowing no more about her than he did, he expected her idealization and adhesiveness would make an eventual ending difficult. When, several months later, the patient did call again, the therapist had an opening in his schedule and, with misgivings, agreed to see her but only for an evaluation. Given the opportunity to talk, the patient poured her heart out. She was desperately unhappy, so needy for relationship that she had alienated all her friends and acquaintances other than the one who had suggested she call this therapist. She was indeed envious of this friend, who clearly was getting her life together, but her friend's success also gave her hope that she too could turn her life around. Working hard and well as acquisitions editor for a major publisher, she had gained great success at her profession. But the rest of her life was vacant and her biological clock was ticking loudly.

In this first session, the therapist was surprised to feel a warm regard for the patient; although the adhesiveness that worried him still seemed present, it seemed less prominent than during the earlier phone calls. The patient also showed a discriminating sense of the genuineness of relationship, and an intolerance of phoniness. She also had a sharpness of tongue that made her a formidable conversationalist and that suggested that it was not just her neediness that turned people off but also her tactlessness in voicing acute observations of the conventional insincerities in which her professional life immersed her.

The therapist decided he would like to work with her; but, instead of the analysis she assumed he would recommend, he offered to continue the evaluation on a twice-weekly basis until they each had a better idea of the basis of her difficulties and what might help. She agreed, reluctantly, because she was in a hurry to get into treatment but felt enough confidence in the therapist to accept his proposal. This extended evaluation, of course, was a psychotherapy but the format was one in which the therapist felt he could comfortably stress its instrumental character and limit his commitment if that should prove necessary.

The patient fell into the rhythm of their meetings, used them to associate freely, though without any instruction to do so, and soon made it clear that she could use a psychoanalytic treatment and, indeed, had already constructed one. She no longer raised the question of when "real treatment" might begin. The therapist pondered whether things would go better if they met more frequently and used the couch, and he decided for the time being to leave well enough alone.

He thought that the first test of her ability to sustain this treatment would be when he informed her about his plan to attend a meeting out of town. It turned out that, although she was reluctant to mention his leaving lest he see her as too needy, the patient also had been worried about how she would fare with any absence. Could she tolerate even the weekend breaks? She was afraid her "clinginess" might drive the therapist away, as it had some friends. To her surprise, while therapy was always on her mind, she was able to tolerate the weekend interruptions as hardly more disrupting than the intervals between sessions. Her worries about the longer break evoked memories of early interruptions of family unity by the "mysterious disappearance" of one or the other parent that to this day she could not make sense of. Only by asking an older sister did she clear up the mystery of her father's bouts of tuberculosis and why it was necessary for him to remove himself from the household when the disease was active.

The therapist was reassured to find that his earliest concerns about the patient's narcissistic vulnerability were not borne out by experience in treatment. Again, he wondered if it would serve the patient better to "convert" the treatment from a twice-weekly psychotherapy in which the process essentially was psychoanalytic to a more formal psychoanalysis, with four-times-a-week meetings and the patient using the couch. After reconsidering the pros and cons and still unable to convince himself that the change would benefit the patient, the therapist decided to maintain the treatment in its current format.

In about two years, the patient achieved considerable success, transforming her social life from a near desert into a near garden. Several men were interested in her, including one with whom a relationship seemed to promise serious commitment. The usual signs of flagging interest in treatment in favor of life outside informed the therapist that they were in an ending phase. The patient concurred with his observation that she had obtained what she had hoped for and more and felt no need for continued therapy at the moment.

As she considered stopping, the expectable anxieties erupted, and a termination process ensued that was similar in many respects to that described for Mr. H but without any emergence of disappointment and resentment. As happens in most successful therapies, the patient's expectations of life heightened. Although highly successful as an editor, she had put aside her earliest ambitions to be a writer for reasons that no longer made sense to her. If she were to continue therapy, that would be a topic to get into. On the other hand, if her new romantic relationship developed as she hoped, having a family would be her first priority. The therapist had the impression that, perhaps fearful that she might find a worm in her apple, she specifically did not want more psychotherapy right now. She wondered about undertaking an analysis some day, and the therapist agreed that if she wanted to take up therapy later on, psychoanalysis would be an option.

## The Ending of the Psychotherapy of Mr. E

The patient's insistence on accepting "hollowness" as his fate softened as the therapist expressed interest in that state and how the patient could have come to such a dismal conclusion about himself. The patient told of his many failures at relationship because he "wasn't interesting enough to attract anyone he would like to befriend." While the therapist accepted these stories as valid in the sense that the patient really felt that way, he contrasted the stories of failure with the relative ease with which the patient had engaged with him. Seeing the therapist's puzzled acceptance that the patient felt that way about himself, the patient began to offer increasingly feeble rationalizations of his conviction. As he tried to justify his self-description, more of his history emerged. For the first time, the patient mentioned the younger sister who had come along just in time to knock him from his perch as the center of his parents' life. He soon found out that he could not compete with his charming sister; the tricks he used to draw attention to himself drew only ridicule.

Later disappointments accreted to this theme and confirmed that he was a loser. As it turned out, the crisis that led him to call for an appointment in the first place was that he had felt tempted to respond to an overture by a woman at work to whom he felt attracted and who responded to his apparent appreciation of her by inviting him to a party she was planning. He sweated over the invitation—he "knew" she didn't really mean it and was only taking pity on him. But was it possible that he was wrong about himself? He could not resolve his doubts and only at the last minute phoned his acceptance and that night had an attack of anxiety. After calling the clinic for the appointment, he felt better and talked himself back into the resigned position he described to the therapist; he expressed his conflict by forgetting to cancel the appointment. As the patient came to grips with this conflict and the way he had organized his life around preventing feared humiliation, he was emboldened to take more chances, and, as he gained more success, his world expanded.

After a little more than a year of therapy, the patient's life opened up enough to allow some acquaintanceships to ripen into friendships, and he felt freer to approach openly the woman who had shown interest in him. He seemed more restless in session now and kept looking at the therapist as if trying to divine what he might be thinking. When the therapist finally commented about this behavior, the patient said that he was satisfied with the results of his treatment and that it seemed to him about time for him to spread his wings and to see what he could do with his newfound confidence; he had been wondering what the therapist thought about it. When the therapist said that it sounded reasonable to him, the patient accepted without further inquiry that degree of approval as an endorsement. He agreed with the therapist's pro forma suggestion that he might have other problems to work on, but for the time being he would like to see what he could do on his own. He agreed it would be wise to take a little time to test out this new sense of himself; during the next few sessions he spoke openly of his doubts and anxieties and was pleased to find them unfounded. His relationship with his new girlfriend also provided emotional support. On the date patient and therapist had set, the patient thanked the therapist, shook his hand, and mentioned as he left the office that he realized he could call if he felt he needed to. As of this writing, some years later, the patient has not called back, but a Christmas card again expressed thanks and announced his marriage.

*The Ending of the Psychotherapy of Mr. F*
Two months after discharge from the detox program she had requested, the patient contacted the attending psychiatrist to ask about the possibility of outpatient treatment. She now wanted to kick her habit completely and take back her life. She recognized that the divided opinions the ward staff held about her mirrored her own divided opinions about herself— was she worth the effort? The kindness of some staff members and the example of other patients who were getting their lives together inspired

her to attempt to break out of her despairing way of life. This time kicking the habit was easier. In fact, she had almost completed it before turning to ask for help.

In outpatient therapy with the attending psychiatrist, she regained more of her sense of worth, enrolled in community college, earned good grades, and took increasingly responsible jobs that supported her sufficiently (if not as well as her former profession had). She was able to pay for her treatment and insisted on paying for it as a private patient. She ended her psychotherapy when she earned acceptance at the state university on the strength of her performance at the community college.

She had been wait-listed and was finally accepted quite close to the time of registration. She felt some conflict about leaving her therapy and therapist for this opportunity but believed she could now move on. She and her therapist agreed that more treatment could be useful but that she could defer it until she settled herself at the university and had a job. There was barely enough time to work through the feelings of gratitude that he had not let the staff turn her away when she requested only a partial detox, but she had come to realize that, by presenting herself in that way, she was daring the staff to reject her. She was of a generally stoic character and had regained enough self-confidence so that she experienced, or at least admitted to, little anxiety about ending this episode of treatment. She was convinced she wanted more therapy because she wanted more out of life and would ask her therapist for a referral when she was ready. In the meantime, she wanted only to be certain that he would want to hear from her about how she was doing from time to time.

This example illustrates another variety of the confluence of beginning and ending. Having been given the treatment she wanted, finding it useful, and ending it electively according to her own plan, the patient felt free to begin again when she was ready to strive for new goals. That outcome should not surprise us; an inevitable consequence of successful psychotherapy is the heightening of the patient's expectations of life.


### Final Thoughts


These examples of how psychotherapy may end and terminate hardly exhaust the variety one will see in clinical practice. It may at first seem paradoxical that patients who demonstrate widely different ways of beginning go through endings that seem more alike than different. We could say that any patient who stays in therapy long enough for it to be effective is able to form an attachment to the therapist sufficient for that therapy.[4] If the therapist is sensitive to the nature and degree of that attachment and can work with the patient on the extent to which separation from the therapist is problematic, the actual ending is likely to approximate the model of working through and mourning that I presented in detail for Mr. H. If the therapist is sensitive to the patient's reactions to the many interim separations that any therapy affords and takes advantage of the opportunity to work on these "miniendings" to prepare for the ultimate ending, both he and the patient will find that ultimate ending less troublesome.

Although the same principles apply to all patients, therapists must apply them with greater sensitivity when working with patients who are especially vulnerable to regression (Schlesinger, 2003). I refer especially to patients whose sense of self is insecure and who feel that they must guard against becoming lost if they get too close in the relationship. They organize their emotional lives around the need to defend against the perceived dangers of relatedness, especially intimate relatedness, and for reasons that could be described as structural, not merely dynamic. I will discuss the application of the general principles to such patients in Chapter 6.

---

[4] This is not to say that patients who leave early necessarily do so because they are unable to form a sufficiently strong therapeutic relationship.

# 6

# Ending and Termination in the Treatment of Vulnerable Patients

We turn now to vulnerable patients, those who are uncertain about who they are. They are described as having an insecure or unstable sense of self, or as being fragile. In consequence, they are also uncertain about the stability of the others around them, a condition sometimes termed low object constancy. They have difficulty forming and maintaining close relationships, that is, relationships in which they feel and fear a demand to reciprocate the warmth and affection offered them. These patients are found mostly in the diagnostic categories of borderline personality disorder through the spectrum of schizotypy.[1]

You may sense that I am picking my way carefully through the vocabulary commonly used to describe these patients. I believe some terms, for example, fragile, give rise to misleading imagery in both patient and therapist and hence to mishandling. These patients are not fragile like a porcelain cup that will shatter if dropped on the floor. Their experience is closer to feeling "unsolid"; they might become unglued or dangerously fluid when anxious. Such patients find it difficult to hold themselves together especially when tempted into a relationship that demands more intimacy than they can tolerate. Susceptible to being influenced, they feel in danger that others will define them for their own purposes. Thus, they try define themselves safely by exclusion, as it were, in terms of who they are not, for example, "I am not my father" (Greenson, 1954). We can analogize their situation to that of a diabetic who needs insulin to survive but is allergic to insulin.

---

[1] These diagnostic labels may help you locate yourself among familiar terms. My focus is on the treatment of patients whose vulnerability to regression is based on a disturbed sense of self. I do not believe that a special psychology of self is required to understand or treat them.

Various conceptualizations have been offered for the psychopathology of these patients. All of them presume that the disorder results at least in part from faulty childhood development, but they differ in the strategies for treating them (e. g. Knight, 1953, 1954; Kohut, 1971; Kernberg, 1975; Searles, 1985; Gunderson, 1996). I will not discuss the merits of those strategies. For my present purpose, I stress one aspect of the psychopathology and the treatment. I assume that the therapist recognizes that the growth of a secure sense of self in therapy takes place much as it should have occurred but, for some reason, failed to occur during childhood. This growth usually occurs through processes we sum up as identification with the key figures of that time. The processes in therapy that lead to the repair or replacement of identifications also take time, time that permits trial identifications with aspects of the therapist as well as anxious withdrawals to check for safety. Successful therapy leaves the patient with a strengthened sense of self and, consequently, with a increased ability to remain safely in relationship. The more successful the treatment in accomplishing these goals, the more closely the processes of ending and termination will approximate the "classical" model presented for Mr. H. It remains then to discuss the ending of treatments that for one or another reason fall short of this ideal.

*Example: Mr. I*

The patient is a young man who, complaining he was bored and wanted to get on with life, dropped out of college just short of graduation. His grades were good when he was interested in the subject. Then he would get intensely into it, read everything he could find, and then, just as suddenly, lose interest and drop it. In this way, he had successively been a poet, an engineer, and a labor economist, finally deciding he could not find out what he wanted to be in college but would have to do something "real." Leaving college, he used his remaining savings to wander, hitchhiking across the country and, when he had run through his funds, found work as a laborer. His family finally found him and persuaded him to consider a psychiatric consultation. Worn out by laboring and feeling no better about himself, he went along grudgingly to pacify them and, as a practical matter, to ensure their continued financial support. He was unconvinced there was anything wrong with him.

The consultant found Mr. I likeable, if at first difficult to reach. He noticed, in the course of a desultory conversation, that the patient's eyes searched every corner of his consulting room and returned frequently to the bookcase. He commented that the patient seemed driven by great curiosity. That casual but empathic remark served to make a connection between them. The patient relaxed and seemed more interested in telling his story although his gaze still alternated searchingly between the bookcase and the eyes of the consultant. He said that he had always been a "different"child. Unlike his older brother, he had few friends and was socially reclusive. The consultant observed to himself, however, that the patient had a certain awkward charm.

Mr. I mentioned that he had an easier time with things than with people, could always figure out how things worked, and could repair anything mechanical or electronic after studying it for a while. The self-observations he reported led the consultant to add to his earlier conjecture about the patient's curiosity. He wondered if the patient was curious about how the consultant did his thing, what he employed as his "technology." The patient flushed, then grinned at having been "caught," and agreed that he did not think it possible for one person to understand another. The consultant nodded as though accepting that understanding and added that was a difficult feat to imagine but certainly worthy of curiosity. He suggested that, if Mr. I were willing to have some conversations of the kind they were having now, maybe he would be able not only to figure out the "technology" but also find out something useful about himself.

With that tentative but promising beginning, a therapy ensued that lasted several years. The therapy was interesting in its own right, but for our present purpose it is enough to note that the therapist, with eventual termination in mind, was on the lookout for how the patient would react to interruptions. He found little reaction to the ending of sessions or to weekend breaks until quite late in the therapy, when Mr. I, for the first time, expressed interest about where the therapist was going for a planned interruption. He noticed that the patient was engaged in a continuing struggle with, against, and about identification with him.

It was clear to the therapist that the patient was modeling himself on him and was aware of doing so and worried about it, though denying its significance, often in ways that were transparent but that the therapist was careful not to challenge. For example, on one occasion, when the patient had just bought a recording of a piece of music the therapist had mentioned in passing, Mr. I supposed that the therapist was interested in working with him because his musical tastes were similar to his own. He became especially concerned when he felt that the therapist was getting too close as, for instance, by seeming to take for granted his presence in, and commitment to, therapy. Indeed, for a long time, the patient acted as if he had decided at just that moment to attend each regularly scheduled session.

Mr. I gave the first hints that he was thinking about ending his treatment when, after about two years of therapy, he began speaking regretfully about having dropped out of college. He raised the topic diffidently, and the context suggested to the therapist that he was thinking, regretfully, that finishing college would be what his parents wanted him to do. The therapist noted that it would be difficult for him to know whose idea it was. Would it be an expression of his new-found independence or a caving in to his parent's expectations? The therapist did not voice at that moment the further concern he thought the patient had: what does he (the therapist) think about it? Would he also approve, making it difficult for him to say no; or, just as likely, would he refuse to allow the patient to leave him and live his own life?

Soon the patient brought up the subject in his own way. He came to a session in a funk, "depressed" because "it" would never work; he never could be sure he was his own man. The therapist was able to help him see that until now being independent had meant he would have to foreswear connection to anyone. The patient could voice that conflict now because he found it possible to recognize and appreciate relatedness, but he was still not certain that having feelings for another person would not trap him. Much of the work of the therapy was replayed in this termination phase as Mr. I increasingly was able to test whether he was having his thoughts or the therapist's or his father's. Was he self-directed or unwittingly a pawn in another's game? Repeatedly, he had to work through and "detoxify" his awareness that he was in a significant relationship with the therapist; and, each time, he came to see that, although he was connected, he was not entangled with him. This core issue was the background for working out the more familiar issue of termination: the fear that if he separated from the therapist, all would be lost.

To the extent that a patient strengthens his sense of self during the therapy, his reactions to the impending separation from the therapist will approximate those of the general run of "neurotic" persons. In less favorable circumstances, the patient will deal with the ending in his characteristic way. For instance, the patient may break off treatment during one of the "crises," such as an anxiety attack when he is feeling threatened by having moved too close emotionally to the therapist or when the therapist overreaches interpretively and inadvertently leads the patient to fear that the therapist is closing in on him. The patient may justify his flight by thinking or saying, "It was no good, anyway," or by a paranoid fear of seduction.

A general suggestion for such critical moments is that, if denial or projection is the best defense the patient can muster under the circumstances, the therapist would do well to offer support to the extent possible. By doing so, he may make the premature ending, if it comes to that, the least destructive of the work done as possible. The therapist may avert a threatened breach if, in a sense, he is willing to "go along" with the patient's threatened action, that is, if he acknowledges the seriousness of the patient's worries and the belief that the only way to suppress those worries and avoid the danger is to leave. In effect, the therapist accompanies the patient as he contemplates flight. In this way, the patient's "flight" may be accomplished symbolically in words and in the session. Feeling that the therapist believes he has both the power and the reason to leave, the patient might be relieved of the previously felt necessity to act on it.


### Crises Related to the Fear of Ending "Half-Cured"


It is a common experience that, after a period of seeming progress, a therapy seems to "get stuck" and go nowhere. The tendency to slow down and tread water may arise for many reasons. Recall that in Chapter 3 I listed brief episodes of slowing down and disengagement as possible indicators or "markers" that a patient has come to the end of working on a topic or task and may be fearful about going on or fearful that the therapist might believe he is finished with therapy. A case may get "stuck" in a lengthy "impasse" or "stalemate" because of issues related to other fears of the patient that are not acknowledged by the therapist.

In Chapter 7, I discuss the impasse that develops when therapist and patient avoid raising sensitive issues in their relationship (the "elephant in the room" phenomenon). Such avoidance may reflect the presence of unanalyzed mutual transferences, or it may be an aspect of the "transference neurosis." Both the brief slowdown that may serve as a marker and the much lengthier slowdown of an impasse have in common that, although both the patient and the therapist may be aware that "nothing is happening," neither draws the other's attention to the phenomenon.

A brief slow-down (perhaps so brief that the therapist may not have noticed it) may erupt into a crisis when a borderline patient who has become engaged in the therapeutic relationship suddenly fears being dropped. In such an instance, the patient does not call attention to any feeling that nothing is happening. Most often, the patient complains loudly that the therapist has lost interest in him, that he is worse off than before, or that he is being left "half-cured." I am including such phenomena in this chapter because they represent fearful intimations of eventual ending. They are anxiety attacks about being abandoned that occur not during the actual ending phase of psychotherapy or even at a point close to it, but at an intermediate point, somewhere in the middle of treatment. They generally occur when the therapist was not thinking of an imminent planned ending and was unaware of the patient's concern inasmuch as there was "no reason" for it.

Some patients, however, become frightened enough, and discouraged enough, to interrupt treatment at such points. And some therapists, when barraged by this complaint, seem prematurely ready to acknowledge failure and give up, thus confirming the patient's fear. Here is an example taken from a time when I attempted to explain what I thought was going on to a therapist who was downcast by the sudden and unexpected regression of a borderline patient who, until that moment, "had been doing so well."

*Example: Ms. J*
The young woman was a college student, doing well in her studies and nearing graduation. Two years earlier, with a long history of suicide attempts, binge eating, self-cutting, and academic failure, she had been hospitalized for several months. She began psychotherapy with her current therapist while still in hospital and, with only a few setbacks, began to progress. When discharged from hospital, she started to live on her own and, while still in therapy, resumed college.

The relevant background is that she was an older sister convinced, not without reason, that her younger sister was the mother's favorite. Her envy of the favored sister had colored her relationships with her ward mates, and she would measure herself constantly against the actual and imagined achievements of her therapist's other patients.

Recently, the therapist, who still held a hospital position, undertook new duties that required her to wear a beeper. Then the therapy hit a snag, an impasse developed in which the patient seemed convinced the therapist must have volunteered for the new duties in order to get rid of her. Each time the beeper went off during her session, Ms. J would explode, and, between interruptions, the patient tensely anticipated the next provocation. The therapist finally was able to arrange to be undisturbed during sessions, but the patient's anger hardly abated. She was now sure the therapist was fonder of another patient who had won honors at her school.

These themes of being the unfavored one, expecting imminently to be eased out of her family, were familiar. But the intensity and persistence of her feelings were new, and it seemed ironic that they flared up just when things were going so well. The patient had all but convinced my young colleague that she was a bad therapist. Maybe, unconsciously, the therapist thought she had provoked the patient by not refusing the new assignment; maybe Ms. J was right that she was no better now than when she had entered the hospital; maybe she had been blinded by her own ambitions for the patient; maybe she did prefer her other, less troublesome patients. While the patient kept denouncing her to her face and to anyone else who would listen, she never missed an appointment, was never late, and was furious when the therapist was delayed by some hospital emergency.

As we reviewed these facts alongside the therapist's doubts about whether anything useful had been accomplished, the therapist was able to see the parallels between the accusations she had all but agreed to and the accusations the patient typically had leveled at her mother. But why had they flared up now?

The problem seemed to be not that so little had been done, but rather that so much had been done. From "the outside," the patient looked fine, and sometimes she even felt fine "inside" as well. But she was suddenly and uncomfortably aware of how dependent she had become on the therapist. For the longest time, she had been able to deny the depth of her attachment to the therapist. She would reassure herself, when she found herself thinking about what she would tell the therapist in her next session, that she could quit any time she wanted to. After all, she had been in therapy many times and therapists were like buses—if you miss one, you could always catch the next one, or walk.

With the sudden fraying of her denials, Mr. J became aware of some other uncomfortable truths. She no longer felt like the "stable–unstable" borderline of her familiar old self. She was no longer cutting or bingeing, and no longer felt much like doing either; although, off and on, when she felt a twinge of anxiety, she played with the idea of trying to see if she could do it again. But the old sense of urgency and inevitability was missing. Worst of all was discovering that really, she no longer wanted to, that the anticipation of cutting was no longer exciting and that the act no longer promised the certain relief it once did. She felt as if her "will" had been undermined; and this was especially frightening.

Further, since she had **"made progress"** and looked so well to others (and even to herself), she no longer felt entitled to claim the **"rights"** she felt were due her when sick enough to be hospitalized. Soon she would end her college days with a respectable record and would have to decide what to do with her life. She now had some new friends who were not fellow inpatients. She was even murmuring about a young man who seemed interested in her; formerly any such possibility would have terrified her and would instantly be repelled by humiliating the fellow. And she was aware that the therapist had relaxed and no longer seemed worried about her making missteps. Rather, the therapist was encouraging her to venture out into the world, even to take some social risks.

As we reviewed the patient's complaints about her therapy and her therapist against this background, we constructed a scenario that made sense of the patient's episode of flailing about. We could then appreciate the patient's fury that she had been deceived into "getting better" and see the merit in her charge that she was worse off than before treatment. After all, she no longer could convince herself that she was being cheated by life, as she believed she formerly had been, and it was only the conviction that she had been cheated by life that entitled her to the rewards of victimhood. Now, just because she had "done a few little things without failing," she was sure she would be ignored, simply "taken for granted." Meanwhile, everyone's expectations of her would continue to mount. She insisted she had no inner resources to draw on, and soon she would be deprived of external resources since the therapist was getting bored with her and wanted her to go off on her own. Inevitably, she would run out of steam and fail. Thus, these temporary successes ultimately would lead to crushing humiliation and abandonment.

No one any longer was worried about her, certainly not her therapist, she felt. Since nobody cared, and nobody ever had cared, why should she continue to strive? She was stuck out on a limb, neither sick nor well, but in a kind of limbo that had the worst features of health and illness—all the responsibilities of health and none of the rights of illness. And it was galling that the therapist seemed so pleased with what *she* had done, so smug about *her* success. Of course, the therapist would like to get rid of her, to trick her into "quitting while she is ahead." But she herself would no longer be the person she was accustomed to being. Perhaps she had limped through life like a wounded bird, but she had somehow functioned and had gotten along. But, in any case, she would never be the ideal person (i.e., like the therapist) she now wanted to be. She was in a pickle, no longer herself and not the therapist either; she was about to be abandoned "half-cured."

Between the lines one could see that the patient's fears of abandonment were projections of her own secret wishes for autonomy as she entertained the idea that she one day might finish her treatment and "have a life." This ambition would, of course, involve separation from the therapist, and that frightening implication soon became paramount. Her wish to get on with her life had become transmuted into the therapist's wish to get rid of her. What is more, the desire to have a life aroused the more or less unconscious belief that the only life worth having was the therapist's life; she really wanted *to be* the therapist and have the therapist's life, not just to be *like* her in some peripheral respects. And the thoughts she secretly had been playing with—that after college she might go to graduate school, or even medical school, and then become a professional—suddenly were exposed as meaning that, no matter how hard she tried, she would be condemned eternally to being second rate, only a pale imitation of the therapist, never the therapist herself.

One of the precipitants of the crisis was the sudden inkling that she had been lending herself to the deception. As soon as she felt the first hint that she liked coming to sessions and liked the therapist, she deceived herself into feeling secure because she knew that, as in her previous bouts of therapy, nothing important would happen; she was permanently, invulnerably "sick." Behind the screen of her denials, the patient was able to remain in a close relationship with the admired therapist and could let herself imitate her attitudes and mannerisms, as it were, to try them on for size.

As she allowed herself to internalize aspects of the therapist, she was able to resume the processes of growth and development that had been interrupted by the arrival of her sister and the loss of place in the family, among other formative experiences. It was as if behind the screen of denial the patient had allowed herself to become identified with the therapist, that is, "to become as one" with the therapist.

When the veil of denial suddenly wore thin, she became frighteningly aware that she had changed irreversibly, that she could no longer go back to being as she was. She realized, despairingly, that the therapist and she were separate persons and that she herself never would be the therapist (Schlesinger, 1993, 1996).

Let us deconstruct the crisis in the therapy of this patient. Her anxiety reflected fear that something dreadful *might happen in the near future*, while she complained *in the present tense* about the bad treatment she was getting. Her therapist reacted guiltily to the barrage of complaints, considering that perhaps the treatment she had provided was no good. So nothing useful had happened, and something even worse might happen if she did not back off.

The lesson to be learned here is that, in contrast to the patient's literal complaint, this phenomenon actually reflects that *much has happened, more than the patient welcomes. The patient is reacting to what has happened, to the progress (read change) that already has occurred*. To be sure, for the patient, what has happened has implications that are both fearsome and exciting.

The therapist's immediate task, once his conscience recovers from the probably unwarranted spasm of guilt, is to identify what happened recently and to help the patient come to terms with the progress that has been made and to the patient's fear of rising expectations and certain disappointment that success implies.

For a borderline patient, as for all of us, progress brings new problems as well as new opportunities, and both outcomes may amount to the same thing. These reactions must be distinguished, of course, from the fortunately far less frequent regressive episodes that signify that therapy is seriously overstraining the patient's adaptive and defensive capacities.

The general form of this crisis, with the angry subtext that the patient was tricked into changing only to be abandoned halfway through, is far from unusual. I have heard the story often enough to feel safe in proposing that it may to be an inevitable event in the psychotherapy of a borderline patient who gets deeply into treatment. Appelbaum (1996) has described several such patients in this situation.

Another characteristic of patients with borderline and narcissistic personality organizations has relevance for ending and termination. Some of these patients come to therapy because life is a mess and also because of a sense of moral obligation (perhaps reinforced by family coercion) that they really "ought to do something about themselves." For some of these patients, just "being in therapy" is sufficient for them to satisfy their good intentions, to assuage their sense of obligation, and to get relatives off their back (Schlesinger, 1978; Appelbaum, 1972).

These patients are convinced they are "hard core," and sooner or later, the sterility of the therapy will confirm that it is just another exercise in futility. Oddly enough, they do not find anticipated failure unwelcome, especially if they can put it off indefinitely. They are willing to come and to pay (or have someone else pay), but they neither expect nor desire the therapist to be powerful enough to influence them. Although they do not expect anything worthwhile to happen, merely being in therapy is an end in itself, a kind of sanctuary of low expectations. They have a relaxed, almost cheerful sense of hopelessness, so that the inevitable failure of therapy will yield no more than token disappointment. The conviction of being incurable is, of course, a compromise between hope and fear. For some, however, the presumed certainty of ultimate failure also holds permission that eventually they can commit suicide, a fantasy they keep in mind as the inevitable but postponable conclusion while they are allowed (and allow themselves) to dabble in therapy.

When such a patient (for example, Mr. I) finds that something did indeed happen and fears that what happened might be irreversible, the reaction is analogous to a fish discovering the hook: a crisis composed of surprise, dismay, and efforts at flight. Unlike the fish, however, the patient was not totally unaware of what was going on and was not totally rejecting of what happened; indeed the patient may be secretly pleased that there may be hope for a better life after all. During the crisis, however, the patient guards that secret jealously.

The therapist, of course, must be on the lookout for signs that the patient is conflicted about what is happening and be ready to hint at it, although only when it would be tactful to do so. If he points to the secret pleasure too soon and, as it were, rubs the patient's nose in it, the patient will likely experience it as a humiliating exposure. A nontraumatic opportunity to expose this hidden side of the patient's experience may arise when the patient hints that perhaps some aspect of changing would not necessarily be an unmitigated disaster. There might be room then for the therapist to agree mildly that sometimes even a seemingly troublesome situation may not be as bad as it seems at first. The therapist comments diffidently because it is important to minimize the tendency of the patient to attribute any change in himself to an unwanted influence by the therapist or other authority. In the first few encounters of this kind, the therapist should expect no more than a mild grunt of assent by way of acknowledgement for his tentative comment.

## The Expression of the Fear of Ending in Less Vulnerable, Better Integrated Patients

All patients, not just the vulnerable ones, however eager they may be for change or ending, may have mixed reactions to the experience of changing (as well as mixed reactions to ending therapy). Although the fear of being left half-cured tends to be expressed in dramatic form by borderline patients, attenuated expressions of the same fear can be seen even in patients in analysis. Any patient who has been "progressing nicely" may do a kind of "double-take" when he realizes that more has happened, that is, that he has changed more than he previously had noticed, and fears that the change may have unforeseen risks. For instance, the patient may notice, with some alarm, that now he is driving directly home from work, that he is "forgetting" to stop off at the local bar, his hitherto invariable custom.

The therapist will not yet have heard about this surprising development. During the next session, this patient might express his as yet unvoiced concern so subtly that the therapist might overlook that something important is going on. How might the therapist recognize that something unusual is occurring? How do better integrated patients, those who are not given to dramatic announcements through crises, manifest this phenomenon?

While the same content, ideas, and reactive moods are present in the treatment of better integrated patients, these moods will be expressed with little intensity, and most likely indirectly. The patient may show only a slight withdrawal and turn inward; he may come late or find a reason to cancel a session, or he may express his concern in dreams. The patient may express his sense of uneasiness only metaphorically in words, perhaps words that imply potential or imminent action in other contexts; but there will be little of the tendency toward the kind of disturbed behavior that disrupts treatment and may even endanger a borderline patient. There may be a mild depression-like state with a grudging admission that, unaccountably, things are all right, but that won't last. A common form of expression is difficulty maintaining continuity of topic.

These reactions are the same as those I called "markers" in Chapter 3, and they have the same implication here. The patient feels at a loss; he has come to the end of some line in therapy because he noticed an unexpected change in how he feels or in his behavior and does not know what to make of it. The change may be something he has "sort of wanted" but he was not expecting it so soon or not in the context in which it occurred.[2] The patient's reaction is muted, unlike that of the borderline patient, because he has a clearer cognitive sense that what happened was not categorically bad but was surprising and unsettling. He is reluctant to acknowledge it openly and go on lest he confirm it as a step taken that cannot be reversed. While such muted reactions slow treatment down, they may not seem disruptive, so that the therapist may not consider that the patient is withholding some news that disturbs him and that he has a serious conflict about the possible consequences of changing.

As a matter of technical principle, the therapist should be prepared to consider such seemingly trivial episodes as possibly significant (not, for example, "Oh well, the patient will soon get over it") and be ready to investigate and interpret it, especially if he has come to recognize that this reaction is part of the patient's repertoire of defensive postures. The stance I recommend is the same as I suggested earlier, for instance, to conjecture, "Something must have happened to throw you off stride." If the therapist fails to intervene when his clinical sense should have suggested it, the patient likely will get over it and in time return to the status quo ante,[3] and the therapist will have missed an opportunity for effective work.

---

[2] Notice the allusion to the unsettled question, "Does insight follow or precede change?" (Schlesinger, 2003).

[3] Alternatively, the patient's behavior may escalate; some impasses begin in this way.

Following is an example of this pattern of reaction taken from a psychoanalysis. Note that some of the dynamics of this patient are much the same as for a borderline patient, although in comparison, for instance, with Ms. J the expression of conflict and anxiety about impending loss and abandonment are relatively inconspicuous. This patient is far better able to deal with the anxiety about the degree to which he has changed, and his reaction causes no obvious disturbance of the therapeutic relationship. It would be easy for an analyst to wait out the muted expression of conflict and mild dysphoria as too trivial to bother with, and with the expectation that they soon will pass, as they will. But by doing so the analyst will be encouraging the development of a pattern in which, when the patient signals distress through slight withdrawal, he is regularly be ignored, a pattern that is likely to be repeated endlessly. While one would hardly refer to this patient's reaction as a crisis, it does reflect in *form fruste* an important dynamic, his fear of allowing others to be emotionally significant to him. To accept pleasure from others would be to establish their "right" to a permanent place in his life and their right to make emotional demands to which he would have to yield. To ignore the subtle indicators that this conflict has been aroused and to fail to follow up the patient's response to intervention would be to waste an opportunity for analyzing and possibly set up the conditions for an impasse (Schlesinger, 1996).

*Example: Mr. K*

Mr. K, a lawyer in his late 20s, is a newly made member of a prestigious law firm, and in the second year of an analysis. He opens, in his usual dutiful fashion, by reporting on his emotional state, that he feels tired and unengaged today. He felt lazy the night before and had let his wife make oral love to him; he always feels very guilty about letting her do this because he thinks she does not like to do it. The weekend was nice and relaxed and he felt at home. However, last night he felt tired and burdened. He came home feeling exhausted and complained to his wife about his bad day at the office. She was sweet and loving. They went to bed early, but he just was not in the mood for sex, turned over, and went to sleep. He woke up, however, and she took the initiative. They had had intercourse four times the previous week. That was a kind of breakthrough because the sex was increasingly good and his wife said she had felt more—their enjoyment of sex was more mutual. He used to think that sex was good only with someone you did not love and didn't have to think about.

The session continues in this generally complaining and withdrawn mood. The patient mentions how very uptight he felt during a conference with the lead attorney on a case; the attorney had even commented that his voice sounded tense. The analyst senses that the patient's transference position, as expressed in the material thus far, is to pull away from him because he expects and fears that excessive demands will be made of him, much as he felt when he went home to his wife the previous night.

The analyst comments that he began the hour by mentioning how tired he was and that sex the night before had left him with feelings of shame and guilt. The patient agrees and goes on to repeat some of what he said earlier and elaborates a bit. The analyst adds that the patient seems to expect to be criticized unjustly for being withholding and selfish and that, like his wife, the analyst will ignore how worn out he was, that he gave his all at the office, and that he was left with nothing more to give. The patient agrees and elaborates his feelings of exhaustion and his dread that by coming today he would be imposed upon. The analyst then guessed, "When you achieve a degree of mutuality, as you mentioned you did last week, you feel it has to be that way all the time; no backsliding is permitted. As with toilet training, once you get it, no more slips are allowed."

The patient concurs and goes on to fill in the details of his fantasy about expecting demands in this hour as well as condemnation for what he did last night.The analyst says that playing it out that way could help him restore the familiar feeling of being criticized unjustly and that, once again, whatever he does will not be enough. Again, the patient agrees and connects this realization to the way that he had expected such treatment from his mother. He then extended the comparison to the way he is with his young son and how lucky he is that his wife is such a good mother who handles toilet training sensibly. Over and over again, he compares his early experience to what he presumes to be happening with his son and decries the noxious effects of making demands for precocious cleanliness and sharing. The analyst comments that the patient is using his own experience here to inform his raising of his son. Then he stops, noting that he feels he is withdrawing; he is starting to feel just the way he did last night with his wife.

The analyst says he thinks that, at first, the patient felt his comments were helpful but that soon they seemed to demand that he reciprocate by doing even better. The analyst adds that he cannot accept anything from anyone without feeling he has to match it immediately. The patient agrees emphatically and spells out how intolerable that demand feels to him. The analyst is then able to add that it must seem inconceivable to him that his wife could have enjoyed making love to him as she did, that is, even if oral sex was not her favorite way, she could still enjoy indulging him. The patient seems to relax at this point, and the analyst adds that it must be an enormous strain to feel that something was helpful to him, yet at the same time feel that it was poisoned by the implicit demand to respond instantly and at least in kind.

The patient's associations go back to the experience with the lead attorney who differed with him about how to deal with a difficult and angry client. He is sure the client felt some hostility toward him as well as toward the person she was suing; she did not seem to care if she hurt her case and her lawyer as long as she hurt the defendant as well. He thinks the lead attorney's advice was not worth much. It was ad hoc and plausible, but no better than his own ideas. Again, he says he felt he was withdrawing. The analyst notes that his associations suggest that he was trying to diminish the value of what the analyst had just said. Indeed, if what he said was worthless, the patient would not feel under pressure to reciprocate instantly or at all. Taking a deep breath, the patient agrees, and goes on to say, "Actually, what the lead attorney said to me was true; the advice I rejected was good advice and well intended, and there is probably also something hostile in what I am doing to you." The analyst agreed that if the patient could lead him to believe that the ideas he was offering were worthless, the analyst would feel less good about himself.

The patient goes on about this theme for a while and then returns to feeling compelled to reciprocate. He visualized an image: "You and I are connected by a steel rod—if you move, I have to move; there is no elasticity in the system." He elaborates this image and, at some point, the analyst takes a chance and adds that everything he offered the patient has strings or hooks attached to it.

Starting to review his history, the patient wonders when all this began. He does not think he was this way when he first came to the city; maybe it began after he came back from the trip abroad and took his present position. At first, he was praised for the way he did things, but from then on he has felt that he has to be perfect; he has to grow up instantly and never backslide. The better he does and the more he lets himself enjoy life, the greater the risk that he might slip or be unable to meet the next demand. And then rejection will follow. Better to withdraw first and bring about the separation he fears. He fills the rest of the hour with allusions to what we had just come to understand about this characteristic attitude; he finds analogies to it in memories of childhood and in other areas of his current life.

We could look at the treatment of this patient from the vantage point of how to handle instances when a better integrated patient is changing positively. In distinction to the advice about treating a borderline patient who can permit a degree of improvement only as long as he can overlook or deny it (to support the denials as long as the patient needs them), a better integrated patient is likely to have other reasons for feeling diffident about improvement. For instance, the patient may superstitiously fear that improvement might not be permanent, or perhaps it arouses conflict with a moral stance that forbids it, or it might expose the patient to new temptations.

*Are These Reactions Native or Iatrogenic?*

It is heuristic, useful, to consider the regression of a borderline patient or the defensive withdrawal of a neurotic patient as partly iatrogenic. To the extent that the therapist, by ignoring the premonitory signs of distress, seems to validate the patient's not yet clearly expressed fears, he invites a louder, more disruptive expression of the conflict. The therapist of the borderline patient, Ms. J, allowed herself, or seemed to the patient to allow herself, to be lulled into believing "the worst was over"; the patient was now coasting along and would continue to improve with less attention. The estimate of continuing improvement might indeed have been correct—in the long run—but not the implication that less attention would henceforth be needed. It was still essential that the patient be able to sense the therapist's continuing presence, even though the attention could be of a different kind (Gunderson, 1996). To the extent that the patient's sense that "getting better" implies eventual separation from the therapist, as it always does, allowing the patient to brood about the intimation of abandonment in the context of the therapist's relaxed attention invites the kind of protest that may feel to the therapist to be a disaster.

The therapist's contribution to the crisis might well include ignoring what the experience of changing means to the patient while the therapist continues to focus on making progress. Or, as happened to the therapist of Ms. J, one might become distracted by new responsibilities or opportunities; it could as well have been taking on another patient in therapy, or taking a vacation, or getting married—anything that would signify to the patient a dilution of interest. Indeed, no outward event is necessary. To a patient fearful of being stretched out of shape, even the therapist's failing to notice a barely apparent moment of anxiety, or a worried silence, could signal that total neglect and abandonment are in the offing.

I am not implying that the "ideal" therapist can prevent such crises. That goal would be as pointless as trying to prevent transference. But with experience the therapist learns to expect that changing may be experienced as dangerous, and, for all his patients, he learns to anticipate the form and severity of the ways they express anxiety. For instance, by interpreting the likely and understandable presence of fears when the context suggests they are only barely conscious, he may help the patient articulate them and deal with them symbolically in words. In this way the therapist can help the patient appreciate the validity of the anxiety and perhaps preclude the necessity to act on it in the form of a crisis. By interpreting, the therapist can both attenuate its severity *and* prolong the duration of the reaction to allow enough time to discuss and absorb its significance. To reiterate, it is not the therapist's aim to prevent crises, but to help the patient experience fully and safely both the joys *and* the anxieties associated with growth and change. The issue is the same for all patients in therapy or analysis.

## Negative Therapeutic Reaction

The ominous term negative therapeutic reaction comes to the mind of a worried therapist when a psychoanalytically informed treatment, which to all appearance has been conducted properly, not only fails to achieve all its hoped-for gains but also paradoxically seems to be making the patient sicker. Since Freud described it in 1923 and again in 1937, the phenomenon has preoccupied the field, with well over 100 references to the term in the literature. Many authors have described treatment failures that justify the ominous tone that the term has come to imply (e.g., Glover, 1971; Asch, 1976; Castelnueva-Tedesco, 1989). At the very least, the range of reported experiences demonstrates the wide array of guilt-inspired reasons advanced to explain why patients have failed disastrously when the treatment seemed to promise improvement. A few authors (e.g., Brenner, 1989; Loewald, 1972) have seen the need to distinguish the more implacable reactions from those similar in form but with more hopeful implications, such as the examples I have offered.

## The Nature of the Patient's Attachments in the Inner World

If a therapist can induce *some* of these vulnerable patients to tell about what is going on in their minds when they seem to be having particular difficulty allowing desirable therapeutic change to occur, he may hear a patient tell of a set of additional dynamics to those I have described thus far. As the patient describes his inner life, the therapist will gather that the patient has not outgrown the circumstances we presume existed during early childhood before the sense of self and nonself became clearly established; in his mind the patient is still living amidst unassimilated others. We presume that was a time when the images and memories of important others, real and imaginary, who were prominent in the child's environment were not yet integrated into a coherent social context and apart from the self. The result, as the therapist may infer from the patient's current experience, is that the patient, in effect, feels inhabited by a number of disparate personas, each of whom seems to have a claim on the patient and individually or collectively dictate what must and must not be done. Although the situation is terribly painful for the patient, these "beings" also seem familiar and dependable to the patient, far more than real people in his current life who are independent and have minds of their own.

We presume that all of us pass through such a stage and have similar experiences as we integrate our personalities. In these patients, however, development seems to have been arrested at this point. They seem acutely aware that their experiences are deviant, and they are hesitant to admit to them. They are also aware that these inner denizens are afraid of what the patient's psychotherapy might do to them; their very existence depends on the patient's remaining as is. When they feel threatened, which is most of the time when the patient is in therapy, they become a formidable foe. The patient is in conflict, wishing for a more normal and less painful life, but one he has never known; and he is also loyal to this inner group, which includes the only ones he can truly count on to be present and predictable.[4] The patient may seem to be able to obtain surcease from this inner horde by placating them with assurances that he will not change.

Thus, this additional dynamic, the nature and tenacity of the patient's attachment to objects in the inner world, may contribute to his fear of changing. Asch (1976) suggested that attachments to imagos of parents who idealized suffering might be responsible for the formation of a masochistic ego prone to negative therapeutic reactions. Bemporad (1994) emphasized how patients, particularly those with severe characterological depression, may be tied inexorably to representations of childhood figures. How widespread this phenomenon is remains unclear. Gunderson (1996) has called attention to the borderline patient's intolerance for

---

[4] You will recognize that I am describing a group of patients about whom alternative schools of thought have been constructed, for instance, object relations theory (Fairbairn, 1952) and self psychology (Kohut, 1971). I believe that therapists must adapt their technique to an understanding of how these patients, like all patients, experience their world, including how they experience the therapist, but I do not believe we need new psychologies to work effectively with them.

aloneness as an essential characteristic of this condition. He outlined the conditions necessary for an adequate psychotherapy, chiefly the continued availability of the therapist to provide opportunities for the patient to internalize an agency of self-soothing. Indeed, internalizing of aspects of the therapist is a likely mechanism of "cure," but a large part of the problem is not just the absence of soothing imagos but the presence of malignant ones who jealously interfere with the formation of any new identifications, such as with the therapist.

I mentioned at the opening of this section that one might have to induce a patient who seems to react negatively to ordinarily helpful interventions to explain why. When pressed, he may allude, perhaps reluctantly, as if unwilling to betray a family secret, to his fear of alienating inner objects, who become alarmed at any hint of change in the status quo, since they depend for their existence on keeping the patient in bondage. Only occasionally will a patient in a midtherapy crisis describe spontaneously such a personified inner world, and that he is tormented by his "voices," but that it is easier to defer to them than to fight.

Recently, I suggested to a colleague that the patient he was consulting me about might not have disclosed the presence of such an inner life. He asked the patient, whom he had been seeing for several years, if he ever had such experiences. The patient looked at him suspiciously and only after a while said he had never told anybody about them because he thought others would think he was crazy. The voices sometimes invaded his waking thoughts, but they were especially intrusive when he wanted to sleep. Then they would urge him to get up and snack—he would never lose enough weight to look good. They would say, "Who was he fooling? Nobody would give a damn anyway. He'll end up a suicide like his father, so why bother to discipline himself?"

When one sits with such a frightened and defiant patient, the hateful inner objects seem to have the awesome power to convince the patient that any "improvement" would undermine their relationship with him. One might think the patient would welcome a diminution of their power. But he is afraid to let go of them; they are "the only ones who can be counted on to be there." Indeed, they are "family." And the only way he can preserve them as his reference group is by remaining steadfast as the person they have defined as complementary to them.

Generally, since some point in childhood, the patient has been regarded by his family as a hopeless failure whose ambitions must be squelched and who must be kept in place at any cost. As in a tyrannical political system, the "overclass" of the "inner world" requires the unquestioning loyalty of a subjugated "underclass" consisting solely of the patient. For the patient, suicide, with its perhaps unconscious subtext of wiping out everyone, may seem to be the only alternative to passive acquiescence.

Such patients may say they worry that remaining in treatment only prolongs their misery and serves merely to postpone this inevitable act of freedom, atonement, and revenge. The patient described below is one who managed to outlive a reputation as having a negative therapeutic reaction.

*Example: Ms. L*
The patient came to therapy at age 30 as a last resort. She has been in treatment intermittently since adolescence and "none of it has helped." The thick medical chart bears out her story. She complains of depression and numerous physical symptoms but, if any therapist had inquired more closely, he could have heard that her inner state was not so much depressed as, as she put it, "I feel empty. There's nothing inside. I'm not solid, there's nobody home." She was considerably overweight from trying to combat the feeling of emptiness by bingeing.

Therapists soon tired of her because she failed to follow through on their treatment suggestions. After a short time of enthusiastic compliance and seeming progress, she seems to lose interest in the program, stubbornly goes on strike, and after a while breaks off treatment as unhelpful. She has just about written off herself as well. "If nothing works this time, I always have my stash of pills to fall back on."

No therapist would be eager to begin with a patient who quietly announces that her reserve option is suicide. However, the patient obviously is bright and has a certain ingratiating charm, and there is something appealing about her persisting at psychotherapy despite her series of failures. Her talk of pills does not seem threatening, but rather is a recognition that she does not have to agree to a life that seems to hold nothing for her.

She summarizes her history briefly, much as her chart recorded it. The oldest child of an alcoholic father and a long-suffering, depressed mother, she was both "parentified" as a youngster—given charge of the new babies that came along regularly—and abused sexually by her father until her teens. Although she has told the story to a succession of therapists, she still tells the sordid details haltingly, with much shame but with less resentment than one might expect. Her younger siblings owe their lives to her care of them but have written her off, as her parents did, for enrolling in business school in an effort to break out of the family's "white-trash" tradition.

She lives continuously with pain, though being in pain is not a major complaint. A congenital orthopedic defect and injury from a difficult birth required a series of surgeries beginning in childhood. Walking now was difficult, partly a result of unsuccessful surgeries. To the therapist's surprise, however, she continues to seek the "master surgeon," the one who can perform the miracle that will make her body whole again. Each time she was able to convince a surgeon to remove some supposedly offending body part, she would feel better until the period of convalescence was over, and then she would slip back into her usual state of empty futility. Between surgeries, she obtains some relief from her mental anguish by cutting herself.

As in her previous therapies, she attends regularly and is compliant and eager to hold the therapist's attention. She seems to want nothing more out of therapy than to be in therapy; earning her place by being a "good patient" makes her feel better so that she does not have to cut herself or binge. However, changing is not part of her program. When the therapist catches on to the regimen she has prescribed for herself and observes that there seems to be nothing about her life now that she wants to change, the patient's face darkens and she insists that things are OK now that she is in therapy. When the therapist observes mildly that once she held some ambitions for herself, succeeded at business school, and thought of going on to higher education, the patient protests that all that is behind her. Now she is a permanent invalid ready to be declared eligible for public assistance.

From time to time, the therapist has occasion to mention the contrast between her abilities and her refusal to consider any life other than as a chronic patient. Each time, it seems to him that the patient's stubborn expression comes close to panic, and at one point she seems ready to flee the session. He notes that he frightened her by wanting to understand what led to her adamant refusal; there must be very good reasons for it. She slumps in her chair, shakes her head, and mutters, "You couldn't understand." He waits as the patient starts to speak and then stops herself several times. Finally, she looks up at him appealingly, begging to be excused. The therapist had guessed what her problem must be and told her softly that she didn't have to tell what is holding her back.

As she looks relieved, he voices off-handedly his conjecture that she is not alone in this fix; there must be many interests that have to be satisfied by what she does with her life. She looks startled, as if he has guessed her secret, and when he adds, "They don't want you to tell me about them," she breaks down and cries for the first time. The therapist goes on to say that he is aware that she has a very serious dilemma and that there is no easy way out of it. He acknowledges that she feels she has very few moves open to her and suggests they might be able to find a way so that nobody loses. The therapist leaves it at that and allows the patient time to pull herself together. The patient says no more but looks at him gratefully, he thinks, as she leaves.

In the subsequent sessions, the patient feels safer, and the therapist remains receptive and nonintrusive and quietly maintains his position that everybody's interest will have to be respected. The patient tells more about her mind as being a kind of occupied territory. There are many of "them," how many she isn't sure, but more than a few. Occasionally she thinks she recognizes a voice, but she cannot be sure. Mostly, they are mean and accuse her of not doing enough. They say she is lazy and good for nothing, always thinking about herself and ready to betray them. She is not to think of changing, for she owes everything to them. As long as she was content to remain as she was, they stayed pretty quiet; in fact, she could come to therapy only by promising them she would not change anything.

As the therapist maintains his even-handed stance toward the patient and her inner entourage, the patient gradually becomes bolder, seeming to take courage from the therapist's interested tolerance of her situation. She has taken a part-time job that makes use of her business skills and no longer urges the therapist to qualify her for public support. She admits that "they" are no longer so active when she wants to sleep and so she has had several uninterrupted nights. Now that they are quieter, she has begun to show some interest in who they are and where they came from. The therapist ventures that they sound to him like her own reproachful voice repeating the same things she told him about her basic unworthiness that made it reasonable for her parents to abuse her and to punish her so severely in childhood. The patient seems struck by the idea that "they" are part of her, a way of keeping connected with the adults she then needed to survive by becoming the slavey they needed her to be. She can also see that was why she took the "good" parts of herself, her concern for others, and made them into a kind of psychopathology; her willingness to put herself out for the sake of friends who simply are unwilling to do for themselves amounted to submitting to exploitation.

As she starts to identify herself with the therapist's tolerant objectivity for her situation and his obvious warm interest in her, it makes increasing sense to her why she turned out as she did. She has come to see that she did the best she could under impossible circumstances. She no longer mentions feeling empty. Periods of tentative movement, trying new things, attempting to lose weight, and making new friends alternate with far briefer periods of what seem to the therapist to be deliberately slowing down and almost clumsy efforts to do things the way she formerly did. She looks guardedly at the therapist when she reports that she "backslid." He guesses she is wondering if he will think she is being disloyal to him. He supposes, too, that she has to be sure that just by allowing some change to occur she has not lost her ability to get by in the old way. She admits sheepishly that sometimes she does wonder if what is happening to her is real. At the same time, she realizes (with the therapist's help) that the very fantasy that she might have to get along with only her "old ways" means that she can imagine a life some day without a therapist and is fearful that she will not be able to take her new abilities into that new life.

Thus, intimations of eventual ending and termination appeared even as the patient was beginning to develop a sense of an independent self, to challenge the noxious assumptions she had adopted about herself, and to try out new ways of dealing with herself and others.

Treatment ended with a phase of termination when the patient was offered a better job out of town. The patient calls the therapist every few months to check in, to report that things are going well and getting increasingly better, and to make sure the therapist is "still there."

It seems axiomatic that the therapist ought to consider the malignant objects of the patient's inner world the enemy of the treatment. They certainly regard the therapist as archenemy, since he intends to change the patient's definition of self, which has always been the jealously guarded privilege of the inner objects. But this array of object representations, while assembled out of unpromising and painful developmental experiences, has still served several important functions for the patient. It has provided an identity, a limited and impoverished identity to be sure, but a sense of self nevertheless. As for all of us, this sense of self is defined in relation to the sense of "others" who provide a stable reference group. Would it not be foolish of a patient who had been raised in the matrix of an abusive family to surrender the miserable certainties guaranteed by the fantasized relationships with the abusive denizens of the inner world for the ambiguities of ordinary life and the possible fickleness of actual others?

When a therapist first encounters a sicker patient who develops such a middle-phase crisis, he faces a new diagnostic problem. At least the first time the patient exhibits such a reaction, the therapist will have to locate the patient's reaction on a continuum whose poles are mild resistance to change and malignant negative therapeutic reaction. If the patient was reasonably well selected in the first place, there is only one way to find out, and that is to assume, heuristically, that the reaction is toward the milder end and will be analyzable until proven otherwise. My concern is that factors within the therapist may tend to lead him to a dim view of matters, as did the earlier therapists of Ms. L. However, while remaining hopeful, the therapist must respect the patient's loyalty, coerced as it may be, to the inner objects and respect the courage involved for the patient to let go of the only thing that has worked for her in order to risk the uncertainties of changing.

### *"Crises" Viewed in the Context of Ending and Termination*

The therapist of such a patient will be subject to all the transference and countertransference factors I sketched for the therapist of Ms. J. The difficulties engendered by these factors also may be augmented by simple ignorance. As I discussed in Chapter 5, therapists who have been trained in programs that provide little if any experience in ending psychotherapy electively will also have had no experience in engaging in the work of termination, that is, in helping patients to separate the gains of the treatment from dependency on the therapeutic relationship, and to work through the implications of growth and separation.

As noted, most psychotherapy conducted in training institutions ends at the convenience of the therapist rather than according to the needs of the patient. Thus for some years after graduation, young therapists may not correctly understand the range of phenomena that typically accompany growth, change, and ending in psychotherapy. They tend to view with alarm phenomena that are expectable and even salutary. In particular, they seem to regard as a new idea the fact that the patients tend to show such negative reactions *after* therapeutic change has occurred rather than while they are in fearful anticipation of it, and that testing the continued involvement of the therapist, and other aspects of working through, generally are embedded in the reaction.

The eruption of a crisis in a patient's treatment always involves a jolt to the therapist's conscience. Even experienced therapists will have at least a momentary worry about what they did wrong or overlooked. And a therapist *should* have such reactions as spurs to sort out what is going on and how it might have come about. But guilt, particularly inappropriate guilt, can cloud judgment. It is not unusual to find that psychoanalytic candidates of good conscience are especially vulnerable to transference and countertransference centered on the fear of making a mistake that unwittingly inflicts pain. The worry that the candidate has done something harmful to precipitate the crisis leads him to abstain defensively from further interventions that he fears may be even more harmful. The candidate then becomes preoccupied with patching things up with the patient rather than exploring the meaning of what is taking place. It is as if, ironically, the therapist mirrors the patient's fear that the treatment might actually "do something."

It is a diagnostic challenge to distinguish the patients whose "flight into ill health" represents a sudden awareness that unexpected change has already occurred, with positive and negative implications that have to be worked through, from the patients who adhere to self-destructive modes of adaptation and are desperately loyal to persecutory inner objects. For the first kind of patient, the "crisis" represents a backhanded acknowledgment that more progress was made than was anticipated, and that, as usual, every solution brings new problems.

For the second group, an additional diagnostic step is needed; the "crisis" might signal that the therapist made a diagnostic error in accepting the patient into a treatment the patient cannot cope with and that further treatment will have to respect the unsuspected weakness in the patient's adaptive capacities.

The presence of a world of inner objects in itself, however, does not discriminate between the groups. Many people, including those whose midtherapy crises arise out of positive change, are aware that they carry with them representations of the important figures of their past that serve as reference points to be called on at the anxious moments when crucial decisions must be made, and who may comment on the action from time to time. Patients in analysis or psychotherapy frequently carry with them an imago of the analyst or therapist who generally intrudes as a rather stuffy and moralistic guide when the patient would just as soon be unobserved (Schlesinger, 1978).

A more promising discriminator is the nature of the world of inner objects. My tentative formulation is that the patients with more favorable prognoses are those whose inner objects are still particular and personified; their voices are identifiable. These objects have not yet been fully "metabolized" or internalized; one might say they have not yet become fully "structuralized." In contrast, the patients whose path to wholeness seems more difficult seem to carry with them a masked Greek chorus of woe-singers and nay-sayers; the voices are no longer those of individuals but come from disembodied shadows who know the patient well but are not known in turn. Patients refer to them as "they." I have only a couple of instances to support this suggestion, and I propose it only as a topic worth pursuing. Still, you will notice that the patient Ms. L was one whose treatment, while difficult, ultimately was reasonably successful. In contrast, here is a much milder example of the presentation of these dynamics taken from the psychotherapy of a neurotic patient.

*Example: Ms. M*
Now in her late 30s, Ms. M studied art here and abroad with noted teachers and is widely regarded as having great talent. She sought

treatment because of chronic anxiety but without any idea that her anxiety is related to her difficulty establishing a career. With great effort, she seems to achieve only minimal success. Over time she has come to recognize that she always gets in her own way and that her failures are calculated, obedient to the belief that her parents did not want her to succeed. They practice successfully in the same field of art, and she believes that they feel her to be an unwelcome competitor. She experiences them as looking critically at her and the work on her easel and shaking their heads ruefully, as if to say, what a mistake we made. The youngest of several children, she was born late in the lives of her parents.

After about a year of therapy, she understands her conflict well enough to price a piece of work appropriately and was amazed and delighted when it sold. She arrived at the session in which she announced this success with eyes sparkling and wearing a red shirt instead of her usual drab outfit. After telling the news, she burst into tears and wailed, "I'm so scared. I'm afraid I'll always need my parents, and the thought of their retirement terrifies me."

As she told her story, the images of her parents, images she could always count on to look on critically while she worked, faded. It took only a little interpreting to help her connect her joy about the sale with the not fully conscious wish to dazzle and shame her parents, and the fear that they will punish her by withdrawing. With this first, defiant success, she feels she vanquished her parents, and they in turn have rejected her. While the loss of their familiar, imagined presence disturbs her, she is able to hold on to the idea that she has the right to succeed on the basis of her own abilities and can also continue to investigate how she came to the strange idea that her success would be an anathema to her parents.

### Do the Principles of Ending Apply to Patients in Presumably Endless Treatment?

Earlier, I promised to continue the discussion of whether or not the principles stated in this book apply also to the severely and chronically mentally ill patients who may need lifelong care with medication and supportive psychotherapy. Such patients have always been with us. When I resumed my education after World War II, I found that the outpatient clinic in a Veterans Administration hospital had been designed for such patients; mostly they were the aging veterans of World War I. Green as I was, at first I could not understand the treatment regimen we were expected to apply. We were instructed that the patients had come to be treated by the hospital, not by us. The office we would occupy during this rotation had been arranged just so for many years, and we were not to change a thing—not move the furniture, not put up any new pictures or personalize it in any way. Neither were we to individuate ourselves more than was absolutely necessary. The patients, we were told, had come to this office for many years and were accustomed to being seen by someone sitting in that chair who would ask how they were doing, would make sure that nothing adverse had happened since the last visit, and would renew the prescription for whatever medication they were on.

The theory on which this regimen was based was later named "transference to the institution" (Reider, 1953). We were told not to expect, and certainly not to encourage, transference to the therapist, as we might have felt free to do in other forms of psychotherapy. My recollection is that, however awful this description of care may sound from a current vantage point, it did serve reasonably well to keep this severely disabled population out of hospital and engaged at least marginally in society.

My impression is that, despite firm instructions to the contrary, most of us young therapists had a hard time to keep from individuating ourselves and from offering a humane presence to the patients. I must admit, however, that the instructions we received were a useful warning that these patients would have difficulty remaining in contact with anyone who wanted to urge them into a relationship with more "warm fuzzies" (to use the vernacular of that time) than they could stand.

Years later, I came across a similar system in a university hospital. Some patients with chronic psychiatric illness steadfastly refused psychiatric care but would accept medical care. The program designed for them provided the psychiatric medication they needed and supportive care in the "Medical H" clinic ("H" for hypochondriasis). Unlike the instructions given in the VA hospital of ancient times, residents now were told to evaluate each patient anew—the condition of some might have "burned out"; others might have recovered sufficiently to permit a more expectant treatment. In any event, their chronicity was not to be taken for granted. Indeed, under this regimen, a few patients each year were graduated to an outpatient program offering psychotherapy that potentially was endable and terminable.

Each patient was reevaluated at least yearly when the new resident rotated in and the evaluations of these rather sicker patients were conducted much as I described for patients Mr. A, Mr. B, and Mr. E in Chapter 4. The governing idea was contained in the admonition to the residents, "Do not take the chronicity of the patient for granted." Each patient was given the opportunity to enter a new treatment relationship with new possibilities and new risks, and, depending on his readiness and the skill and personality of the therapist, new developments might occur.

*Resistance to Change: A Recap*

Resistance to change is a regular and expectable feature of all psychological treatments (Castelnuevo-Tedesco, 1989). Personality, like other bureaucracies, prefers the familiar status quo to the unknown risks of changing. Rigid and brittle personalities, like their governmental counterparts, may exhibit extraordinary, even violent, reactions to any well-intended proposal to alter seemingly self-defeating arrangements in the interest of improving efficiency or effectiveness or to achieve greater good or pleasure. When social reformers or therapists challenge such arrangements and raise the possibility of altering them, it always seems to turn out that the authorities consider the disputed arrangements to be vital to the maintenance of stability and good order, and therefore quite impossible to change.

In the consulting room, the therapist must be able to distinguish the reactions warning that measures are needed to avoid exposing the patient to excessive risk from the reactions indicating that some therapeutic change has already occurred and that working through its implications is in order. The diagnostic problem will be more complicated if the therapist is unfamiliar with the normal accompaniments (that is, the natural history) of growth and change in personality and patients' intimations of readiness to end therapy. A further complication is that therapiststs are subject to transference and countertransference attitudes that make it difficult for them to allow the patient to experience the pain (as well as the pleasure) intrinsic to therapeutic growth and development.

# Impasse or Stalemate?
# The Problems of Ending
# and Termination

Elsewhere (Schlesinger, 2003), discussing the optimal therapeutic relationship, I promised that I would take up the phenomena of impasse and stalemate[1] in a forthcoming work.Now is the time for that discussion. Impasse, generally considered among the most troublesome of the miseries of middle-phase analysis, may develop at any point in therapy when the two parties believe that uncomfortable stasis is preferable to risky movement. It is, however, especially likely to occur when the perceived risk is that forward movement might lead to the ending of the therapy and the feared dissolution of the therapeutic relationship. Before we proceed to a discussion of impasse as it relates especially to ending and termination, a review of the topic in general will be useful.

A psychotherapy is at an impasse when, although both parties are present, what goes on between them seems (to therapist, patient, or both) to be unproductive and has been for a significant amount of time. There does not seem to be consensus about how long the situation must persist to be considered significant. Schwaber (cited in Wallerstein, 1994) refers to "microimpasses," but seems to have in mind what most therapists regard as the ordinary ebb and flow of the treatment process. Mitchell (1997) described a case that effectively was stagnated for several years. When the impasse is so quiet as to be analogized to the doldrums, the question might better be put as, how long does it take the therapist" (or his supervisor) to catch on to the fact that for some time nothing has been

---

[1] Clinicians use the terms impasse and stalemate interchangeably. I use only the word impasse as it conveys more accurately the state of being stuck. Being at an impasse does not have the chess-derived implication of stalemate that, because neither side can defeat the other, the game is over. Therapy is not a zero-sum game, although it may seem at times that at least one of the parties is intent on defeating the other. Being stuck is not necessarily a hopeless situation, as this chapter discusses.

happening? As I have noted elsewhere (Schlesinger, 2003), when viewing psychotherapy, it is never correct to say that nothing is going on. A great deal is going on, but the nature of the activity may not be obvious, and it probably is not what the therapist consciously wants to have going on.

Descriptively, we can array impasses along a continuum from "noisy," with "transference psychosis" (Wallerstein, 1967) at one extreme, and "quiet," doldrumslike stagnation at the other. An impasse in which the patient is so disturbed as to be described as being in a "transference psychosis" is more likely to occur in one of the more vulnerable patients I described in Chapter 6. (I discuss the relation of impasse to the transference neurosis in Chapter 8.)

From a technical point of view, we may regard the impasse as an unsettled disagreement or argument between therapist and patient. The parties may be well aware that they are at odds, though each may have a different version of the origin, basis, or "cause" and desired outcome. Occasionally, however, one hears of an impasse in which—oddly, since I have described the situation as an argument—the parties (or at least the patient) may be aware only of being in a deeply unsatisfying situation with no idea how it came about and no idea how to get out of. All they, or at least the patient, is certain about, is that treatment is not helping. I attribute most of the uncertainty to the patient because the therapist may be convinced (probably wrongly) that he knows what is going on and what should be done to make it right, if only the patient were not so stubborn. In the impasse that Mitchell (1995) described, the analyst persisted in interpreting along a line that the patient persistently rejected while feeling that the analyst had something he wanted but refused to give to him.

Let us, then, regard the impasse as a chronic argument, whether verbally explicit or obscure, whether noisy or still, and whether or not the terms of the argument have been spelled out clearly by the parties. Finding out what the argument is about, why the parties involved cannot settle it, why it erupted when it did, and why it has lasted as long as it has are the immediate tasks of the therapy.

I am concerned particularly with the impasse that occurs when it would be plausible (for any or all of the interested parties, including those outside the consulting room) to consider whether the therapy has gone on long enough and now ought to end. For therapies that we expect to end with a phase of termination, impasses are mainly of the quiet variety, and the dominant mood is sad to sullen.

Occasionally, however, one hears of an impasse that is openly argumentative. A common version is one that comes to light when the therapist is disquieted by a growing awareness that the treatment seems to have bogged down, and he faces the embarrassing possibility that maybe it has been so for some time. If so, however, he cannot recall when it started to slow down. Nothing dramatic has occurred; the patient continues to attend faithfully, speaks more or less fitfully about familiar things but does not seem to have much of importance to say about them, does not complain vigorously but occasionally may utter statements about feeing mildly uncomfortable. The therapist notices (or perhaps his supervisor points out to him) that occasionally he comments dutifully about whatever the patient says but does not address the obvious stagnation that is present. Neither party seems to want to rock the boat. The situation, while mostly quiet, is not easy; the tension in the room is palpable. By analogy to a boxing match, the two parties are in a clinch, each afraid he will be hurt if he lets go. We could say that, considered from the point of view of regression, the level of discourse between the parties has lowered from symbolic speech to symbolic action—in their tense inaction, each inarticulately, but eloquently, says, "No."

## The Therapist's Contribution

Clearly, an impasse is a creation of both parties. While the patient often is held to be the source of the problem, an impasse requires the therapist's active or inactive[2] collaboration. Therapists of higher level patients who lapse into the more common "quiet" impasse generally contribute inadvertently by an error of omission, that is, by failing to act in the sense of observing and interpreting the unverbalized state of affairs that is developing between them. The noisier episodes tend to occur following errors either of omission or commission[3] by the therapist.

To refer to actions of the therapist in this context as "errors" is misleading. For therapist behavior to conduce to an impasse of either variety, the impasse would have to fit dynamically with the unconscious predicament of the patient. Thus, we regard the therapist as colluding unconsciously (probably) with the patient to produce the impasse as a desired outcome, at least the lesser evil. The therapist's "errors" in colluding with the patient to produce an impasse are motivated ones that arise in transference or countertransference of the therapist (Schlesinger, 2003). By viewing matters in this way, we can include impasse in the larger category of symptomatic behavior that requires a collaborator and view it figuratively as a form of folie á deux.

---

[2] Descriptively but not dynamically "inactive." The therapist is never an inactive ingredient in the treatment (Schlesinger, 2003).

[3] As viewed by the patient.

Here is an example:

Consider the predicament of a therapist who found himself "stuck" with a patient, Mr. N, whom he had been treating for some time and who had made considerable progress with some of the issues that had brought him to seek help. Having worked on the connections of his inhibitions to his relationship with his overbearing and infallible father, he no longer was quite so shy and began to report success in meeting women.

One problem remained; Mr. N could not deal with the awareness that at his office he had been passed over for promotion, and he brooded about it continually. The therapist was of an activist disposition and eager to help. Also, he was more than dimly aware that the patient's ineffectuality in this matter offended him. He found himself thinking at all hours about the patient's problem. He devised strategies to help him confront his boss without endangering his existing position. Aware that his investment in Mr. N's dilemma was excessive and that perhaps it had something to do with the slowing down of the treatment, he sought consultation and reviewed the situation. As is often the case, the therapist had all but figured out what was causing the difficulty by the time he presented the case to the consultant. The consultant, in turn, observed that the therapist seemed already to have figured out matters and merely summarized what the therapist had told him.

Hearing his own words spoken back to him succinctly, the therapist "got it," that is, he understood that the difficulty he had presented was an expression of the transference neurosis and that his sense of powerlessness stemmed from having become part of the patient's "problem" that he was trying to "fix." He was aware, he said with some chagrin, that the intention to "fix" his patient's problem was a milder version of *furor sanandi,* which had gotten in his way since residency. He knew that the proper stance of the analyst is to put aside his expectable professional intent to relieve pain and remove the cause in favor of trying to understand why the patient has put himself into such a state of discomfort and pain; to assume that there once was a good reason for the patient to accept this compromise solution to his conflict; and to avoid taking sides in that internal conflict. The therapist will, or should, seek to understand why the uncomfortable arrangement also serves the patient' interests. He recognized that he had been viewing the patient's problem as he might view a cancer, or a foreign body in the eye, something that is not part of the patient and can be extirpated, rather than seeing an arrangement the patient had devised, mostly out of awareness, to solve a problem he was also mostly unaware of.

The consultant could well understand that, despite his knowledge about the dynamics of the therapist's and the patient's contribution to the impasse, the therapist's instinctive reaction to "getting it" was to resolve instantly to stop doing "it"; he could hardly wait for the patient's next session to apply his new understanding by behaving differently. Fortunately, the consultation was not yet over. After allowing the therapist some time to demonstrate his new understanding and his renewed confidence by rehearsing the next session with the patient, the consultant cautioned restraint. He pointed out that the wish to fix things immediately is analogous to his actions that contributed to the very problem he had brought to consultation. The transference position the therapist "bought into" was the role of "fixer," the clueless outsider who heedlessly would disturb the delicate balance the patient had achieved.

Much as the patient would like to be relieved of the burden of the painful solution he had resigned himself to, anxiety warned him that things could easily become much worse and that there might be more to lose than gain by heeding the blandishments, persuasions, and implied threats of the now internalized analyst/helper, a kind of live-in enemy, to give up his hard-won compromise in favor of who knows what. The consultant stressed that the position the patient attributed to the therapist is one side of the patient's own conflict, not a new position, and it was a shifting position that depended on the nature and intensity of the patient's anxiety.

As the consultant reviewed why he thought the patient believed he had to cling to the painful and inadequate solution he had arranged, he pointed out that, now that the therapist had been brought into the patient's unconscious fantasy, he was actually in a privileged location, uniquely positioned to influence the fantastic arrangements in a way that he could not when he was only an "outsider." Now, as an "inside outsider," so to say, he could speak from this position, not merely act blindly from it, as he previously had done and had found so frustratingly ineffectual. However, "inside" and "outside" may be misleading terms if taken literally; having taken the therapist into the transference neurosis, the patient now enacts its script "outside" in the session.

The consultant then offered a demonstration of how the therapist could use the impulses that formerly led him to try to override the patient's fears by putting these same impulses into words. He explained that he would not be modeling actual statements the therapist could use with the patient but, rather, illustrating a stance from which, and in context, the therapist could generate more useful interventions. He offered several trial statements that had the general form of, "What you just said made me feel that I ought to persuade you to stand up to your boss—as if I wouldn't know how dangerous that might be and how often you tried to do it and to no avail."

The consultant illustrated that putting into words that the therapist felt drawn to play a role, that is, to act in the patient's unconscious fantasy rather than acting on it, served several purposes. First, putting into matter-of-factly spoken words that described the position in which he felt himself, that is, feeling impelled to interfere in the patient's carefully arranged solution, and by using words that manifestly are noncritical and appreciative, invites the patient to respond also in words and to reflect on the new turn that the therapy is taking. Second, putting matters into words always has the effect of slowing things down. Words, that is, untendentious symbolic expression, always take longer to utter than the actions they describe, and they draw for understanding and thoughtful response rather than instant reaction or a dismissive retort. Third, the therapist brings a new dimension to the discussion, a description of his inner state and attributes it to an effect the patient has had on him; he acknowledges that the patient has some power to influence him.

The consultant's account might sound as if he considered the position of the therapist in this situation to be like that of a "mole," a spy embedded in an institution to serve an alien purpose—hardly a palatable image for a beneficent therapist. However, the patient may well view the therapist in that way when he feels forced to compare the painful stasis of the impasse to the danger of changing. Perhaps we can imagine the analyst as a "friendly mole," one who allows the patient to view him suspiciously and even voices these suspicions for the patient as well as voicing his own inner reflections about being viewed suspiciously and about being pulled this way and that to do things that feel alien to him.

The advantage of viewing matters in this way is that it helps any therapist understand why, so much of the time, his patients seem to place themselves in sullen opposition to his well-meaning efforts to extricate them from the situations about which they complain. This version of the patient's dilemma is the same as I have proposed for all neurotic difficulties (Schlesinger, 2003) but it does not account for why the therapist, who also understands this much only too well, is at his wits end. All the therapist just discussed finally "got" from the consultation is that, willy-nilly, he has been co-opted by the patient (that is, has been molded by the patient's transference, aided by the therapist's transference to the patient and by his countertransference) so as to become an actor in the patient's unconscious fantasy as the patient enacts it in the script of the analytic session.

*Anticipating Impasse*

One lays the groundwork for an impasse at any stage of a therapy by allowing two components in the patient to remain unanalyzed: a dependent sexual transference and a deep attachment to the therapist.

This last statement contains a theoretical position and points to a direction of clinical activity as well. The theoretical position is that we should understand the episodes of noisy or quiet regression that form the impasse neither as accidents nor as inevitable occurrences with this particular kind of patient. Rather, they are emergents, if not emergencies, that result from the failure of the therapist (and perhaps also the patient) to appreciate the nature, intensity, and significance of the current state of the transference, or perhaps of a recent shift in the nature or intensity of a transference demand or expectation. I use transference here as an omnibus term to include not only the patient's transference toward the therapist, but also the therapist's transference toward the patient. It may be necessary in this connection to distinguish the therapist's transference from what we usually think of as his countertransference (Schlesinger, 2003).

I have described episodes of impasse as emergent but not as sudden. The therapist may be surprised, if not shocked, to discover that he and the patient are "suddenly" at an impasse, especially when a noisier one erupts. However, if one has an opportunity to query the patient, one may hear a different story, perhaps, "I was trying to tell him for weeks, but couldn't make him understand." For others, the patient also (I believe in collusion with the therapist and out of a wish to protect him) reports the episode as having a sudden onset. A careful review of the material may indicate that prodromal indicators were available for both parties to see and hear.

I do not want to leave the impression that impasses involving severe regression are inevitable in the treatment of vulnerable patients. Of course, when one undertakes to treat such patients one runs the risk of unproductive regression if the treatment is at all involving. If a significant relationship with the therapist develops, the patient will experience the temptation to regress. As the patient's conflicts are mobilized, tendencies to act in and out of the treatment situation will be as likely as with any other patient, but with a greater danger that the regressive swings might get out of hand. The therapist may find, however, that he can work most effectively, as it were, when the patient is on the risky edge of acting or regressing (which may amount to the same thing). For the therapist, the task here, as always, is to maintain the therapeutic situation and to help the patient experience and verbalize experiences rather than aborting them or short-circuiting them with regressive acting, whether overt or inhibited. Regression may be inevitable, but the situation need not settle into an impasse.

*Impasse and Regression*[4]

Although it is useful for the therapist to use his skills to preclude full-blown episodes of regression, he should not attempt to suppress the premonitory stages of such episodes, for instance, the patient's responding to a correct and well-timed interpretation with a sense of being moved, even shaken, and momentarily even feeling that he has lost his bearings. These feelings, which may be frightening to the patient, indicate that the patient is changing. If the treatment is at all effective, it is inevitable that the patient will experience such moments of change as unsettling. The therapist should be ready to interpret them in the sense I am describing, to help the patient understand why he feels as he does and to "normalize" the experience. The patient's response to the experience that something fundamental about him is changing (usually experienced by the patient as being changed by some external force) especially needs the therapist's interpretive attention (Schlesinger, 1996). These premonitory phenomena may take various forms, varying from tearful experiences of poignant affect, minianxiety attacks, a glazed look in the patient's eyes, or a more obvious "spacing out." These outward signs may be the indication that a change in self- and object concepts and a shift in the transference is occurring.

It is important that the therapist be secure enough to allow the patient to have these experiences safely, painful as they may seem to be. The empathetic therapist realizes that the patient's experience is complex, confusing, enlightening, painful, and also pleasurable and that part of the pleasure is the patient's sensing that he can "stand it" and can welcome that he is mastering matters that he formerly could not tolerate. The hazard for the therapist, as well as for the patient, is that the patient's transference is so coercive.

The patient's cry for help, embodied in his transference reaction, may polarize the therapist and force him willy-nilly into a position of acting or counteracting—with or against the patient. One common position is that the therapist identify himself with the patient and strive, first of all, to relieve the patient's (and his own) pain. Another common position is that of the helpless, would-be rescuer, sensing the danger to the other

---

[4] The following discussion rests on the several chapters on regression in Schlesinger (2003).

but standing frozen, unable to help. Every therapist has been in this situation, feeling "over a barrel," therapeutically impotent, perhaps seeing what the patient is doing but unable to help the patient or himself. We may think of all these therapist emergencies as counterpart experiences to the severe regressions of the patient but as experienced by a person less vulnerable to regression.

Calling attention to the parallels between the patient's severe regression and the therapist's crisis of impotence helps us to seek generality in what would otherwise seem to be a collection of particulars. If the therapist can entertain the possibility that, when he is feeling "in a bind," his patient may also be on the verge of feeling helpless, then he can consider that his experience may have been evoked by the patient in an effort to mitigate his own sense of helplessness. Then he may be in a better position to help both the patient and himself. The main point is that, when one is conducting a psychoanalysis or dynamic psychotherapy, matters should not be allowed to settle into an impasse; the therapist should not regard regression or the impasse itself as the "enemy" but as an occasion for useful work (Schlesinger, 2003).

## The Phenomenology of Impasse: A Clinical Example

Generally, when the therapeutic situation is moving toward impasse, the patient will be experiencing something like an "attack" of helplessness-hopelessness and rage. There may be a coloring of homo- or hetero-eroticism as well. The patient will be feeling "in a bind," "over a barrel," "in a crack," let down, even furiously disappointed. At the same time, or alternately, the patient will be feeling guilty for failing the therapist's expectations that he should be getting better, or at least not be a nuisance; and he is enraged about the therapist's "demands" that he should behave himself, no matter what and about the unfairness and injustice of it all.

What is going on in the therapist while these feelings are intensifying in the patient? Generally, in the situations that develop into impasses, the therapist will either be unaware of the patient's fearful sense of being in a bind or, more likely, will be highly defended against recognizing the extent of the depth and intensity of the patient's feelings and his desperation about them. The therapist's defensiveness may mirror that of the patient; it may stand for his fear that if he could recognize what is going on he would either have to yield to it or give it up.

Possibly, the therapist may be more or less aware of what the patient is experiencing, but he does not know how to interpret it without hurting or shocking the patient and hence is fearful about touching it, a fear possibly fed by the rage induced by the high level of mutual frustration. The therapist will not likely experience rage as such and, if he does, is likely to displace it and even deny that it has any relationship to the situation with his patient. Each party will be unwilling to face up to the nature and intensity of what is going on. This collusion of the therapist in the patient's defending against his own rage may increase the patient's sense that a loved and needed, but now untrustworthy, person is betraying him.

Here is an example of a therapeutic impasse of the quiet variety, which a resident presented at a case conference.

*Example: Ms. O*
The therapist is a psychiatric resident nearing the end of his outpatient year. He describes his patient, who is in her early 20s, as "not his most attractive patient, but close to it." She presented to the clinic because she is sleepless and cannot keep up her schoolwork following being "dumped" by a boy friend. She tends to fall into swift infatuations with unsuitable men and breaks off the relationships almost as rapidly as they were formed, but she is not accustomed to being dropped herself. The bit of history presented to the conference included that the patient hates her mother, whom she regards as "intrusive;" during her adolescence, she said her mother stole her first boyfriend and had intercourse with him.

The treatment has been underway for less than a year. Early on there were clear indications of erotized transference. The therapist said he had "worked on it," with the help of his supervisor, and "it had gone away." The therapist confided to the conference that he was having a painful time now. He had his own sense of attraction to the patient to deal with as well as her attraction to him.

From the anxious titters in the group as he told about the situation, it was clear to all, and later articulated by several of the residents, that the situation was not only painful. Even now that things had quieted down and "nothing" seemed to be happening, it was clear that the therapist still looked forward to seeing this patient. He described their sessions as quiet, even desultory. Ms. O is always prompt, never misses a session, and pays her bill instantly. She is also very exacting about the therapist's attendance and obviously is hurt when he is late. She spends much of each session with her head down, looking at the floor, often after only a few minutes of talking about nothing in particular. The therapist said that, while he had planned to continue this treatment after graduating, now he was not sure because he was uncertain that they were "getting anywhere." He said his supervisor had warned him that sometimes these conditions take a long time to resolve.

In the conference, we could help the therapist see that the "work" he had done with the patient's erotic feelings about him had only driven these feelings underground, which we might assume was the therapist's more or less unconscious intent. The patient was strong enough to suppress her feelings and not talk about them openly, while giving clear indications that, although she was able to inhibit them, she was unable to do anything else. Rather than "nothing happening," a great deal was happening; the therapist's account led all those attending the conference to feel the tension in the office.

Although the situation was manifestly uncomfortable, neither patient nor therapist was willing to move from his or her position. They were colluding to preserve what both of them valued and could have in fantasy as long as neither of them talked about it. Both patient and therapist were at least potentially aware that, if they talked about their relationship, they would risk losing the sense of excited but restrained involvement they were enjoying.

During the conference the therapist caught on to what was happening and kept saying, "But I thought I had dealt with that issue." At the same time, he recognized that the very way he had presented the case told of how he and the patient had colluded in constructing the impasse. We did not hear enough of the clinical material to demonstrate the presence of rage, but I believe all the other elements of the impasse were present.

We may also infer from the example that the therapist's transference to the patient, as well as his countertransference, were involved in producing the impasse (Schlesinger, 2003). As the resident came to see, the problem was his (and the patient's) wish to continue their relationship although the distress that had led the patient to apply to the clinic had long since been relieved. Clearly, one could see ample reasons why she might have wanted to continue in treatment, but they did not seem pressing to her and she did not offer them as reasons to continue. Rather, she and the therapist were not ready to face the realization that, while she had gotten what she had come for, neither of them wanted to stop seeing each other. The alternative to impasse, of course, was for the therapist to help the patient end and terminate this episode of therapy.

## Impasse and Ending Phase

Occasionally, a therapist, fearing that an impasse is impending, will be concerned when treatment slows down. However, matters may slow for good reasons and with no implication of stagnation. Paradoxically, this phenomenon is likely to result from successful analyzing. Consider the following example:

*Example: Ms. P*
The patient is a professional woman in middle age, widowed and without children. Her childhood was happy; her recollection is that she was a "winner" until puberty. In school, she quickly showed herself to be extremely bright. She surpassed all her peers in studies and was good at all sports but never was able to win consistently in tournaments. She was a third child; a brother two years older was as much trouble to the parents as she was a delight. This brother has been a chronic failure at life while envious of the patient's success.

Ms. P had a period of analysis once before when she was undecided between college and marriage. After a brief period in analysis, she broke off to marry and, after a while, resumed her undergraduate education. She sought further analysis when she realized that, although her career as an editor for a woman's magazine was successful, it was not fully satisfying as it used few of her many talents. She thinks she might have had a low-level depression for many years without fully being aware of it. In college she wanted to be a writer, wrote many stories and had even started several novels. She submitted only a few of her writings for publication, and, although several were accepted, she gradually stopped writing—she feels it was something she should not be doing but does not understand why. She applied to professional school, did very well, and is now firmly established in her field.

Her marriage, too, is not fulfilling. Ms. P resents her husband's failure to recognize that she has her own interests, although she does not push very hard at pursuing them. She thinks that, if he had not died prematurely, she probably would have divorced him. She has made many tries at establishing relationships with men but, although some lasted several years, she would not have wanted any of them to be permanent.

Analysis proceeded in classical fashion for several years, clearly building on the earlier analysis. The basic problem the patient had to understand and come to terms with was a conflict between her ambitions and her fear of loss of relationship (Shengold, 2002). To be everything she might be would be to surpass and in fantasy to destroy the persons she felt dependent on. Her pattern with men was to attach herself to a man whom at first she would idealize as powerful and authoritative and then gradually discover that he was not as smart as she required him to be. She would be embarrassed at the discovery and resentful that her needs in the relationship were not being respected, the inverse of the facet of the man that first attracted her, his single-mindedness.

As the core conflict became salient, Ms. P began writing again but mentioned her writing projects only in passing as if they were matters of no great interest. Once it slipped out that she had been looking for an agent and, at another time, that she had presented a book proposal to a publisher. Her social life had livened up, and her sense of depression diminished, only to be replaced by occasional bouts of anxiety. Dreams, too, displayed anxiety; she might go over a cliff, or she would be unable to stop doing things she enjoyed doing while her parents, waiting impatiently for her, became increasingly angry.

During this time, the pace of the analysis slowed perceptibly. Ms. P became more sensitive to the therapist's interventions and felt bruised by the kind of interventions she formerly had welcomed. She bristled at his intrusiveness and brooded about his insensitiveness and his failure to take her feelings into account. She became afraid that she might be influenced by him to change in ways that would make her no longer herself; there might even be dangers that she and others would be exposed to if she became less inhibited. She began to worry that the therapist might be smarter than she and that she might then be "stuck" with him, unable to leave a relationship that inevitably would distort her. On the other hand, if she proved to be the smarter one, he would become resentful and withdraw from her. Clearly, Ms. P foresaw dangers associated with continuing in analysis and dangers in not continuing.

The analyst recognized that, rather than sliding into an impasse, the patient was absorbing and working through the implications of the analytic work that she had done and was testing out the implications of letting herself begin to write again and extending herself in other ways. The analyst stayed on the interpretive line that she feared he would either insist that she become like him or withdraw from her if she persisted in going her own way. Gradually, the patient came to accept, both from the interpretations and from his behavior, that the analyst was willing to let her take her time and move only as fast as she felt safe. In a few months, it became clear to both that the analysis was in an ending phase;.

This case example typifies the situation after psychotherapy has brought about useful change in the patient's personality organization or in the way the patient deals with problematic situations. The patient will generally feel less distressed and more at ease. As the patient becomes more comfortable and tries his wings, rather than triumphantly announcing his successes, as a naive observer might expect, and then looking forward to ending the treatment, the patient will ignore them, possibly mentioning them in passing and ignoring the obvious implication that he may have had enough treatment. If the therapist does not comment on this astounding omission, the relationship may slip imperceptibly from an instrumental one designed to bring about change in the patient, into a relationship that is its own reason for continuance. It is as if the patient were saying through this behavior, "We got together to conduct a treatment, but now I want us to stay together because I want to be with you (or because I am afraid to be apart from you)."

When the treatment seems to slow down, the therapist will have to distinguish whether the patient is engaged in a needed period of practicing new-found capacities that requires the analyst's forbearance or is settling into a state in which no further change is expected or desired, least of all that the therapy should end. One clue is that, unlike the ordinary, clearly identified impasse in which there is a high level of tension, as befits an unspoken argument, this seemingly more benign situation may be relatively free of working-tension (Schlesinger, 2003). Of course, the patient may be anxious, as was Ms. P, about whether the analyst really will let her progress at her own rate or will join the patient in settling into a relationship for its own sake. In the latter case, the atmosphere tends to be quite comfortable; the participants may be pleasantly engaged with each other. There may be hardly a dull moment and few moments of silence. But, if our naive observer were permitted to look in, he would be hard put to say why these people are getting together, why one of the parties continues to pay for the attention of the other, and why that other accepts payment. It is difficult to recognize that any professional service is being rendered.

You might question the usefulness of lumping under the heading of impasse two phenomena of distinctly different import. One of these phenomena is inevitable in any normally progressing treatment: slower moving times and relative stasis alternate with periods of more rapid movement. When the patient has made progress, he may arrive at a plateau; he may need time to assimilate the changes recently brought about and properly is not yet ready to take on a new challenge. After a period during which he has accomplished important change, the patient might well find himself relatively comfortable and with the unaccustomed leisure to reflect on where he has been and where he might go. The contrasting phenomenon feels ominous, a stagnant situation with or without tension that seems to have no exit. Indeed, it might take careful observation to differentiate the two situations. The reason to put both situations under the rubric of impasse is that in both, for the moment, the patient is in what I have called an "ending phase" (see Chapters 1 and 3).

The question facing the therapist of both patients is, has he done enough so that we ought to be thinking about ending or is the patient taking breath (or a breather) before taking on a new challenge? When these phenomena occur in the treatment of a patient who has accomplished what he came for and more, the therapist will naturally consider if this is a time when they could end the treatment. The therapist could presume, even though the patient has not mentioned it, that thoughts about ending have occurred to him too while he hopes they have not occurred to the therapist. If the therapeutic relationship has acquired a value of its own, as it usually does, that very thought might motivate the patient to want to stay put. The state he is in is certainly more comfortable than the one that preceded it, and possibly, too, the one that might follow it.

My point is that it is useful to consider the situation of the patient in an ending phase—a phenomenon that occurs many times during a therapy—as if it were a variant of the quiet form of impasse, or perhaps consider the impasse to be a version of the ending phase phenomenon only writ large.

The therapist who is aware that the patient has accomplished something useful has no pain, and, perhaps only for the moment, has lost his sense of urgency. He will also be aware that this comfortable situation could lapse into an impasse. Allowing enough time for the patient to resume the lead, he can help the patient to recognize what is going on, take stock, and decide whether or not the therapy is worth continuing. If the therapist does not interfere, the patient (rarely) may raise the issue himself, may even (more rarely still) stop unannounced, or (most likely of all) settle down in this relatively comfortable but seemingly purposeless state as if it were its own reward. There is, of course, a purpose to the seemingly purposeless chatting, but it is covert. The purpose is to maintain the relationship and to avoid anything that might threaten it. Additional therapeutic change might be desirable for its own sake, but the patient is willing to forego it because pursuing it might put the valued relationship at risk.

## Diagnosing Whether Treatment Is Active or Stagnating

How can one tell if a therapeutic situation is still active, even though for the moment it is quiescent, or if it has become stagnant and tends toward impasse? There are several indicators that one can use to make this important discrimination. These indicators are the same as I proposed for determining if the process between therapist and patient is optimal for therapeutic purposes (Schlesinger, 2003):

1.  There should be an optimal level of "working-tension" between therapist and patient (Schafer, 1982). This optimal level is generally much lower than the intense sense of frustration that characterizes a "quiet impasse" and is certainly lower and different from the kind of tension present in the noisy version of the impasse. But there is a clear sense of a "working level" of the tension of expectation between the parties that is perceptible to both (and to the supervisor, if there is one).

    Other sources of tension may be present, of course: the patient may be dissatisfied, feeling that there is more to do; things may not be going quite right in the patient's life; a nagging problem may bother him. While such matters may trouble the patient, however, the therapist will have the odd feeling that he is uninvolved; he will not feel that the patient is demanding covertly that he fix the unpleasant matter. Of course, if any of these obvious "extrinsic" sources of tension in the patient is present, it will help to reassure the therapist that there may be more to do and hence that the treatment may be presumed to be "active."

    Such external indicators may obscure the fainter signs that the "basic working tension" is absent. If such extrinsic sources of tension are absent, the therapist will find it easier to detect whether the basic working tension is present or absent. That is when a naive observer wonders if the participants have gotten together merely to pass the time in each other's company.

2.  The basic working tension is often a subtle affair, apparent, for instance, in the patient saying, "I didn't know why I was coming today, and then I remembered this dream . . ." or "I thought of canceling this session, but then I remembered what you told me last time. . . ." In brief, there will be evidence of the patient's awareness of opposed transference wishes or opposed transference and reality-based considerations.

3.  There will be a focus in the joint or complementary activity of the participants on some prevailing concern. It may not always be in the forefront of their attention, but they will return repeatedly to it. The patient will likely focus on "something outside" in his life, but something that also finds representation in the therapeutic relationship. The "something" is a troublesome aspect of the patient's life that conceivably is within his power to change or about which he can change his attitude sufficiently so that it no longer will be a problem. In short, while the patient complains about his wife's niggardliness, the therapist will be considering

the metaphoric implications of the complaint, that is, that the patient also resents the therapist's withholding from him. If the therapist loses sight of the metaphoric quality of the complaint and agrees with the patient who is complaining about the weather that truly, "the weather is at fault," we may suspect that an impasse is close at hand.

4.  The flow of a patient's material generally takes a predictable course. If the therapist follows the stream of associations, he can discern whether the direction suggests involvement in the therapeutic process or in some other form of interaction. Indications of involvement in the therapeutic process include that the patient tells of events outside the treatment, usually current events of the patient's life. As these become exhausted for the moment, the patient's attention turns next to events inside the session, and from there to events in the past (Menninger and Holzman, 1973; Schlesinger, 2003). This pattern is typical of a patient's communication when transference is a major controlling force in psychic life. Events in life, if not governed in some sense by transference, are selected for recounting by it. Those events then lead associatively to more or less direct expressions of the transference in terms of actual or fantasized interaction with the therapist. These interactions then lead associatively to the recall of events in the more distant past, even childhood, that resonate with the current transference disposition. When the patient's associations do not flow in this way, but remain stuck in one or another of the three areas, or oscillate between two of them only, these patterns suggest that the treatment too is stuck.

It is important that the therapist recognize when the pace of the treatment has slowed and then to attempt the differential diagnosis of process. Perhaps the patient has had enough for the time being and needs a little time free of pressure to absorb and integrate his accomplishments before going on, or perhaps he has done enough so that it is time to consider interrupting or ending treatment. Or it may become clear that the patient is about to settle down to a steady state that is intended to sacrifice further change in order to put off ending the relationship with the therapist. This alternative, of course, is an impasse aborning, and now is the best time to deal with it. Another possibility is that, after the analysis has done all it can do, both parties agree that it would be useful for the patient to remain in a supportive relationship with the analyst, with relatively infrequent visits.

*Dropouts*

The way in which patients end treatment that is most troublesome to therapists is by "dropping out." Seemingly without warning or discussion of any kind, the patient fails to show up for a scheduled appointment and may refuse further contact altogether. The experience may traumatize the young therapist in the training clinic particularly if he is a recent arrival and, as sometimes happens, several of his newly assigned patients disappear in this way. The supervisor, in an attempt to be helpful, will reassure the therapist about the "kind of patients we see these days," and he will tell the therapist about the administrative procedures the clinic has developed to formally end the clinic's treatment responsibility for patients who miss too many sessions or who absent themselves, without sufficient excuse, for a statutory period. The therapist will gather that the clinic is quite used to such misbehavior, but, if he is at all sensitive, he may wonder if it is a sign that he is not suited to the field. If he carries on, likely fearful of losing another patient, he will treat all his patients more tentatively and perhaps more cynically. Supervisors and colleagues will commiserate and do what they can to reassure the therapist to restore his confidence.

The young therapist generally will not be helped by reassurance to understand why some patients behave in this way, and it is even less likely that he will be helped to see how some of the ways he may have dealt with his patient, his acts of commission and omission, might have contributed to the problem. We may suppose that he did nothing out of the ordinary range of what young therapists are taught to do about how to engage with the generic outpatient. Nevertheless, his way of working with the patient may have had the side-effect of giving unintended, possibly frightening messages that may have made it seem to the patient that it would be safer to leave without discussing his plans.

Before taking up the matter from the point of view of technique, I must review two implications of the previous paragraphs. First, we cannot dismiss out of hand the reassuring remark of the supervisor about expecting this kind of behavior from "this kind of patient." In my experience, students in the mental health professions, other than perhaps social workers, do not study the sociology of the populations from which their training cases are drawn. Nor do they learn about how their patients experience contacts with the social service and public health care services they must depend on, may be grateful for, but also often resent.

Patients' anticipations about a new "provider" will be mixed for reasons that have to do with their previous encounters with "the system" as well as their character and dynamics. Let me note that, if the therapist who was stood up by his patient had been sensitized to the circumstances and experiences of his patient, he might have noticed that, at a certain point, the patient began to withdraw from him and could have taken up whatever it was that implied imminent detaching. The hints of imminent detaching are the same, of course, as those I listed as markers of accomplishment, task completion, and ending phase in Chapter 2.

We can reject another implication: if the therapist had done everything properly, the patient would have, and should have, stayed in treatment. Without knowing much more about the case and the treatment, we cannot rule out that it might well have been the right time, or at least a reasonable time, for him to leave. What is troublesome about the dropout is the *way* of leaving. I assume that the patient did not leave impulsively but that the therapist missed the patient's hints that he was thinking of leaving. Since the therapist missed these hints, he could not help the patient to verbalize either his doubts about what was going on or that he was no longer feeling any need for therapy. Unwittingly, by leaving unverbalized his fear that he might be coerced into staying, the patient may have felt he had no choice but to "vote with his feet."

Another common determinant of dropping out is that the therapist overestimates the patient's attachment to him and to the therapy. Some patients sense that they mean more to the therapist than the therapist means to them and that, for his own reasons, he desires them to stay and to engage in an emotionally painful process. Other patients may leave without warning because the therapist has missed the hints that they already got what they came for, or at least no longer are driven by the sense of urgency that first brought them. For their part, they are done with treatment and are ready to leave while the therapist seems to be out of phase, planning a new treatment for them. They may feel too intimidated to raise the matter and find it easier just to split.

Clearly, the problem of the early, nonconsensual ending can be traced to the way the treatment was begun. Whether a stalemate or a dropout eventuates depends less on the dynamics than on the personality characteristics of therapist and patient including frustration tolerance, impulsivity, intensity of attachment, and, not least, common sense. Consider that the treatment that comes to a dead halt, either through paralysis of the parties or the decamping of one of them, might be a treatment that would discontinue for other reasons. Good sense on the part of the patient might dictate departure on the grounds that the therapist seems unlikely to "get it," while the patient feels unable to help him get it.

Lack of urgency, loss of "tension" in the process, and other indications of anxiety not obviously related to the problem that brought the patient— while not exclusive indicators of impending dropout—should inform the therapist that the patient is experiencing emotions that are not part of the explicit conversation between them.

Dropping out has multiple meanings. A culture of irresponsibility, resentment, getting back at indifferent social systems, insufficient relationship with the therapist, excessive libidinal demands by therapist, feeling better, and so on should alert the therapist to become aware of the likelihood that a patient will not come back the next time. If he does, they can take up in session what the feelings and attitudes of the patient are, providing an opportunity for him to put them into words rather than action.

# 8

# Interminable Analysis

This ominous-sounding term refers to the unfortunate tendency of some psychoanalyses as well as psychotherapies to drag on endlessly and unproductively, to the despair of therapist and patient and the uncomprehending dismay of all classes of third parties.

The phrase interminable analysis may give rise to a range of associations. The more philosophically minded may entertain considerations of an existential sort. "Isn't analysis a kind of education? After all, Freud (1917) even called it 'after education.'" One never finishes one's education; there is always more one can learn. As I discussed in Chapter 1, in principle, perhaps, both psychoanalysis and education should be considered as unending. Both are, in essence, lifelong projects. Unfortunately, educators, and philosophers can more easily take comfort in this line of thought than analysts and therapists can. Analysts recall the pessimistic tone of Freud's (1937) late paper on "analysis interminable" and may also have personal associations to the experience of neverendingness. With a cold twinge in the heart, one recalls the analyses and psychotherapies begun with such high hopes but that for mysterious reasons later bogged down. No longer guided by a goal, they followed some weary logic of their own while getting nowhere.

I will return later to consider whether the existential position may have some validity for analysts after we have examined some issues exemplified by the cases each of us has had that seemed, for one reason or another, to get stuck, to arrive at an impasse that threatened to become permanent and perhaps ultimately did so.

A reader who has not yet been in this painful situation might wonder at such a point. As I suggested earlier, he might inquire naively, when viewing an impasse at any time, "Why is the situation so problematic? If the analysis is getting nowhere, why don't they just stop? Why doesn't the patient just get up and walk away? I hasten to caution that in some company the answer to that question is likely to be unfriendly. If a civil answer is indeed forthcoming, it will likely be preceded by a burst of sullen resentment and the thought, if not the expression, "You've obviously never been there, or you wouldn't ask such a question."[1]

Let us look a bit closer at the phenomenon captured in that bit of dialogue. It is the essence of feeling stuck that one feels unable to move forward or backward, unable to go on and unable to extricate oneself. Like the spouses in a bad but stable marriage, both parties seem to hate it but neither can give it up. Something seems to hold them together even as it prevents them from accomplishing their other ostensible purposes. Life being finite, sooner or later one or the other party will come to an end—but the marriage need not end, and frequently it is not ended by the death of one partner any more than it is necessarily ended by a divorce. We all know of persons who are still very much married to the spouses they have legally divorced, while others are psychologically divorced from the spouses to whom they are still legally married. So it is with some psychoanalyses. The treatment we call interminable will end eventually, at least in the narrow sense that the patient will no longer attend sessions, but it may never terminate in the specifically analytic sense of that term.

While conducting the second or subsequent analysis of such a patient, one may hear his bitterness about not having been understood that tells that the previous relationship never ended. The analyst must hear the metaphoric implications of such recollections, of course, but it is noteworthy that they remain as points of reference.

To make sense of these assertions we will have to recall the discussion of the distinction between ending and termination in Chapter 2. The terms are not synonymous.

You may have heard in these musings an allusion to the aphorism attributed to Freud to the effect that the neurosis is immortal. Indeed, the phenomenon of a treatment that seems unable to stop does seem to be a case in point. To jump ahead in my argument, I propose that the impasse that leads us to invoke the term interminable analysis, like any impasse, is an expression of the neurosis[2] that brought the patient to us in the first place. It is the revival of the patient's neurosis in the analytic situation, or, in other words, it is a version of the transference neurosis.

I must digress here to firm up the link between interminable analysis and the transference neurosis. For all the importance we assign to the

---

[1] Kubie (1968) reviews the problem in resolving transference that lead to interminability and recommends that another analyst be called in to effect termination.

[2] I use "neurosis" as an omnibus term for the patient's conflict-based psychopathology.

transference neurosis in clinical psychoanalysis it is remarkable how slim the literature is on the topic.[3]

Freud (1914) stated clearly that if a patient is able to conform to the regimen of psychoanalysis, a transference neurosis regularly appears in which the symptoms of his illness acquire new meaning. In 1917 he further clarified his understanding that the original neurosis is replaced by a "newly created and transformed neurosis . . . which lies in relation to the transference" (p. 444). He warned also that one should not expect to reconstruct from the manifest transference neurosis the dynamics and economic conditions of the infantile neurosis. The transference neurosis is a new construction (p. 455).

Glover (1971) and more recently Cooper (1987) spoke for those who doubted that the transference neurosis is a universal experience. Glover held that it is seen in characteristic form only in hysterical conversion reactions and obsessions. He even listed a number of conditions under which the development of a transference neurosis should not be expected. However, Glover also took a position quite like the one I advance: that it is possible for an analyst who is not alert to such phenomena to overlook the subtle manifestations of the transference neurosis. Glover offered many examples of what one might say are "uncharacteristic" transference neuroses that, at least for a time, can escape the notice of both patient and analyst. He thought such oversight likely when the patient is able to conceal ambivalent attitudes about the analyst through identification with the analyst and when an apparent impasse in the analytic work is in itself the unrecognized indication of the transference neurosis.

For our present purpose, citing Freud, Glover, and Cooper may be sufficient to sketch the range of thinking about the transference neurosis and justify using it to understand the phenomenon of interminable analysis. Notice that I have brought together two issues necessary for an understanding of interminable analysis: the transference neurosis and the impasse. My argument can be restated to the effect that an impasse in analysis can be, and I believe usually is, an expression of the transference neurosis. If not recognized as such and if allowed to continue, such an impasse eventually may be renamed interminable analysis. To be sure, this simple construction is easier to describe than to modify.

This formulation has at least one potentially misleading implication that I would like to disown. Linking the transference neurosis and the impasse that in some cases may be its major manifestation with interminable analysis does not imply that these phenomena necessarily interfere with analysis only toward the ending phase. Neither the impasse

---

[3] See *Psychoanalytic Inquiry*, Vol. 7, No. 4, for a review of the topic of transference neurosis.

nor the transference neurosis is purely a characteristic of the closing phase. As discussed in Chapter 7, both may occur at any time.

It is usually held in the oral tradition of analysis, if not in its literature, that it takes some time for transference to develop and particularly for the transference neurosis to develop, if indeed (as some authorities doubt) it ever develops. The counsel I received from certain supervisors during my candidate days, and an opinion I have heard expressed many times since at case conferences, is, "It is too soon to be expecting a transference neurosis. You should be patient, interfere minimally, and allow the transference and transference neurosis to develop undisturbed. Psychoanalysis is, after all, an expectant treatment."

Under any circumstances, it is dificult to fault advice to be patient. But it is utterly wrong and frequently destructive of the analytic purpose to link the prescription of patience to the general expectation that transference and transference neurosis are late-developing phenomena. That erroneous expectation in itself could well lead to a treatment's becoming stuck.

While it is often asserted that the appearance of the transference neurosis ushers in the middle phase of analysis, it can appear quite early, chronologically and does so much more frequently than is commonly recognized. I believe that most of the problems that we link with interminable analysis are problems not of the termination phase but of an analysis that has become stagnant. One may justly say that such cases include analyses that were never properly begun along with analyses that are having trouble ending. To the extent that we can link the dismal prospect of an interminable analysis to the common phenomenon of the analytic impasse, we will have opened a way to deal with the problem.

The debate still continues as to whether or not the transference neurosis is an essential aspect of psychoanalysis. Some authors (e.g., Cooper, 1987) ask if there are not cases in which we do not see a transference neurosis. My categorical answer is, No, we do not see such cases in psychoanalysis. Much as I would like to stand pat on that categorical statement, I hasten to add some qualifications. First, we must agree to include only analyzable patients who are in analysis; not every suffering person has the necessary ego (and other) resources to be able to profit from analysis. Klauber (1977) described cases that he found impossible to terminate; he finally concluded that they also were not analyzable. Regardless of what may be written on the monthly bill, not every person supine on a couch in the benign presence of an analyst is necessarily "in analysis." But asking if analysis is actually going on begs the question at issue here (see Schlesinger, 2003).

It may seem like a play on words if I say that the essence of the problem, indeed, is that we may not "see" such cases in analysis (Schlesinger, 1994).

Glover (1971), who was one of those who doubted the universality of the phenomenon, also suggested that the problem might well be that the analyst literally does not see what is going on, so to speak, under his nose. From years of supervising candidates' analyses and being consulted by colleagues, I am convinced that is frequently the case.

The cognitive root of the problem is that we are accustomed to thinking of the transference neurosis in terms that are much too narrow; we are misled by the expectation that only certain obvious clinical manifestations deserve the name. We tend to think of transference neurosis as necessarily implying an exaggerated version of ordinary transference phenomena—livelier, noisier, and more boisterous. When the patient's associations revolve solely about the person of the analyst, when the patient is exigent, importunate, and generally impossible, then a transference neurosis is unmistakably present. When we see these same phenomena in their most flagrant form, we may even elevate them to the status of "transference psychosis" (Wallerstein, 1967). A far cry indeed from those murky, stagnant pools we call impasses in which patient and analyst are up to their necks in desperate inertia.

We forget that being at an impasse—being in a painful state of frustration, inexpressible yearning, boredom, and rage, being "stuck"— is a quiet, sullen version of the transference neurosis, expressing the same variety of unconscious fantasies as does its noisier cousin. When one is up to one's metaphorical elbows in alligators or quicksand, it is hard to remember that these are the very conditions that psychoanalysis was designed to treat. Recall that the psychoanalytic situation was contrived to convert a chronic neurosis or chronic disorder of character into an acute disorder. It was designed to facilitate the open reenactment of issues of the infantile neurosis or later development on a new stage, that is, in the analytic situation. The "lytic" function of the psychoanalysis operates on the transference neurosis. We cannot treat the infantile neurosis in its historical locations, only as it becomes transformed and displays itself in the here-and-now of the analytic situation.

I have reminded you of matters that for the most part are well known. But the persistence of the problem suggests that the major cause is likely not to be a lack of information about the problem. Let me now take up again the questions conveniently raised earlier by our naive reader, which I summarize as, "Why don't they either get on with it or quit?"

You will certainly have surmised that the reason for the "stuckness" of the impasse is that the parties are in a transference–countertransference bind and cannot extricate themselves because they are each in conflict, bound by ties of love and hate, committed to the conditions of a replica of the very neurosis that the patient brought in the first place. Like Laocoön trying to free his children from the snakes, the analyst and the patient have become emotionally entwined with each other in a neurosis transformed by the analysis itself into a folie-á-deux. Either form of the impasse—the frighteningly noisy and threatening one, or the quiet, stagnant, mutually frustrating one—implies, first of all, that the psychoanalyst has become a coconstructor of the transference neurosis. The analyst, willy-nilly, has become part of the problem he set out to fix.

This account of the unpleasantness may seem to place the blame for the situation on the analyst, and under the circumstances, it would be hard to find anyone else to blame. Nevertheless, I am actually describing a most hopeful situation. For, if one understands the impasse as resulting from a transference–countertransference bind, it is a situation that is likely to yield to analyzing.

Perhaps this is the place to mention that not all apparent impasses are of this kind; consider the following alternative possibilities. First, it is the analyst's responsibility to rule out that the stasis may represent an earlier diagnostic error, for instance that the patient was improperly selected for analysis in the first place. In this case, the stasis might be better understood as a last-ditch effort by the patient to defend himself against an even more severe regression. Second, both the analyzable stalemate and the diagnostic error may be signaled in other ways as well, such as the so-called flight into health. Precipitous acting out (better called acting up) or flagrant attention-seeking, social misbehavior implying a wish to be rescued, suicidal gestures, and other intercurrent emergencies also require the analyst to make this differential assessment of the treatment process. Third, for completeness' sake, I should mention once again that occasionally a seeming impasse may simply imply that the patient has had enough for the moment, is trying to assimilate analytic work done previously, and may be defending against being overloaded by a zealous analyst. In this instance, forbearance is called for.

You will have noticed that the question raised by our naive reader has given rise to a new and better question, What keeps the patient and analyst from analyzing so that they can either get on with it or quit (or find a more appropriate treatment)? We can offer a useful answer only in connection with a specific case example that illustrates the complicated ways in which the neuroses of patient and analyst interpenetrate. This sort of information is rarely available other than in the setting of the analyst's personal analysis, and it is usually necessary to make do with a reported vignette from which one may be able to make plausible inferences about the underlying unconscious factors of both parties. Before I introduce such an example, a sketch of the general conditions that guide the formulation of an answer is useful.

### The Effect of the Transference–Countertransference Bind on the Therapeutic Split

The presence of a transference–countertransference bind interferes with analyzing in several interconnected ways. Perhaps the most important impediment occurs when the analyst (and perhaps the patient, too) loses his therapeutic split (Sterba, 1934). This split is the capacity that permits the analyst to experience what is going on in depth and at the same time to observe himself clearly; it is a capacity essential for analyzing. It is also a fragile capacity that easily becomes impaired when the analyst is in the grip of a strong affect, whether anxiety, guilt, lust, or fear. When the analyst must defend himself against the awareness or expression of any strong affect, the split becomes "rewelded." If I may use a metaphor drawn from movies about the old West, when the settlers are threatened, they no longer can afford to spread out to explore the terrain but must prepare to defend themselves. Defense demands that they draw the wagons in a circle and await attack. When so preoccupied with defense, the analyst surrenders for the time being the abilities both to experience his own state of mind and to empathize with the state of mind of the other. And with that surrender, the analyst's sense of potency and his therapeutic leverage diminish sharply.

When such a situation is brought to consultation, it is generally after the analyst has struggled alone for some time. He presents the material diffidently, ashamed and chagrined that he allowed things to get to such a pass. However, he presents the case clearly and concisely, and invariably present is the phenomenon for which there is no universally accepted term but only local descriptors. In Denver, near the foot of the Rocky Mountains, an analytic audience would have no trouble appreciating the situation of the patient and analyst if I were to say that they were behaving as if there were a dead elk in the room getting older and smellier by the hour. Neither party dares to comment on the presence of this large, strange, and noisome obstacle that has somehow come to fill the space between them.

When one calls the attention of the analyst to the presence of this unremarked and presumably uninvited hulk, the effect invariably is salutary. The analyst has "sort of known it all along." Yes, he knows that the patient is probably equally aware of it, and both are aware that each of them is avoiding saying anything about it. The reasons offered for this mutual restraint may be of several kinds and speak to the underlying (unconscious) reasons for the inhibition, for instance:

"The patient is sensitive about that issue; she has recently lost her father."

"The last time I tried to interpret that, there was a huge blowup, and the patient stopped coming for a week."

"I can't think of a way to interpret that without sounding critical."

"I'm reluctant to interpret her attraction to me because I think I may have inadvertently encouraged it, and it doesn't feel right to blame her.

Each of these reasons or rationalizations illustrates the "involuntary participation" (Menninger and Holzman, 1973) of the analyst in the patient's transferences; countertransferences are interfering with the analyst's ability to split therapeutically and hence to analyze. It is my general expectation that the analyst who offers one of these excuses is at least half-aware that it is an inadequate reason for nonanalytic restraint and that it rests on a personally motivated avoidance. When the analyst recognizes that his personally based avoidance is contributing to the impasse, he is close to beginning to solve the problem. Not infrequently, the analyst brings the case to consultation when he has already arrived at that awareness, is ready to do something about it, and wants to have his judgment confirmed. In that event, the consultant, like the supervisor of earlier times, gets the undeserved credit for solving the problem.

Of course, the amount of time that is allowed to pass before the analyst recognizes, however reluctantly, that he has a problem and decides to do something about it varies enormously. If the time is brief, the threat that the analysis will drag on interminably hardly arises as a realistic possibility. But I believe it does arise as a haunting eventuality whenever impasse is present or impending. I speak of it in this imprecise way because the possibility contains some ambiguity. After all, the threat of interminability may also conceal a wish by both parties to go on forever.

While we speak loosely of interminable analysis, we should put the matter more precisely: the interminability (that is, the prolonged impasse) has come about because the parties are not analyzing. By not analyzing, the parties have surrendered the instrumental character of their professional arrangement, and so the relationship, but not the analysis, becomes interminable. Recall that I mentioned that a feature of the transference neurosis and of the impasse that may express it is that the attention of both parties is centered on the relationship. One of the main conscious and unconscious motives of the resistance expressed in the impasse is a fear of loss of the object, whether through death, abandonment, or rejection. One might say, somewhat circularly, that the "purpose" of the impasse is to prevent movement since movement implies change and change implies loss (Shengold, 2002). Thus, the impasse is in every sense a conservative operation. It is "designed" not so much to "accomplish nothing" as to "prevent everything."

We might return now to the existential musings with which I began and see that we need not reject the existential view of an unending analysis. We can say that it is the unconscious motive of the patient at impasse, and also, if possibly to a lesser degree, of the analyst, to prevent change in order to keep from losing the relationship. Is this not a strange fear? We do not need to be reminded, after all, that the actual current relationship between analyst and patient does not end when the patient stops attending sessions. Ending an analysis no more ends the relationship than leaving home ends the relationship between parent and child. As I noted earlier, we may think of both analysis and education as lifelong processes. When a patient terminates an analysis, he does not have in his possession a product called "analysis" that he can demonstrate, but rather an enhanced capacity to analyze, to stay in touch with himself in depth, and to be more respectful of the human condition of others.

The anxieties that lead to impasse are not about loss of the "real" relationship but, rather, about loss of fantasies of the infantile relationship. In the patient's unconscious fantasy, personal growth, development, and change are conflated fearfully with loss, abandonment, and death and lead to defensive efforts to freeze time in the form of the analytic impasse. Thus, the impasse typically represents a fulfillment of the conditions of the unconscious fantasy. Its reenactment amounts to a "return of the repressed" (Freud, 1896). Both the wish and its punishment are represented—a fantasized immortality is one of the imaginary gains resulting from surrendering the opportunities for real growth and development. The analytic impasse, as a version of the transference neurosis, like all other symptomatic behavior, achieves the illusory satisfaction of a fantasy by surrendering satisfaction in reality.

The analytic impasse, then, is not the analytic equivalent of the doldrums. It is not a windless lull when "nothing is happening" but rather a period of apparent stasis brought about by the subtly balanced dynamism of opposing forces within as well as between analyst and patient. The impasse represents a coconstruction, or collusion, depending on the imagery you prefer, between patient and analyst. It is a time of great tension, if little apparent movement. The impasse, as a version of the transference neurosis, is the clinical situation that psychoanalysis was designed to treat, and the painful situation generally is analyzable.

# 9

## Ending, Termination, and the Life Course of the Analyst

It may seem strange to arrive at this topic close to the end of a book on ending and termination of psychoanalysis. Thus far, my attention has been on the experience of the patient before, during, and after treatment. I have given some attention to why patients come to analysis but none so far to why analysts do. To round out the discussion of termination, which mostly has been about what we hope the patient will get and hold on to from treatment, let us consider now what the analyst gets out of the experience; after all, he repeatedly experiences ending analyses. What are, then, the analyst's rewards from analyzing, and what happens when analyzing is no longer rewarding?

In previous chapters I have stressed that doing psychotherapy and analyzing are serious matters requiring years of study and practice to develop an effective level of skill. By the time they graduate, most analysts are in or are approaching the state commonly regarded as middle age. One might infer that this is a very difficult profession to enter, requiring years of prior academic and professional preparation; that practice is full of hazards and pitfalls; and that what analysts do is hard work made even harder by difficult patients. Moreover, a central theme of this book is that success and change are always accompanied by loss as well as gain and that patients are not always eager to give up the illusory gratifications embedded in illness for the more mundane gratifications available in reality. Analysts, too, face loss of a valued relationship when they help a patient end a successful treatment. One might wonder what attracts would-be analysts to a field so marked by trouble and loss and what keeps them engaged in it? What rewards induce an analyst to take up the grave responsibilities of the profession?

### The Rewards Intrinsic to Analyzing

Beyond the obvious fact that it is the way the analyst earns his living, I have hardly mentioned the intrinsic rewards of this profession; nor have I considered the effect on the analyst, on his work, and on his patients if those rewards were to diminish or be totally lost. To speak openly of the intrinsic rewards of analyzing—the intrinsic pleasures of analyzing—is to invite misunderstanding on a grand scale.[1] Some of you who have experienced analyzing as I describe it may feel that it is something that should not be spoken about in public. It is tempting to analogize to the way most of us were taught about sex. We were told everything, in exhaustive detail, and with the utmost seriousness; everything, that is, except that it is fun.

I think there are very few analysts who have not experienced pleasure when analyzing, at least some of the time. But we may not feel comfortable using the term pleasure in connection with analyzing—which is, after all, our work.[2] I suspect that, if we were to discuss this point at greater length, even those who might be offended by my using the term pleasure in connection with analyzing would agree that a pallid synonym like "job satisfaction" offers greater dignity but quite misses the essence of the experience.

These observations imply a question: what is the nature of the pleasure in analyzing? What keeps us listening, attentively and mostly quietly, to the same few patients, day after day, week after week, for years? What is so absorbing about analyzing? Clearly, it cannot be the content alone. Fascinating as it might seem to an outsider to hear the secrets of interesting people, it cannot be that alone. After a while, one has heard it all. There are few surprises, in the sense of hearing something one has never heard before; after all, there are few original sins. The same sorts of things disturb most people. In any event, analysts hear them over and over again; considering only the content, analysts hear a never-ending refrain.

### Pleasure and Analyzing

The importance of the experience of pleasure in analyzing is that one of the reliable indicators that a psychoanalysis is going well is that the analyst

---

[1] I refer to analyst and analyzing only to avoid the ungainly construction therapizing for what therapists do.

[2] I am omitting further consideration of the economic motive; after all, there are many easier ways to earn a living.

is enjoying his work. You may object that the analyst's enjoyment certainly cannot be taken as the sole indicator that all is well. We are all painfully aware of potentially enjoyable experiences that would be worrisome. Perhaps for the sake of clarity I should invert the assertion. Let me propose, then, that one of the surest ways of knowing that a psychoanalysis is *not* going well is that the analyst is *not* enjoying his work.

The major implication of this point is that to do analysis effectively, the analyst must allow his mind, in both its cognitive and its affective capacities, to operate freely, to "play" in the sense that a fountain plays, allowing its functions to be exercised naturally (Alexander, 1958; Greenacre, 1959). The analyst's mind should be minimally constrained; that is when it functions best as a therapeutic agent.

Notice that I have used the words work and play in several different ways. Clearly, we cannot do without the term work for what the analyst does for a living. We need the term work, at the very least, to answer our children's questions about what we do at the office all day. It would hardly do to call it play, even though, as I hope you agree, the essential activity of the analyst's mind is much closer to play than work. You may recall that Freud (1908) viewed the play of children as opposed not to seriousness (that is, to work) but to reality. And yet the playfulness I allude to is not at all divorced from reality; indeed, it may provide a safe way for a child patient and analyst to approach essentials,[3] (Solnit, 1987).

Winnicott (1968, 1971) put the importance of playing in the context of psychotherapy or psychoanalysis most strongly. In 1968 he noted that, "we must expect to find playing just as evident in the analyses of adults as in the case of our work with children. It manifests itself, for instance, in the sense of humor" (p. 592). He also observed, "Playing is *essentially satisfying*. This is true even when it leads to a high degree of anxiety. There is a degree of anxiety that is unbearable and this destroys playing" (p. 598). In 1971 he asserted:

> The general principle [is that they occur] . . . *in the overlap of the two play areas, that of the patient and that of the analyst.* If the analyst cannot

---

[3]Among analysts, the child analysts have dealt most extensively with play, its significance in development, and its place in treatment. A child analyst expects to enter into the play of the child during sessions and in that way to facilitate the communication of feelings and thoughts that the child cannot put into words. A skilled and secure analyst of adults will also be willing to enter into the indirect modes of expression of the patient, whether verbal metaphor or (analogous to the play of the child) enactment, and for the same reasons. This technical use of the child or adult patient's "play" is important, but it is tangential to my current argument.

play, then he is not suitable for the work. If the patient cannot play, then something needs to be done to enable the patient to become able to play, after which psychotherapy may begin. The reason why playing is essential is that it is in playing that the child is being creative [p. 54].

If we admit the use of the term work to describe the analyst's vocation, the activity for which he gets paid, how should we think about the colleague who tells us that he "is working very hard" with a particular patient? He certainly does not get extra pay for the extra effort; analysts do not generally get paid for overtime. I am inclined to accept in part such self-description as an honorific complaint, a tribute to the moral imperative that we sedentary types also should earn our bread by the sweat of our brow, and as a covert plea for admiration. But I am concerned when I hear it from a candidate in supervision. After all, it is not self-explanatory or necessarily virtuous for an analyst to experience himself as working hard. The situation is analogous to that of a patient who describes himself as working hard. The patient's hard work nearly always represents resistance, especially when the ostensible goal of the effort is to overcome resistance. Consider, for example, the protestation of a patient, made with the full expectation that the analyst will consider it praiseworthy, that he is "trying very hard, working really strenuously, to try to overcome my inhibitions." The experience of working very hard suggests a violation at least of the spirit of the "basic rule," essentially to give voice to everything that comes to mind.

This pattern can be seen in supervision when a candidate seems to be straining to learn how to analyze. He concentrates very hard to understand the patient but regularly misses the point. As he follows the patient doggedly, sticking close to his heels as if to keep him from getting away, the essence of analyzing escapes him. When an analyst is fearful about losing the patient, or worried lest he fail to catch every word to report to the supervisor, he cannot let his mind wander or take the skips and leaps it should be free to take (Schlesinger, 1994b). Neither can he permit himself to sit back and sense the absurdity of what the patient is doing and then try to help the patient appreciate the absurdity. My use of the word absurdity here may jangle; let me clarify what I mean by it.

Understanding the patient and the analytic interaction is a serious matter for both patient and analyst. But seriousness of purpose does not require an atmosphere of solemnity or sterility. During psychoanalysis the patient will experience a wide range of moods and emotions, from gloom to elation, from hate to love, from finicky aloofness to passionate involvement, and from apathy to excitement. Tears are common, of course, but sessions are also occasionally punctuated by laughter. I want to focus on the moments of laughter, since I believe the phenomenon of laughter in analysis has a systematic importance in our understanding of the analytic process and is not commonly given enough weight.

To be more precise, I think that whatever laughter does occur tends to be ignored in "official" reporting, as not fitting our canonical expectations. The laughter is not usually at a joke. It occurs spontaneously and quite naturally when the patient catches on that there is something ridiculous about what he is saying, or has just thought, or perhaps when he becomes aware of the contradictory premises in his argument and realizes suddenly that his strongly held position is untenable; it is absurd. The ability to catch on and to respond emotionally and appropriately to such absurdities may, indeed, be of the essence in analyzing neurosis. The patient's laughter, of course, may have various qualities; frequently it is rueful, sometimes sardonic and occasionally joyful. With not a few patients— until they catch on that it is all right to laugh, that analyzing is not a solemn ritual that would be profaned by laughter—one may hear suppressed or aborted laughter, an embarrassed snicker, or see a furtive smile, an odd grimace, or a sneaky grin.

I have used the word absurd here in the same sense as in the theater of the absurd. Like Ionesco's actors, patients are driven to reconcile incompatible premises. The license of the psychoanalytic situation allows patients (although they may feel forced rather than permitted) to express themselves freely. Inevitably conflict emerges, and the efforts at reconciliation yield strained and lumpy compromises. After all, the essence of the idea of neurosis is a conflict in which "A" and "not-A" collide in the same time and space, when an unconscious wish and the defense against it achieve representation simultaneously. The result is usually an absurdity, but one that is not always immediately obvious to the patient. For as the patient attempts to "tell his story" in free discourse, he steers a careful course, balancing among the requirements of expressing impulse, respecting defense, and observing reality, while constantly seeking adequate representablity for his ideas.

Under the most facilitating of circumstances, it is difficult to affect a compromise among these claims. And the psychoanalytic situation, by encouraging continuous rather than discretionary expression, is marvelously designed to make compromising even more difficult. To draw an analogy from the highway, the more skilled a driver is at steering, the less obvious will it be to a passenger that the driver is attempting to avoid imaginary potholes. One might say that offering the patient the basic rule is analogous to suggesting to a nervous driver that he take his hands off the wheel so that we may see where the car will go on its own. A linguistically skilled patient is better able to conceal illogic or avoid obvious self-contradiction by lapsing into vague references, by slipping into generalizations when specificity is called for, or by sliding gracefully off the topic.[4] Linguistic skill may make the intrinsic absurdity of his position nearly imperceptible (Schlesinger, 1994a, 2003).

Much of the analysis of resistance, and much of our technique in working with such material, has the immediate intention of slowing the patient down so that the effort he puts into defensiveness becomes more obvious. At the same time, we encourage the patient to listen to himself. As the pace slows and as the analyst helps the patient hear the inconsistencies and internal contradictions, the patient first may feel forced to rationalize them. It may take some time before the patient is able to see the non-sense in the contrived order. It is, of course, a matter of clinical judgment in each individual case whether to wait for the patient to discover the absurdity for himself or to confront him with the contradiction as soon as the analyst becomes aware of it. I have stacked the deck, of course, by putting the choices so baldly, for it is my own preference, and I think better technique, whenever possible, to allow the patient the right of first discovery.

The point of this digression about the analysis of resistance is that, if the analyst is able to stay relaxed, he will be more sensitive to the subtle signs of underlying absurdity that inevitably emerge as opposing forces vie for expression. If, instead, the analyst fosters an atmosphere of solemnity, the intrinsic absurdities might not be noted and appreciated for what they are—perhaps not until they hit him on the head. If not expectant of absurdities, one might tend to overlook or excuse them as forgivable lapses in English usage, rather than understanding them as the essence of the patient's communications (Schlesinger, 1994a). If he maintains a stifling atmosphere, he might forego much of the therapeutic leverage of the analytic situation. The stance the analyst takes strongly affects the way he listens to the material and how he understands what he hears, just as it influences the patient's understanding of what is truly permissible to think, feel, and say.

It is essential that supervisors be able to help young analysts appreciate the absurdity in the material, particularly as it is expressed in the transference, that is, in the patients' verbalizations and behavior with respect to the analyst. It is equally important to help candidate analysts welcome awareness of the absurdities in their own responses to patients' behavior. Absurdities do occasionally appear in a candidate's technical interventions (and other behavior). I do not mean the clumsiness that results from the expectable awkwardness of inexperience, although that does play a part, but, rather, the compromise formations that stem from

---

[4] "Man devised language to conceal his thoughts" (attributed to Talleyrand).

the candidate's unwittingly assuming the position of the object of a patient's transference fantasy.

The absurdity will show even more clearly in an analyst's unspoken thoughts, to the extent that he allows himself to be carried along by the patient's material. The supervisor hears about these previously unspoken thoughts, of course, only if the candidate feels safe enough to voice them in supervision. If the analyst is sensitive to faint signals of counter-transference, he will also be able to participate minimally but still perceptibly in the absurdity of the neurosis. It is useful for the analyst to do so, for by splitting analytically (Sterba, 1934) he will be able to experience and view the absurdity and underlying conflict at the same time. The analyst must be free to observe from these several perspectives in order to help the patient appreciate the complexity of his experiences.

## The Several Theories of Pleasure

To discuss these issues further, it is necessary to clarify the meaning of several other key terms besides work and absurdity. Let us consider briefly the psychoanalytic theory of "pleasure." Freud's (1911) early idea was approximately that pleasure equals discharge. You will recall, through, that, if the equation is true at all, it is true only in the reverse. Rather than pleasure equaling discharge, it is more accurate to say that the inhibition of discharge may lead to the experience of "unpleasure." That early theory, of course, uses the terms pleasure and unpleasure in different senses than we require for our present purpose. While the reflex arc might conceivably serve as a model for some of the experiences of the neonate, we now need a theory suitable for mature and complicated human beings for whom pleasure does not imply merely release of tension but is, rather, a complex affective and cognitive experience conditioned by many internal and external factors. When we consider the experience of analysts, who have a large proportion of their needs met and their pleasures fulfilled by the psychological treatment of others, we are at quite a remove from the reflex arc.

Ideally, an analyst experiences at low intensity both the feelings he originates (including the transference) and the feelings evoked in him by the patient's transference. His ability to do so is an additional benefit of maintaing the analytic (therapeutic) split" (Sterba, 1934).

The intrinsic pleasure in analyzing is not a direct function of experiencing evoked affects, even affects at low intensity. In the first place, the affects evoked in the analyst are not generally pleasant; dysphoria of some degree is far more common. The evoked feelings generally conflict with those the analyst would comfortably recognize in himself.

Transference attributions, if understood fully, are not usually flattering, and the emotional position and attitudes assigned by the patient to the transference figure are seldom those one would care to endorse for everyday living. They are not ordinarily narcissistically enhancing.

## The Duality of Process

Elsewhere I have discussed (Schlesinger, 2003) the psychoanalytic view of "process." Here I consider how becoming immersed in it can be a source of continuing fascination for an analyst, enough to provide a lifetime of fulfilling activity. The concept of process in psychoanalysis includes two contrary trends. On one hand, process implies the idea and ideal of progress, and it is linked also to the theory of development. Observing the process of development, we observe an accumulation and reorganization of small changes that build eventually toward a new synthesis. On the other hand, an analyst expects to see the familiar recycling of self-defeating behaviors as the patient relives the script of an unconscious fantasy. The analyst tries to influence this pattern of endless repetition so that new events may occur in the patient's life. In other words, he tries to reduce the hold of repetition on the patient so that development may reclaim its normal place in the patient's life.

One reason that analyzing is so difficult is that, in a sense, recycling through an unconscious fantasy is a sort of guarantee of immortality—life never changes; Peter Pan never grows older. On the other hand, restoring the natural course of a developmental process permits maturation and aging to resume. As we grow older and presumably wiser, and give up being victimized by an ever-repeating, familiar past, in which there are no surprises, we allow new, risky, and exciting things to occur. Analysis, after all, is a method for opening a hermetically sealed personality, a chronic neurosis, to the possibility of new experience. The structural changes in the organization of the personality that we seek are merely the guarantees that openness to new experience will endure.

After this circuitous digression, you might ask if there is a relationship between the patient's achievements and the *analyst's* experience of pleasure in analyzing. First, another digression: it may not immediately be obvious that the patient also may enjoy the process of analyzing. I do not mean enjoy in the sense of the lady of hypochondriacal disposition who was described as "enjoying ill health." Neither have I forgotten that neurosis is a painful condition and that psychoanalytic treatment frequently involves a good deal of pain for the patient. It is not the pain that should be enjoyed. Neither is enjoyment to substitute for or compensate for the pain. Rather, the conditions of the analysis should be such that it is possible (and worthwhile) for the patient to experience the pain fully, not simply put up with it. The pain is not simply an inconvenience, or even a necessary evil that lies on the path to a higher satisfaction. The pain is not instrumental, and there are no prizes for suffering. Rather, the pain is part of the process. The patient comes to understand and accept that much of the pain he experiences belongs, in fact, to painful memories and that the recovery of those painful memories is intrinsic, if not essential, to the treatment. It might be better to speak of reconnecting current pain to the appropriate memories; to derive some satisfaction, if not pleasure, from discovering that today one is capable of bearing that pain; and that, by the patient's bearing it and working through the old connections, the pain diminishes and his strength and possibilities grow. The appreciation that the pain of memory is linked to painful realizations in the present is an experience one cannot avoid if one is to live fully.

There is pleasure, too, in achieving mastery and pleasure and legitimate pride in permitting oneself to risk experiences that previously one had to avoid. In this sense, the well-analyzed person has available a wider range of pleasures than before and can take deeper pleasure in the ordinary experiences of life. The lesson all patients must learn is that banishing one feeling generally banishes or attenuates most feelings, including pleasurable ones.

I have alluded here to some ideas presented more fully elsewhere (Schlesinger, 1995a, 2003) when I highlighted the technical importance of bringing into the analysis the complex of emotions, surprise, dismay, anxiety, and also pleasure that follow an effective interpretation. These experiences, which regularly accompany a moment of insight, must be recognized and acknowledged by the analyst and extended as long as possible. It is at these all too fleeting moments that increments of intrapsychic change occur, changes that potentially could become structuralized. The feelings that infuse such moments are generally mixed. They include an element of pleasure that is likely to be overlooked by the patient unless the analyst recognizes it and helps the patient to validate it. The intervention should be designed to help the patient appreciate the complexity of his response to the interpretation and help link the feelings of pleasure and discomfort to their context.

We welcome the situation when a formerly dour patient finds it possible to laugh during a moment of discovery, discharging the tension that accompanies sudden insight, even while he simultaneously experiences emotional pain. Any psychoanalysis will yield many such mixed emotional states, and the analyst must help the patient to experience the complexity fully, to appreciate the pleasure and pain separately, see the black as black and the white as white, rather than defensively blending them into a bland, neutral gray. The patient then comes to appreciate the special qualities and distinctiveness of each of his feelings, as well as the significance of their emerging simultaneously. And, of course, the occasional flash of humor may also signal a welcome increment in objectivity.

It is interesting to note that, when talking with new patients about undertaking psychoanalysis, analysts considerately enumerate the likely duration, the expense, and the possibility of painful times. I have never heard of an analyst who has ever mentioned that the process might also be enjoyable. Indeed, some might consider the suggestion frivolous; and, since the patient is sufficiently distressed to consider undertaking a psychoanalysis, it is at the very least, beside the point. Perhaps it is best that the enjoyment of analysis remain a secret for each patient to discover for himself—that analyzing and achieving a new mastery, coming to understand himself and his circumstances better, seeing new choices emerge where formerly compulsion reigned, constitutes an adventure, one replete with "heady" experiences. There is enjoyment and gratification in achieving mastery and coming to understand oneself, and enjoyment also in appreciating the absurdity of the solutions that conflict-governed, compromised behavior formerly entailed.

To return for a moment to the theory of pleasure: if we put to one side the old discharge theory of pleasure–unpleasure, we can recognize that in mature persons pleasure, as well as wisdom, derives from the various ways and the various paths through which they delay and channel, rather than inhibit, the discharge of drive. For mature persons, the experience of forepleasure, figuratively as well as in the specifically sexual sense, is linked both conceptually and psychologically with anticipation of end pleasure of various kinds. At the other end of the pleasure spectrum, aesthetic pleasure, whether achieved through artistic creation, through the appreciation of the artistry of others, or through the appreciation of nature, also depends more on what happens on the path of discharge than on the fact of discharge itself. This brief excursion around the theory of pleasure is merely an allusion to a larger treatment of a theory of affects that I cannot develop here as fully as it would need to be.


## Pleasures, Legitimate and Nonlegitimate


To return to the couch and to the chair behind it, perhaps it is time to ask if pleasure is an unqualified "good" in analysis. We can recognize that there are several legitimate sources of pleasure potentially open to the analyst and that each of them may be experienced appropriately, or insufficiently, or to excess. Let us consider some of the sources of pleasure we have all experienced. A common one comes with the feeling of hatching a brilliant interpretation. Akin to the pleasure one takes in a sparkling bon mot, or a masterful tennis shot, a well-formed interpretation may be enjoyed by the analyst as much for its intrinsic brilliance or elegance as for its usefulness to the patient. I have chosen my words here to suggest that admiration for one's productions, pleasurable though it can be, is not the main source of pleasure I am asking you to consider.

A second source of pleasure derives from the relationship itself. There are few human relationships that match the analytic relationship for closeness, intensity, and intimacy. There is pleasure in knowing one is trusted to an extraordinary degree and knowing also that one is trustworthy. To be sure, the enjoyment of closeness and intimacy is tempered by the recognition that it is an extraordinarily unbalanced relationship. The two parties do not have comparable power or matching expectations. When analysts lose sight of the stratified nature of the relationship, which follows from its professional purpose, and value attributions of magnificence and the perquisites of illusory power for their own sake, the pleasure taken in the relationship can become nonlegitimate or, perhaps, illegitimate.

A third source of pleasure available to the analyst is akin to that available to a good parent: the enjoyment of observing and participating in the growth of another person. Good teachers also have this source of pleasure open to them and, considering the economics of education these days, it may soon be the main pleasure available to them.

But pleasure in facilitating another's growth is also not the essential pleasure I am asking you to consider. Perhaps its importance, and the importance of the pleasures taken in intimacy and openness, might be captured best if I inverted the propositions. For example, I think we might feel more comfortable with these ideas if I suggested that, if a clinician finds intimacy and intensity in relationships distasteful, or if he is often made envious by the growth of another, then he probably should not be doing psychoanalysis. It is a delicate matter to talk about, and perhaps all I am doing is letting you see that I have not fully resolved my uneasiness in talking about pleasure in the analytic situation. Perhaps I protest too much, fearful that you might get the impression that I believe doing psychoanalysis is one long, unbridled joy.

### The Unique Pleasure in Analyzing: Function Pleasure

The main source of pleasure to consider now is of a different order. It has been called in other contexts "function pleasure." The child who masters walking, or crawling, experiences pleasure not just from getting somewhere or getting there faster, although that is not unimportant, but also from the sheer enjoyment of being able to move. Children clearly enjoy themselves not only when they are going some place but also when they merely are in motion. For grownups, it is more difficult to separate function pleasure from goal-attaining pleasure, although, considering the sweating hordes running in circles around the park, it is not impossible to separate function from goal. But even while drenching a sweatsuit one may have a goal. For some the goal may be as concrete as running six miles. Others may be working off the guilt of overindulgence, or paying for it in advance. For some, I imagine the goal is the certainty that they will either live forever or die healthier than the rest of us. But for an increasing number it is simply the awareness that they enjoy running. Running, they tell me, is in itself pleasurable; for some it is even addictive. In any event, and without prejudice against heavy exercise, I imagine that the healthier we are, the more are the areas of life in which we can achieve function pleasure.

All the sources of analysts' pleasure I have pointed to in the analytic situation can be found in other activities as well. But there is a source of function pleasure that I would like to think is both intrinsic to the analytic situation and perhaps also unique to it. It derives from the opportunity the analytic situation provides the analyst to allow his mind to play fully, untrammeled by the necessity to solve problems, achieve goals, or promote survival.

The analyst's source of function pleasure can also be thought of as coming from the free use of what Isakower (referred to by Balter et al., 1980) called the "analyzing instrument," that is, the analyst's ability to allow his mind to run free, to "hover evenly," to associate freely, to dip in and out of the patient's experience and his own, to allow bits of his own history to emerge, to do all those things that we summarize inadequately as "being intuitive." Then, or perhaps even at the same time, and with another part of our mind, he tests the adequacy or truth or plausibility of what is occurring to him about the patient. He formulates an intervention, an interpretation, and tries it out in his own head. The analyst may (but does not always) offer it to the patient as an inspired guess. Then he listens and watches more or less disinterestedly for confirmation, for rebuttal, or even for refutation.

The analyst can indeed enjoy being partially, or even thoroughly, wrong, especially if he is wrong for the "right" reasons. This paradox deserves more thorough discussion, but consider, by way of illustration, the not uncommon experience of being "misled" by a patient (through transference and countertransference) so that one proposes a particularly wrong idea. One may surprise, annoy, even shock the patient—"How could you think of such a thing?" Early in one's career one may retire in confusion, vowing to bite one's tongue the next time a bright idea surfaces, while hoping only that the faux pas will not come to mind during supervision. But if one does not expunge the idea completely, one may find at a later time, and perhaps at a deeper level, that it was in large measure correct, although perhaps offered prematurely.

The process of understanding, listening and associating, developing hunches, testing them in one's own mind before voicing them, allowing an idea to emerge and change, to be reformulated and refined, allowing oneself to be the instrument of a creative process as patterns of layered meaning emerge and take shape is as close as I can come to describing what I think of as the essence of the function pleasure of the analyst.

As we allow our minds to play in this way, sooner or later we find, as we expected we would, that the scenery of the patient's mind becomes familiar; we see that we are retracing old ground. In this way, without our searching for it, and without our attempting to force the patient's material into a standard paradigm, a sense of the structure of the patient's personality emerges. We catch on to the plan of the unconscious fantasy that drives his repetitive, self-defeating behavior and why he got into it. We also modify and confirm out developing formulation about how the patient can alter it or escape from it, and with that, how the analysis is likely to terminate. There is aesthetic pleasure in arriving at this understanding and in appreciating the intricacy of the delicately balanced unconscious arrangements that maintain the neurotic structure. On close inspection, it may look much like a Rube Goldberg (Marzio, 1973) device to accomplish a simple purpose in a most complicated way. Depending on one's outlook, one may think of that structure either as a work of art or a work of nature, but it is a marvel to behold in either case, and like one of Rube Goldberg's contraptions, in its elaborately creaky way it works. We may consider too that, while playing, the mind of the analyst has produced an aesthetic product.

It is a well-kept secret that this process of analyzing, this way of letting one's mind play rather than work, can be not only therapeutically effective, but also distinctly pleasurable for the analyst. It is a secret that is continually rediscovered by people learning to do psychoanalysis and is seldom written about, as Ernst Kris (1956) did in his classic article about the "good hour." Only occasionally does one actually focus on the fact that one is enjoying the process in this way. Most of the time, I believe analysts take the enjoyment for granted and do not notice it unless it is missing for some reason. But when it is missing, potentially it creates havoc.

Cooper (1986) discussed how important it is for the analyst to permit his mind to indulge in "playful inventiveness." Some analysts are "naturals"; permitting playful inventiveness comes very easily to them, and one does not have to teach it to them. At any rate, the combination of function pleasure and pleasurable awareness of one's effectiveness with one's analyzing instrument may both be unique to the analytic situation and essential to the development of the analyst. As with most skills, whether in music, art, or sports, it is impossible to become really proficient without an irreducible minimum amount of talent or "gift." Fortunately, like the gift of empathic understanding, the freedom to let one's mind play is widely distributed although, as in talent for art and music, there are not many who have it to an extraordinary degree. But most persons who want to become analysts have it to a sufficient degree so that, with good teaching and supervision and lots of practice, they can get to the analytic equivalent of Carnegie Hall. Others need much less practice to develop intuitiveness; indeed some need "taming" to keep their exuberance within bounds and to develop the necessary inner discipline.

As I was thinking about these ideas some years ago, that is, while I was still playing with them, I heard Arnold Cooper (1986) speak about the hazards of analytic life. He discussed some of the reasons for, and some of the consequences of, the loss of this vital capacity. We will want to consider, additionally, the effect of the loss on the analyst's ability to terminate analyses.

## When the Pleasure Is Missing or Runs Out

I believe, with Winnicott (1971), that those people who do not have enough of these capacities to be developed sufficiently by personal analysis, supervision, and practice ought not do analysis. This is probably an unnecessary warning; if one does not find that analyzing is gratifying, one is unlikely to stick with it, even if one has gone to the great trouble and expense to graduate from an institute. Fortunately, analysis is no longer viewed as the pinnacle of the mental health professions. It is no longer the case that if one is in the mental health field and not an analyst one is a "nobody." We no longer see many applicants who want to *be* analysts but not *do* analysis, who want "the name but not the game."

In years past, this was not the case. I have had in supervision several students who very much wanted to become analysts. They worked very hard, studied long hours, put up with the many deprivations that becoming an analyst requires, including years of personal analysis, hundreds of hours of supervision and the privations that attend taking low-fee clinic cases. They worked at it hard, even grimly, because there was a goal they felt they had to reach. Pride was on the line. I was able to help several of them see that for them the goal was inappropriate and the very doggedness with which they were pursuing it was one of the clear signs that it was wrong for them (Schlesinger, 1995b).

I was able to make clear to these candidates that the one essential ingredient—that they should enjoy what they were doing—was missing, that no matter how well they could do it (and "well," in this context, begs the question), there would never be enough intrinsic pleasure in doing it to justify the endeavor. They did not look forward to what the next hour might bring but just kept "putting in their time." They did not feel effective; they experienced little function pleasure, and they felt that doing analysis was hard work. Once they came to see that what I had said was true for them and that it was also "all wrong," they were able to weigh whether it made sense to continue to prepare for a career for which they were beginning to see they were basically unsuited. It is easier to come to the decision to leave the field if one is early in one's career and enjoys doing other things professionally, particularly if one can make a good living doing them.

When one is well into one's career, one may also have to reconsider the place of work in one's pleasure economy. Some loss of interest is temporary and situational and may be restored by rest and vacation. But as one ages, one should expect that one's interests may change. Some analysts, like other professionals, plan for this possibility and look forward to retirement either into a life of leisure or into a new career. Others who retain full possession of their intellectual capacities and whose enjoyment of analyzing has never faltered may remain in practice into their 90s. They inform concerned colleagues that it is obvious to them and to their patients that they will not live forever, but death is part of life and their patients will have to deal with it.

On the other hand, some of us have had the sad task of helping patients who were left behind by the death of an analyst who was mortally ill and failing but who could not be persuaded to close his practice while still able to help his patients deal with what was soon to come. We can only hope that when an analyst becomes aware that his own end is imminent, if he has not earlier withdrawn from practice, he will use the accumulated wisdom and skill with which he helped so many patients end and terminate their analyses to help the last few make the best resolution of this necessarily forced ending. It is an occasion when colleagues can help one end one's career honorably.

## Some Causes and Consequences of Burnout

When a mature analyst becomes aware that his professional life no longer feels satisfying, he will want to discover why. The problem may be a possibly partial and reversible loss of the capacity to enjoy analyzing following on a significant loss, or a serious reverse in life circumstances, or because of intercurrent illness. Remediation will depend on the cause. It generally is useful for the analyst in this situation to seek consultation.[5]

A clinician who feels his life is not going anywhere, whose professional work is no longer rewarding, and who has come to doubt his competence can be described as burned out (Cooper, 1986). This term has gained currency in recent years and occasionally has been used to excuse serious misbehavior in mature professionals by comparing it to a form of disease. Perhaps it can be viewed legitimately in that way. But I prefer to compare burnout to boredom, considering Fenichel's (1934) and Greenson's (1949) view of boredom as an equivalent of anxiety. The symptoms of burnout would, then, be understood to represent not only fatigue and the existential dilemma of middle-age, but also the residue of suppressed (that is, defended against) excitement, excitement relating to overt or covert "indulgences" the analyst feels are not legitimate or illegitimate. Cooper (1986) has discussed succinctly, but deeply, some of the factors that could lead to burnout, and I add here only the emphases that link that hazard to disturbances in the "pleasure economy" of the analyst.

I offer the following thoughts tentatively: It may be that the need to suppress one's awareness of guilty pleasures—of enjoyments that imply yielding excessively to countertransference or more or less conscious exploitations of the patient and of the analytic situation—may lead, as suppression often does, to a blanket loss of pleasure and the resulting state of tension and quasi-boredom that characterizes burnout. If I am correct, the solution is conceptually straightforward, if not always easy to apply in practice.

But first let us consider some of the problematic pleasures that I have been hinting at. Burnout, of course, does not afflict only one's professional life. A lessening of satisfaction and a loss of the sense of meaning in one's personal life is part of the syndrome. When one's personal life is not satisfying, a greater burden is placed on one's professional life, since, for most of us, work must go on regardless of what is going on or absent elsewhere. As one's professional life is called on to make up for missing life satisfactions, the intrusion of unfulfilled need is likely to impair an analyst's ability to maintain the therapeutic split.

As I have proposed, this precious capacity is not only essential to analyzing; it is also essential to experiencing function pleasure in

---

[5] An entire issue of *Psychoanalytic Inquiry* (Vol. 22. No. 4 ( 2002) is devoted to "Analysts' Life Experiences and Their Effects on Treatment: Living, Learning and Working Through." See also Gerson (1996).

analyzing. The analyst must be free to observe himself as he dips in and out of the patient's experience and samples the thoughts and affects of the various transference figures as well as his own. He must allow hints of countertransference to rise above threshold and be recognized as such and inform his understanding of what the patient is experiencing. It takes much personal analysis and supervision for the analyst to be able to develop and trust the capacity to split. It is, however, at best a fragile capacity.

One of the reasons to advocate reanalysis or self-analysis for the analyst is to maintain this essential analyzing capacity in good repair. When the analyst is overburdened, when personal needs intrude on his analytic work, the therapeutic split, like truth in wartime, may be the first victim. For the conscientious analyst, this loss may accelerate symptoms of burnout, because secondary modes of defense, repression, denial, and the rest may be called on when simple suppression fails to prevent awareness that one is at risk of enacting transference or counter-transference fantasies.

I assume there is no need to catalog the fantasies that may intrude on our analyzing in this way. It may be worth mentioning, however, that in addition to the garden variety of unconscious fantasies with which we are all familiar, there are some problems to which older analysts are peculiarly vulnerable. It should hardly be surprising that an analyst who feels his life is going nowhere would feel that least attractive of human motives—envy—of the very persons he agreed to help to fulfill their promise. It can be difficult for an analyst to face that he is helping others do what he feels is no longer possible for him. Analysts seldom express envy openly but may do so covertly by subtly depreciating a patient's real accomplishments, or by throwing cold water on the temporarily inflated sense of self that often accompanies the rebirth of confidence. Some analysts behave as if they have just discovered narcissism and see in it the source of all evil. They seem eager to "shoot down" as grandiosity any flowering of self-appreciation by a patient, as if developing appropriate self-esteem were not a goal of every therapy.

The tendency to "spoil" a patient's accomplishments is in itself noxious and also can prolong analysis indefinitely. The analyst who is never satisfied with a patient's accomplishments may fit neatly with the transference role to be the unsatisfiable parent or teacher who is never ready to let a child go (Rothstein, 1984). The analyst who attends to the patient's narcissism to the exclusion of everything else may comfort himself with the belief that he is more thorough in his work than his colleagues, a belief tinged with bitterness that he is insufficiently recognized as incorruptible and painstaking. At the same time, he may fail to notice that his patients tend to adapt to his strictness rather than to analyze. Wanting one's patients to slow down in general, being fearful that their wish to try their wings must represent acting out or "flying into health," may also serve an unconscious intention to "let no one move ahead if I can't."

I am sure all of us have seen examples of this kind. It is unfortunate that it is easy for an analyst caught up in this tangle to rationalize it as serving a praiseworthy commitment to analytic thoroughness. Along with this rationalization of unwillingness to let the patients go one can expect to find at least a covert awareness that one's patients are not being allowed to get better in their own ways and in their own time and to end their period of formal analysis with a phase of termination.

## The Treatment and Prevention of Burnout

If we can agree that the ability to experience pleasure in analyzing is important in its own right and important to sustain an analytic career, and that its loss may seriously disturb the ability to analyze and to terminate analyses, what can be done about the loss? Can the condition be treated successfully or, even better, can it be prevented?

As in most fields, in psychoanalysis prevention is better than cure, if not always easier to achieve. Becoming aware that a condition exists or is incipient is the first step. Not infrequently one's first inkling of this ominous possibility comes from hearing of the misstep or misfortune of a colleague, not infrequently one with whom one once was close but in recent years has had only infrequent and superficial contact. One has the guilty feeling, "If we had remained close, I might have been in a position to help," and one also has the uncomfortable feeling it could happen to oneself as well. Having the support of colleagues, belonging to a psychoanalytic community, in the ancient and most desirable sense of that term, can do much to prevent as well as to repair the condition.

For analysts, awareness that the personal analysis is not necessarily prophylactic against all of life's subsequent vicissitudes should make it easier to return for additional analysis from time to time. Nearly everyone agrees in principle with this recommendation but only a few act on it and, in my experience, not always those who could use it the most. Consultation with a trusted colleague, perhaps someone outside one's own community, can be highly useful. Some psychoanalytic organizations have tried to institutionalize such extramural consultation. Particularly when one's psychoanalytic community is small, so that everyone knows everyone else too well, calling on analytic colleagues outside the fold can be an excellent recourse.

It is worth reminding ourselves that analysis is a lonely profession and that spending all day as the object of transference can be difficult. Many analysts renew themselves by teaching. I think that is why many of us seek a faculty appointment, in addition to valuing the esteem it confers. One mechanism I have found especially useful is for groups of colleagues to meet regularly to discuss their cases. The objectifying powers of the group can help each member keep his own analytic capacity growing and the therapeutic split unimpaired.

As with most problems we face as analysts, taking the first step is most important. Becoming aware that the problem either is present or is incipient should encourage one to take the next necessary steps. These next steps may be tailored to one's individual situation and take advantage of the opportunities and resources one's analytic community affords. But without the initial awareness, nothing is likely to happen. Here, too, one's analytic colleagues can be and should be of help. We are, after all, members of a profession, which implies, first of all, that we are a self-regulating body—we are our brothers' and sisters' keepers in the best and most intimate sense of that term. If we truly keep each other, we may all continue to grow.

In summary, I have proposed that there is a specific and systematic place for the experience of pleasure in the analytic situation that is not merely a version of the culturally sanctioned "pursuit of happiness." The analytic situation is not a place for the analyst to pursue pleasure for its own sake. Pleasure is not the short-term goal for the patient either, although it may well be the long-term goal of the process.

The ability to achieve pleasure, to recognize that one has done so, and to enjoy that state, is, after all, one of the diagnostic criteria we consider for analyzability. Neurotic conflict invariably disturbs the "pleasure economy," to use that ancient but still useful term. That is to say, it interferes with the achievement of pleasure, or the consciousness of pleasure (inhibition); or it imposes special conditions on the achievement of pleasure in order to prevent anxiety, guilt, or shame or to prevent loss of control or other calamities (symptoms, perversions). Thus, we use loss of pleasure (as well as the inability to work) as an indicator of the degree of disability resulting from neurosis, as well to diagnose the nature of (neurotic) inhibitions imposed as the price of adaptation. And we use the regaining of these capacities as indicators of readiness to end and terminate analysis.

Psychoanalysis is concerned with the full range of human emotions, not just dysphoria. The achievement of function pleasure, pleasure in the process of analysis, as well as the pleasure of mastering the tendency to repeat, are legitimate pleasures for the patient as well as for the analyst. More than legitimate, they are systematically important in that they are indicators of progress and achievement in the analytic process. The analyst must expect and be able to accept the full range of emotions in himself. He must also help the patient legitimate the expression of these feelings in the analytic situation and help the patient appreciate their significance when they occur, as well as to enjoy them, and allow the patient to leave when he has done as well as he can.

## 10

# Mourning in the Analytic Situation
## An Aspect of Termination

### The Ubiquity of Mourning

Some truisms apropos ending and termination: first, loss is the single universal and essential human experience. Death and taxes are inescapable; eventual loss of substance and of life itself is the lot of us all. Yet, this stark realization is not pessimistic, for without the ability to appreciate loss it is not possible to experience gain. Loss, or, more precisely, the ability to recognize loss, to accept it, and to let go is the necessary condition for growth and maturation. Appreciating loss is a corollary of being aware of separateness. It is also the essential discriminating factor for testing reality. Of course, in my apostrophizing of loss I have merely turned on its head the concept of object constancy, an achievement that is essential for developing a sense of self and for normal growth and development.

A second truism: coming to terms with limitations, which is to say coming to terms with what is not one or with what one is not, also implies becoming reconciled to surrendering infinitude, an aspect of surrendering omnipotence. When so engaged, the analytic patient is well on the way toward wisdom, or at least to reasonably effective reality testing. Margaret Mahler's (1972) poetic statement that mourning[1] is a lifelong process is literally true for patients in analysis. She did not mean that mourning ought to extend for one's entire life or even that it is uniformly a sad process but, rather, that, for our patients, the experience of loss and the need to come to terms with it may be a daily occurrence. How can that be?

---

[1] I use the term mourning broadly to include grieving, the initial reaction of recognition of loss, and the rest of the process of working-through loss.

Fortunately, losing a significant other through death while one is in analysis is not a common occurrence. But progress in self-understanding often does lead to giving up relationships that one has outgrown, including the relationship to the former self. We may be slow to accept that the nature of our important relationships is changing, and, while we may come to recognize that the change was an inevitable consequence of growth, we are also likely to experience the change as loss and it may be difficult to bear. There are other occasions during analysis when a patient either experiences loss, or, more frequently, ought to be able to experience loss, but defends himself against the experience as a way to avoid the pain involved.

Let us agree, then, that mourning is a normal and adaptive reaction to loss. In the clinical situation, it ought to be experienced for what it is and what it is about. We could say that it is one of the responsibilities of the analyst to protect the mourning process so that it can proceed toward its natural ending. The mourning that is associated with termination is our particular concern, but we must recognize that, like the impasse, mourning figures in the analytic process from the beginning, whenever change is occurring. The analyst may need to intervene to protect the mourning process both against the patient's efforts to minimize the pain by denying the loss, and thus seeming to make mourning superfluous, and to protect it also from problems the analyst may have in dealing with loss. Many of us find it difficult to allow our patients to experience pain, even the "normal" pain associated with mourning the loss occasioned by growth and change. The phenomena associated with mourning are to be seen and appreciated in every analysis, but they may be minimized or overlooked by both analyst and patient either out of ignorance or for defensive reasons. Each of these possibilities may involve different technical considerations, and so I will address them separately.

## Are There Technical Implications of Mourning?

To speak of the technical implications of mourning might arouse the concern that I advocate interpreting the process of mourning itself. Let me disavow that notion at once. Analyzing, at least in its narrowest and most specific sense, interpreting, is the way we inform a patient about the larger or more specific meaning of what is going on. Interpreting is our way of explaining, either by reducing a complicated phenomenon to simpler components or by revealing the complexity of a seemingly simple matter, or both. But mourning, like other normal processes, does not need explaining, at least not while it is going on. Sometimes explaining can get in the way. To take a comic example, visualize the *New Yorker* cartoon that showed a young couple on top of a mountain. It depicted the dismay on the young woman's face as her callow boyfriend lectured about the meteorology of the beautiful sunset they had climbed so far to see. It is much the same in an analysis. After all, neither sunsets nor mourning needs to be explained in order to be appreciated. This occasion is not the only instance, of course, when the proper analytic attitude is identical with the proper human attitude, that is, deference, respect, and simple appreciation of the integrity of an experience a patient is having.[2]

But there are some technical considerations that derive from the analyst's responsibility to protect the mourning process. It often is painful to recognize that one has lost something precious, even when the loss is only the loss of familiar misery, the unavoidable "dark side" of long-sought relief. The following example is similar to those many analysts could relate.

*Example: Ms. Q*
With the help of analysis, and after a long and expensive legal battle, the patient, a housewife in her 40s, finally has won a divorce from an abusive and vengeful husband. Her relief is palpable, but the anticipated joy seems muted, attenuated by an unexpected sadness, tears she cannot understand. She is willing to attribute her mood to weariness from the long struggle—was it all worth it?

Only slowly does she recall that over the months of analyzing her attachment to the abusive husband, she had felt flashes of anticipatory loneliness. She had foreseen the possibility of feeling bereft when finally divorced. She had fearfully tried to balance the humiliation of remaining in an abusive marriage against the fear of being alone, the horror of being the spinster that her mother had warned about, of losing her identity as a proper matron in society, of being "cut loose to drift." Even though it was she who finally was sick enough of being abused to press for divorce, she now berated herself for being a failure as a wife, the only role life had trained her for. She thought ruefully she had already come to terms with "all that," only to find that from time to time she felt as if her worst fears had all come true. But would she really want to be back in the situation from which she had just escaped?

---

[2] This identity may exist from the outset, for instance, from the first hello or handshake. When the analyst believes the analytic attitude must diverge sharply from the ordinary human or socially conforming attitude, he must be ready to justify the divergence in terms of the necessities of analytic technique; he cannot excuse it merely as a stylistic or analytic mannerism.

Most analysts will conclude that the patient's mixed feelings do not indicate that the analytic work was defective but, rather, that it was merely sufficient to get the patient to this point. It is "normal," that is to say expectable, for the patient to experience the loss again and again and to mourn and work through it repeatedly. Again recalling Mahler's aphorism that mourning is a lifelong process, we can draw from it the implication that no significant relationship is ever given up totally. Pfeffer (1993), in his interviews with former analysands, demonstrated how easily a former patient's transference revives. Schlessinger and Robbins (1974) reported similar findings. Many of us can confirm these findings when, for instance, we experience a surge of sadness as we contemplate a painting we once enjoyed with someone who is no longer with us.

Loss is painful and so is grieving and mourning, especially on occasions when there seems to be no social support for expressing such feelings openly; then we may feel silly or self-indulgent and fear we may be embarrassing others and imposing on their patience. Many of our patients, like the rest of us, attempt to mitigate the pain of loss or the secondary social discomfort either by denying or minimizing the loss or by suppressing the processes nature has devised to deal with it. We admire those who can keep a stiff upper lip and get on with it.

There is a technical lesson contained in these observations. It is essential that the analyst be familiar with the natural history of loss and of mourning in general, and the history of relationships of his patient. As the example of Ms. P illustrates, significant loss is never fully expunged, whereas mourning is episodic and is not done once and for all time. Mourning recurs in waves, and, as with all emotions, intensity rises to a peak and then dissipates. This phasic quality, characteristic of working through, should not be confused with intermittent "resistance" against recognizing loss or against mourning. The distinction may be subtle at times, but it is essential to make it. It would be better, technically, to err on the side of assuming normality, for to interpret the subsiding of an episode of sadness wrongly as resistance is likely to induce guilt in the patient for not being sincerely sorrowful.

We may also consider it "normal" for the patient to attempt to mitigate the pain and to titrate the mourning; not all such instances of defense require interpretation. Sometimes an empathic observation such as, "It's hard when waves of sadness come over you," can provide support both for the patient to allow himself to feel the pain and for his reluctance to feel it. Of course, we may have reason to describe this behavior from the vantage point of resistance, but we must be clear that it has no implication of pathology and imposes no obligation that we ought to "do something about it."

## The Several Contexts of Mourning

There are three contexts in which an analyst can expect to encounter mourning. The first is obvious, the second perhaps less so, and the third, which occupies most of my attention, may at first even seem counterintuitive:

1.  when the patient suffers the loss of a significant other;
2.  when the patient loses a part of the self, for example, a body part or an aspect of the self, a job, or a symptom; and
3.  when the patient has resolved some issue of analytic importance sufficiently so that the ensuing change carries with it an intimation that the analysis will someday end and the relationship with the analyst will be severed.

We might think of the last context as anticipatory mourning, which, of course, realistically it is. But we must be careful that viewing it as anticipatory and hence oriented to the future not lead us to overlook the immediacy of the feeling. The patient's sense of psychological loss is now, and so it is necessary to deal with it now, not to put it off until the someday when physical separation will occur.

## Mourning the Loss of an Other

Since occasions of actual object loss are easy to recognize and may seem most straightforward for an analyst to deal with, let us focus on one of the major sources of technical difficulty. When a parent dies or when a spouse or equivalent other dies or leaves, the stage is set for expectable reactions of grief and mourning. If the patient attempts to minimize the pain of loss through denial and avoidance, these efforts will be obvious. But for the seasoned analyst as well as the less experienced one, there are some expectable intrusions on the proper treatment of the mourning patient that are not necessarily related to defensive efforts of the patient. Among the forces that may interfere with the analyst's deciding whether or not to intervene technically or to allow the patient to mourn unimpeded, of course, are his transference and his countertransference. The intrusions may take several forms. Some clinicians have difficulty tolerating the seeming passivity of remaining in a posture of witnessing; they feel impelled to intervene, to "do something, not just sit there." More usual, perhaps, is the wish to spare our loved ones, including our patients and ourselves, pain of any kind and, in particular, prolonged pain, and we may feel impelled to alleviate our own distress by intervening to ameliorate their suffering. It takes self-discipline for the analyst to allow a patient to experience the processes of grieving and mourning fully and to appreciate, and help him appreciate, the importance of doing so. The urge to interpret inappropriately at such times, or even to offer unneeded support, is perhaps better called by its right name, "meddling." It may seem irresistible to an analyst whose empathy has drifted too close to identification with the patient.

*Example: Ms. R*
The patient is a woman of early middle age who, after several years of analysis, has managed to understand and overcome a lifelong tendency to alienate persons whom she at first cultivates and then cuts off for fear that they will "let her down when she really needed them." She met a man at her office who came in from the field from time to time. They took to each other and often would have lunch when he visited. Matters never progressed past that point, but the patient entertained fantasies that this man might be "Mr. Right"; indeed, their meetings were mutually satisfying. She does not dare to find out if this man is married (as, indeed, he is). His attentions to her have always been friendly but correct, and he has given her no obvious occasion to ask the feared question. The analyst anticipates that her hopes will be dashed and has fantasized warning her to lower her expectations. But he cannot think of a way to do so without puncturing her balloon.

One day at lunch the man casually mentioned that he would have to allow time to pick out an anniversary gift for his wife. Ms. R was stunned and can recall nothing further about the lunch. In her subsequent analytic sessions she has been mostly silent, sad, and hopeless: "What is the use of all this when the meaning has gone out of my life." The analyst feels guilty for not having protected her and now wants to make up for his perceived failure by doing something to ease her pain.

Supervision has helped him realize that his need to protect the patient from being hurt and feeling pain is excessive, as is his guilt and feeling powerless to help her. With the additional help of his own analysis, he restrains his impulse to intervene and does not interfere with the patient's despair. Instead, he repeatedly and gently acknowledges her pain. Only when Ms. R starts to blame herself for letting herself fall in love when she should have realized that he was not really interested in her does the analyst address her self-blaming (and implicitly blaming him) as defensive, as a way to divert herself from experiencing the pain of the loss. He adds that, even though she has contributed to her disillusionment through self-deception, and even though she has allowed her expectations to be inflated by fantasy, her involvement in it was real, she allowed herself to be vulnerable to disappointment, and the disappointment, while painful, was not devastating.

His approach, as always, is to emphasize what Ms. R's defensive maneuvers were intended to do *for* her—to moderate the pain she was feeling. He does not do what some inexperienced clinicians tend to do, that is, accuse the patient of resisting: "You are afraid to go deeper," or "You are trying to prevent further understanding." His intention, in bringing her back to the pain is to help the patient discover that she can bear the vulnerability that she has always feared, a fear that for so long has led her to ward off intimacy. He wants her to be able to discover that she can withstand the pain and can work through the sense of loss.

He understands her fantasized affair as equivalent to the adolescent crushes and disappointments that her neurosis precluded at that time, and he understands, too, that she belatedly is reexperiencing a part of once-stalled development that analysis has reopened for her. Her initial reaction to the analyst's efforts is to become furious with him, at first for encouraging (that is, not discouraging) her to become a "sucker," and then for interfering with "teaching herself a lesson." But soon enough her anger dissipates as her sense of humor catches the absurdity of her complaints. She can acknowledge that she has not been destroyed and is even pleased to discover that she can look forward to her friend's next visit.

Transference and countertransference may also interfere with the analyst's appreciation of the patient's experience in other ways. An analyst who has personal reasons to avoid mourning may become impatient or bored with the patient's seemingly endless complaints of loss. The analyst may tend to withdraw and turn a deaf ear until the patient catches the hint and stops complaining, or the analyst may "interpret" vigorously in a covert effort to shut the patient up. Defensively, the patient may collude with the analyst and even invite such mistreatment by blaming herself for "carrying on" unnecessarily and boring the analyst.

As an aside: analysts must resist the tendency to "pathologize" phenomena they want to highlight for the patient. A general tendency (perhaps another instance of the analyst's transference to the patient) seems to be to emphasize what is wrong with an experience and to ignore what is right. By commenting only on pathology, on flaws in reasoning, or on missing or distorted feelings, clinicians inadvertently subscribe to B. F. Skinner's (1938) operant conditioning paradigm: behavior that is ignored tends to drop away. The strategy may be useful if the target behavior is the naughtiness of an unruly child; if you do not pay any attention to it, it likely will stop. However, it can be ruinous for analysis if the analyst remains unresponsive when a patient speaks of enjoyment, satisfaction, or progress. For by paying attention only to pathology, he effectively may indicate to the patient that he is not interested in hearing about what the patient considers progress.

Of course, this last observation is especially applicable to mourning. Since the experience is painful, patients may need encouragement to allow mourning to continue through its normal course. Like all emotions, mourning is episodic and the episodes have a limited duration. Patients who are fearful about losing control, or are fearful that they may never stop crying, may need to hear from the analyst that they do not need to interrupt this emotion or attempt to control it. As is often the case, hearing the truth may be encouragement enough.

### Reactions to Loss of Parts of the Self

Mourning is the expectable response to loss in general, not just the kinds of losses analysts give the special name object loss. A sense of loss also may be experienced when parts of the self have changed because of analysis. To the patient, a symptom, particularly a chronic one, may have assumed some of the qualities of an object, or may have acquired "object-quality." The symptom may have been painful, embarrassing, and restrictive, such as attachment to an abusive spouse or a shameful obsession, something the patient dearly wants to be rid of.

The object quality of an obsolescent aspect of the self, that is, an inhibition or symptom, does not generally become obvious until analysis has rendered the symptom dynamically and economically redundant. Then it begins to lose its saliency in the patient's economy, and may disappear completely. Oddly, the patient may experience its diminution or absence with an acute sense of loss. He may reproach the analyst for taking away an "old friend," a dependable ally, and find it difficult to conceive of how life might go on without the symptom that until then he had complained about as an excrescence. He planned his life to work around the inhibition or to make inconspicuous the special practices demanded of him by the symptom. Now, and to that same degree, life is emptier; he no longer has to think about IT, "But what else should I think about?" One patient, who was losing her taste for her former flamboyant life style, accused the analyst, "You have taken away my grand opera and left me with only plain vanilla." A formerly secretly alcoholic patient who had essentially stopped drinking, though without calling attention to it, suddenly complained, "I can't remember where I hid my bottle. You have ruined my memory."

The process of working through the implications of the loss of a symptom resembles the process of mourning the loss of a significant other, although it is likely to be briefer. Unless the analyst is prepared to witness such experiences, however, the patient may attempt to hide them and thus will forego the opportunity to work through all the implications of change.

*Example: Mr. S*

The patient is a young lawyer whose severe work inhibition manifested itself in his creating ingenious obstacles that serve to prevent him from completing briefs. Somehow, essential files are lost only to turn up at the last moment, often after he has searched under a pile of unrelated documents on his desk. As the analysis progresses, the patient comes to understand the significance of his behavior as a way of arousing anxiety in his superiors about whether or not he will get his work done. In that way, he can force them to keep him in mind, and he can get even with them for their perceived ignoring of him. He has begun to appreciate the self-destructiveness of his behavior and has started to modify it.

At the same time, he has begun to feel waves of resentment. Isn't the analyst only manipulating him to conform to his parent's old-fashioned values, the old Puritan ethic? He feels deprived but cannot articulate how or of what. His associations lead to earlier times of being deceived, and he settles finally on feeling that once again he is being tricked out of something he values, just as when he was cheated by an older, cannier schoolmate who had talked him into trading a rare but worn baseball card for two common but shinier ones.

Further associations lead to his recalling the traumatic loss of a transitional object, by then a tattered, filthy crib blanket, his "Blanky," which was his constant companion when he was a tot and without which he could not nap. Since he had outgrown his baby furniture, his mother decided to redo his bedroom, and with the new furniture came new bed linens. Blanky vanished that day, and the new blanket offered as substitute could not console the child. He searched in vain for Blanky only to be told repeatedly that he must have misplaced it.

As he accuses the analyst of stealing from him the best way he knew to keep his superiors off balance, it suddenly dawns on him that Blanky must have been trashed by his beloved mother; she tried to discourage his searching for it by sneering, "What do you want with that dirty thing? You're a big boy and big boys don't drag around rags." He realizes then that in some way he must always have known its fate but could not let himself be furious with his mother, who was a much more constant source of comfort than his ambitious and distant father. Then he can connect his suppressed certainty about the rape of Blanky with the wish to get even with his boss by hiding essential papers. He will not search for them; if they wanted them, they can hunt for them. Mourning for the lost symptom became conflated with mourning for lost Blanky, and the restored connection began to free the patient from the compulsion to reenact his revengeful and self-destructive fantasies at work.

In that instance, the patient announced clearly how he reacted to the loss of his symptom, but that is a sometime event; the analyst cannot count on such validation. Much of the time, the patient does not make clear that his sad or foul mood has to do with loss, and his defenses against experiencing mourning may be quite subtle. The main evidence may be negative, the relative absence of pleasure or only a short-lived sense of relief following the removal of a tedious burden and the cessation of long suffering. The patient may seem glum without obvious reason, may seem detached, or show loss of interest when the changes in his inner life and external situation suggest to a naive observer that it would be more fitting if he displayed unalloyed excitement at the range of new possibilities open to him.

## Mourning in Response to Therapeutic Change

By far the commonest instances of mourning in analysis are also those that are most likely to be overlooked by both analyst and patient. These are the occasions when the patient is changing as a function of the analyzing. Does that sound contradictory? Are occasions of analytic change such rare events, so rare that some wonder if they occur at all? No, actually moments of analytic change occur frequently, as often as the analyst offers a correct, well-timed interpretation (Schlesinger, 2003). The problem is not the rarity of moments of change, but the failure of the analyst to recognize that his interpretation has affected the patient.

Rather than following up and prolonging the state of flux or ambiguity that always follows a correct and well-timed interpretation, the analyst, having shot his bolt, relaxes and allows the altered neurotic structure to repair itself; he allows time for the induced change to dissipate (Schlesinger, 1995a). If the analyst were to follow up and interpret the patient's immediate confused mixture of positive and defensive reactions to the interpretation, the full reaction would be allowed to flower. The patient would then become more clearly aware of the complexity of his reaction and could start to tease apart the confused mixture of surprise, if not shock, relief, perhaps even a smidgen of pleasure, and also anxiety and dismay. Fearfully, he might ask, "Why am I feeling all this? Is it all right? Am I falling apart?" He may very well complain, "What are you doing to me?"

Obviously, analysts will not see all these elements of reaction quite so clearly in every instance; they tend to appear successively rather than all at once. However, an analyst who is alerted to expect such a response will grasp the patient's immediate and salient emotional reaction as well as the defensive tactics the patient invokes to contain it. The analyst will respond to impede the patient's effort at reversion, and he will slow down the patient's efforts to repair the damaged neurosis. When the analyst follows up assiduously, he may delay the patient's natural defensive reaction to restore immediately the status quo ante long enough to permit the patient to observe this usually automatic reaction while it is occurring. When the analyst interferes and prolongs the state of postinterpretation flux even briefly, the patient has a little more time to adapt to the change and to make room for it. Eventually, the change can become structuralized.

When I described this process of following up elsewhere (Schlesinger, 1995a, 2003), I did not focus particularly on mourning as an aspect of the reaction to experiencing change. After all, we regard change through analysis as desirable, whereas the aura around the term mourning has the dull glow of finality, a terminal condition from which there is no return and one's only recourse is resignation. I am afraid, however, that we are stuck with the term mourning, just as we are stuck with the dismal word termination, with its funereal implications. But while we may have to live and work with "mourning" and "termination," we should not resign ourselves to the inevitability of other objectionable terms, such as the oxymoron "pathological mourning" and the weaker epithets "displaced mourning" and "pseudomourning." I consider these usages objectionable because they assume there is such a "thing" as mourning, or, to put it more precisely, because they assume that mourning is a condition that one can denote with a noun.

With a sprinkling of adjectives we might specify subtypes of the condition of mourning, some of which are so far from desirable that they almost qualify as diseases. But mourning is not a condition; it is a process. It does not have subtypes. We would do better to think of the many ways one can mourn and of the many ways one can avoid mourning. We must understand each of these processes on its own terms rather than naming what the patient is doing as a condition that fails to meet the standards we have in mind for "ideal mourning." We must understand these processes in terms of what the patient is trying to experience and what he is trying to avoid experiencing.

We must ask what does it do *for* the patient to go about mourning in this way or what does it do *for* him to avoid mourning in this way. We must try to understand what the patient *gains* from his efforts, not just what it *costs*. It is essential that a therapist understand that the patient would like to hold on to something important to him in the memory of the object and that he fears losing "the whole thing." The therapist must try to understand what makes letting go so difficult for the patient. What does he fear is being put at risk by his saying goodbye?

Perhaps I *am* alluding to a sort of disease. But, if that is so, we should consider it a disorder of clinicians, not of patients. To dignify it with a name, we might refer to it as "hardening of the categories." We tend to pathologize patient behavior we disapprove of, give it a bad name, and, at least implicitly, urge our patients to stop it. As analysts, we would do better to try to understand the behavior than to banish it.

Let us return to our patient in psychoanalysis who has fantasized how good would be release from the bonds of inhibition or compulsion. Yet, when the patient feels even a bit of release, he realizes that some of its implications are frightening. For every change involves loss as well as gain, and thus each occasion of change expectably will also be an occasion for mourning. In addition to the loss in one's familiar sense of self, there is also the niggling worry that further progress will lead inevitably to the end of the analysis. While, at the outset of analysis, the patient likely wishes devoutly that it would end sooner rather than later, once he becomes fully engaged it may seem impossible for him to think of life without it.

Let me link the phenomena associated with mourning to my version of the process of analysis. I construe the analytic process as a succession of episodes of varying duration during which the patient works on issues (tasks) that sooner or later are "resolved" to some degree. And by resolved to some degree I mean just that, "a degree," not that the whole issue has been brought to a satisfactory conclusion. I mean merely that the patient has gotten a glimmer of what he has been doing, enough of an insight to be disturbed by the possibilities of going even further, and so he slows down or stops; perhaps he has gone as far as he can (or wants to) go for the time being. At such times, the patient's absorption in the formerly salient issue wanes, and he may seem to be feeling at loose ends, momentarily without a focus.

It may be less noticeable that he also is having some mixed feelings, including a degree of pleasure that he has achieved something, even though he may not know just what it was. It may perhaps be more obvious that he seems worried, but it may not be obvious that the worry is somehow connected to his feeling of pleasure. The problem is that the patient is also experiencing a sense of loss, although he probably would not identify it as such, for every achievement in analysis carries with it an "intimation of mortality"; that is, success brings with it the fear that "If there is much more of this 'progress,' the analysis will be over and then I will have to give up the analyst too" (Schlesinger, 1995a, 2003).

For some patients, the fear of losing the analyst as a consequence of achievement may be conscious enough that the patient will hide or minimize his achievement. Indeed the patient may not even let himself realize fully that some positive change has occurred. Recall how often we hear from our patients that others have remarked on improvements the patient has never reported and perhaps even was unaware of. Such a patient may believe he must deny or minimize any positive change lest the analyst get the idea that the patient has "had enough" and is ready for discharge, that is, that the analyst feels he can safely abandon the patient.

Some of these patients seem convinced that only by suffering are they eligible for attention; they do not deserve care and have no right to expect that the analyst would be interested in them if they had the bad luck to be free of symptoms. They have great difficulty grasping the idea that they can remain in analysis simply because they want to and because they find it useful. Oddly enough, they would have to accept that they could stay in analysis indefinitely, if they should want to, in order to have as a goal to decide to end it electively. As Fleming (1969) observed, wryly, feeling that one has the power to decide to leave another for one's own reasons is quite different from dreading being left by another whom one needs and over whom one has no power.

An analyst who has not yet come to recognize the phenomena associated with ending a bit of analytic work, and eventually the analysis, will not usually be helped openly by the patient, for patients do not generally try to make the nature of this problem clear. Indeed, for the patient who is concerned about eventual abandonment, clarity hardly seems desirable. It is like fearing to mention the word cancer when one goes for a physical exam, lest one alert the doctor to search for it and find it. Indeed, rather than displaying any of the phenomena I have just detailed, a patient may display irritation, hypersensitivity, resentment, or suspicion, and through this behavior make it quite plain that he no longer feels like "working." He would rather keep secret the fact that the symptom has remitted, or that things are going better at work or at home, or that he slept through the night or had enjoyable intercourse. For, if the analyst got wind of these improvements, the patient is certain he quickly will be eased out of analysis. An impasse may occur, triggered ironically by unacknowledged progress.

The patient's experience when reacting to the fear of losing the analyst is complicated. Psychologically, of course, there is no such thing as an

anticipated loss. While the ostensible object, the analyst, is actually
present; in fantasy he is experienced as already gone. It is an experience
that is difficult for a patient to explain to himself and it is even more
difficult to articulate convincingly to the analyst or others because it is so
at odds with the evidence of his senses. The situation is akin to the problem
of experiencing the analyst as malignantly punitive while at the same
time knowing cognitively that he cannot be entirely so, and all the while
trusting him enough to tell him of these dire fears.

The sense of impending object loss, like all symptoms, can be viewed
as a form of memory, a revival of an actual (or fantasized, e.g., oedipal)
loss. From the point of view of memory, that sense of loss represents the
patient's effort to prevent a loss that has already occurred. More precisely,
since the unconsciously remembered loss may have been a fantasy, we
could say that the patient is attempting to prevent the repetition of a loss
that did not occur in actuality in the first place. However, the fear that he
will lose the analyst is really felt, and the patient must attempt to make
sense of that fear since memories of the transference figure conflict with
his experience of the analyst as present and not about to abandon him.

Inevitably, the patient's sense of reality is strained by the conflict
between the cognitive and emotional aspects of his experiencing. That
disjunction is embarrassing and painful, a state that the patient can most
easily express by silence. The analyst must be aware that the silence, as
well as the patient's irritability and other discomfort I mentioned earlier,
may have as much to do with the equivocal transference versus reality
experience as it does to the sense of loss itself. The analyst must be
sensitive to the complexity of the patient's experience and not attempt to
simplify it prematurely by interpreting it if, for the moment, the patient
is defensively invested in maintaining the complexity and needs time to
work through the emotional muddle.

*Example: Ms. T*
A young woman has been in analysis for over a year and has made a
good deal of therapeutic progress in the relief of crippling shyness,
the most troublesome of her presenting complaints. Formerly, much
as she would have liked to be free and easy in social situations, she
would become tongue-tied if approached by a man. She was angry
and bitter about her inhibition and avoided gatherings of her peers.
Now to her delight, she has found that she can converse with men in a
way that, while still shy, is endearingly so rather than discomforting.
She has other problems, of course, and her partial success has led to
rising expectations for what else analysis might do for her. Her initial
reaction to discovering that she was no longer so inhibited was to crow
with excitement, and she set about testing her improvement as if to
make up for lost time.

After a few weeks, reports about her expanding social life dwindled and in sessions her manner, which lately has become relaxed and spontaneous, became noticeably guarded again. Now, before going to the couch, she begins each session with a long, searching look at the analyst as if he has become a stranger. The analyst has commented on the change in her behavior in ways that imply that the patient is resisting, even though he has not used that term. Still, it is clear that his intent in pointing out what she is doing is to get her to get on with analyzing.

This form of intervening has proved counterproductive as the patient has become increasingly sullen and uncooperative. The sessions seem barren to the analyst, who feels baffled and frustrated by the way the patient has "turned off." He notes, however, that the patient has missed no sessions, comes early to all, and is unusually prompt in paying her bill.

Puzzled by this odd mixture of overcompliance and what he views as stubborn defiance, the analyst has sought consultation. As he presents this picture, it has become clear that he has not considered that the patient's behavior might be meaningful, even though her message is not couched in words. The consultant raises these questions: Why did the patient look at him so searchingly? What might she be fearful of? Why has she been so "good" about attending, even coming early, and why is she so prompt about paying her bill while at the same time withholding the cooperation that formerly came so easily to her?

Thinking about these Socratic questions, the analyst begins to link the patient's odd behavior to the previous period of the analysis that yielded such dramatic progress. He begins to consider that the behavior he labeled as resistive and (to him) unnecessary, and even ultimately obstructive to the analysis, might be serving a useful purpose for the patient. Reviewing with the consultant what he has learned about her history and dynamics, he tries to construct a plausible case for why it might make sense for the patient to behave as she is.

He supposes that the patient, who has been so grateful for the diminution of her shyness and now wants much more from him, also feels guilty about her "greediness." He might also consider that the way he confronted her with her resistive behavior might well mean to her that he wants her to stop holding back, get on with her treatment, and make way for some sicker, more deserving patient. She should be content with half a loaf because she already has gotten more than she deserved. Thus, his approach could well intensify her feelings of guilt.

Armed with these new understandings, the analyst changes his approach to the patient. He first proposes to her that his repeatedly pointing out how she is behaving makes her increasingly uncomfortable and also to feel much misunderstood. Her posture immediately becomes more relaxed, although she utters little more than some grunts of assent. After a while, he adds that it must seem that he thinks she has no reason to act as she is acting and that he does not appreciate how distressed she feels to find herself behaving so, and yet how impossible it seems to her to behave any differently. The patient begins to sniffle and then, between her tears, haltingly alludes to her feelings of guilt and the high moral expectations she thought he had of her.

The analyst is reassured that he finally is on the right track. He relaxes and allows the patient to continue the story in her own words and at her own pace. She essentially confirms the construction the analyst arrived at with the help of his consultant, but she adds new historical material that helps to make sense of her foot dragging. She relates that as soon as she learned to do anything for herself—to tie her shoelaces, for instance—her mother never tied them for her again. The inevitable result of any developmental achievement was to be left to do it herself from then on, and she could hardly expect anything different from the analyst. Opening up this pattern of expectation permits the patient to feel the abandonment she fears even while safely experiencing the analyst's presence. And she can then mourn the loss of support by her mother in both its real and its fantasized aspects as well as appreciate that she will one day leave the analyst, rather than be left by him, and that too would be both a sad and a happy prospect (Schlesinger, 1996).

## Mourning and Interpretation, Pro and Con

Mourning, like loving, is a natural, normal, human emotional state (see, e.g., Kernberg, 1974; Person, 1988). Mostly, analysts encounter loving in the context of the peculiar, defensive conditions that patients invent to detoxify what they regard as a potentially poisonous state. Analysts attempt to unravel the complications and distortions that are the familiar obstacles that neurosis puts in the way of loving and being loved. As clinicians, we are concerned with distortions so severe that they may amount to an inability to love or to accept being loved.

It is much the same with mourning. We take for granted now that humans are born into relatedness and that loving and also hating are the glue that holds us together. When relationship is threatened, when the premises of mutual attraction and settled attachment no longer are tenable, a more or less subtle process of detachment begins, and a train of emotional responses normally ensues. These include the familiar cognitive and emotional efforts to deal with the pain of actual or threatened separation (e.g., Kubler-Ross, 1969).

Mourning is a normal experience, a way of coming to terms with loss, and, if it is to be successful, it should be experienced fully. A patient's reaction to loss might be excessive in quantity, deviant in quality, or both, and to that extent it is pathological. With a grieving patient, the clinician will want to understand whether the patient's responses to the loss seem mostly to be leading toward normal mourning or mostly toward defending against the pain of loss.

Loss, especially unacknowledged loss, is the major reason patients come to psychoanalysis. The experience of loss, however, is not the "problem." If there is a problem for analysis, it is in the way a patient avoids dealing with the experience of loss, in particular that either the patient's immediate reaction to the awareness of loss or the patient's subsequent efforts interferes with the process of mourning.

Sequences of encounter, attachment, and relationship—and then perhaps disillusionment, detachment, and separation—occur in patients in analysis with perhaps even greater frequency than in the lives of nonanalysands. After all, our patients are constantly having their emotional presuppositions challenged, and relationships, both within the analytic cloister and outside, are held up for examination and reexamination, experimentation, and refutation. There may be much to analyze in these goings on, but it does not include the simple fact that, when relationships dissolve, the tension of impending separation is painful; significant relationships do not dissolve painlessly. These simple facts require witnessing by the analyst, recognition, clarification, and appreciation with empathy and patience, but never relentless interpreting. I am perhaps overstating my argument here for the sake of emphasis, of course, for I can think of no instance when relentless interpreting would be considered good analytic technique.

A patient's efforts to mitigate the pain by putting off mourning "belong" so to speak; they are "normal" and "healthy," and the analyst must be sensitive enough to recognize when the patient becomes intolerant of the pain. Then, rather than remaining fully engaged in mourning, the patient might attempt to "analyze" in order to defend against the painful experience of letting go. The analyst then faces a delicate discrimination, for the process of normal mourning, like working through in general, is not continuous but, rather, is episodic. Periods of deep involvement in mourning alternate with attention to other, less serious matters and to lighter moods. An obsessive patient may even worry that he is not sad enough and that the seriousness of his loss is thrown into question by alternating with moments of levity.

For an illustration, think of the shifting moods at a wake when sorrow about loss and sadness that the departed is no longer with us alternates with the jokes we once shared with him and with sips of wine. Or consider also the shifting moods at a college graduation, when the joy of anticipation of a bright future alternates with tears at the loss of precious relationships and promises to stay in touch. The course of separation, like the course of true love, is not smooth. Again, the analyst must be familiar with the normal, usually bumpy course of becoming attached and of letting go in order to help the patient experience and appreciate the pains and pleasures that go with both. The analyst must reserve his more specific analytic efforts, that is, interpretation, for the excessive or repetitious defensive impediments that patients erect to slow down the process, and even then analysts must leaven their efforts with appreciation that sometimes it feels too painful to bear.

As in other areas, the analyst's main diagnostic problem is to figure out what the defense is for, not just what it is against. Another way of putting it is that the analyst should focus on what (perceived) problem of the patient is solved by this seeming pathological defending, not just on what it costs. The analyst should expect the patient to mourn whenever he experiences or anticipates loss; absence of mourning when it is called for should alert the analyst to consider the possible reasons.

The analyst must be able to discriminate among several possibilities: the "natural" rhythm of the mourning process, the temporary defensive interruptions when it hurts too much, and the more serious interruptions that represent a stubborn refusal to give up the lost object and settling into chronic grieving rather than to permit mourning that would lead to the eventual surrender of the object. These diagnostic skills are not easy to learn, especially if the analyst has not yet suffered and worked through a significant loss in his own life.

# 11

## Is There Life After Termination?

The easy, literal answer to the question, is there life after termination? does not fully capture the experience of a patient who has just left the final session of his analysis any more than it would honor the experience of a grieving spouse at the funeral of his beloved. It is also literally true, if hardly more comforting, to say that one will view life differently after analysis as one may do after coming to terms with a profound loss. Although we draw on all our resources of tact and sensitivity to reassure the survivor, our well-intentioned efforts neither bring comfort nor facilitate an examination of the complexity of the experience.

You may wonder why I called on such an extreme analogy to make the point if all I have in mind is to remind us that the experiences of both the former analysand and the grieving spouse are complex. I do, however, have an additional point in mind. The extravagant analogy applies mainly if the ending is insufficiently prepared for as when a death is unexpected or when an intensive psychotherapy (e.g., psychoanalysis) does not conclude with a period given over to observation and understanding of the termination process.

Circumstances may not permit such a period. Occasionally, an unfortunate conflation of ending and separation occurs when a therapist dies unexpectedly. It then falls to the colleagues of the deceased therapist to inform his patients and to offer to fill in or refer them, as their individual circumstances require. It is also a special circumstance, and unfortunately not a rare one, when a therapist knows that he is terminally ill but insists on maintaining his practice until nature intervenes rather than helping his patients to end and possibly to terminate treatment while he is still able to help them.

A reminder: If the therapist keeps termination in mind from the outset of treatment, he and the patient may accomplish much of the working through characteristic of termination in distributed fashion so that the actual ending will be less traumatic. The preceding chapters have tried to make clear that a major purpose of arranging for a termination phase of analysis is to allow full expression of the wide range of emotions and emotional positions that emerge in both parties when they anticipate ending both the treatment and separating from the analyst. Consider, too, that unlike other separations the patient experiences during treatment, this one is to be voluntary on the patient's part, not imposed by the clock or calendar or the analyst's schedule. It is probably the only time in the patient's life when the main reason for remaining with another from whom he intends to separate is to allow his feelings about separating to flower, to appreciate them and also to examine them, understand them, and work them through.

The point of the process of termination is not to rid the parties of these feelings; the panoply of emotions does not vanish when the analysis officially is declared over. They are not "resolved" in any definitive sense any more than the complex feelings of the bereaved are resolved. We may therefore ask about the fate of these feelings postanalysis. What does each of the parties do about them "internally," that is, privately, by the former patient and his analyst, and "externally," that is, socially or publicly, between the two of them and among their significant others.

We must look into the corresponding processes in both parties to the ended analysis, the experience of the analyst as well as of the patient. It is customary for the analyst to concern himself mainly with the patient; after all, it is the patient's analysis that is ending. Nevertheless, anyone who has done much psychotherapy and analysis knows that working on ending and termination, and finally saying goodbye to a patient he has grown fond of, is deeply moving for the analyst or therapist (e.g., Viorst, 1982). However often he does it, ending a therapy is a significant experience for the therapist, and the sensitive therapist will not allow himself to become calloused to it. It is essential, therefore, that we appreciate that both parties will need a little time to come to terms with the absence of the other. Consider, too, it is a strange kind of absence, for, while both parties are potentially present in a physical sense and are very much in each other's mind, perhaps tacitly, they have agreed to avoid contact with each other for the time being[1]. With these reservations, we may go on to consider the various aspects of postanalytic life as they eventuate, including the possible emergence of a postanalytic relationship between the parties.

---

[1] The ending of a training analysis obviously is an exception.

## Posttermination Contacts

To my mind, the main principle that governs posttermination contacts is that, just as there is no such a thing as an ex-child, there is no such thing as an ex-patient. This admonition refers mainly to the temptation some therapists and patients feel, when no longer restrained by the strictures of the therapeutic relationship, to enact their desire to allow a fuller friendship or even a sexual relationship to flower. The obvious practical issue is that a patient should be able to feel free to return for treatment should need arise; therefore nothing should be done that might impede such return. The more essential reason, to my mind, is that the intense, purposeful, but mostly not reciprocal, intimacy of that relationship, with its built-in power differential, precludes forming a new, untrammeled, and reciprocal relationship of any great depth. Therefore, the possibility that the therapist, even inadvertently, might exploit the patient's transference cannot be ruled out.

I should note that there are other opinions on this matter; the several mental health professions have struggled with defining the professional and ethical implications of the permissible bounds of posttherapeutic contacts. The most recent positions of organized psychiatry and psychoanalysis bar sexual contact with former patients as well as with current ones. Organized psychology has not yet come to that position. An indication of how vexing the problem is can be seen in the delicately forbidding wording of the "unusual circumstances" that might excuse sexual contact between a therapist and former patient in the Code of Ethics of the American Psychological Association (2002).

Section 10.8 of the Code of Ethics of the American Psychological Association (2002), under the heading, "Sexual Intimacies with Former Therapy Clients/Patients," states:

(a) Psychologists do not engage in sexual intimacies with former clients/patients for at least two years after cessation or termination of therapy.

(b) Psychologists do not engage in sexual intimacies with former clients/patients even after a two-year interval except in the most unusual circumstances. Psychologists who engage in such activity after the two years following cessation or termination of therapy and of having no sexual contact with the former client/patient bear the burden of demonstrating that there has been no exploitation, in light of all relevant factors, including (1) the amount of time that has passed since therapy terminated; (2) the nature, duration, and intensity of the therapy; (3) the circumstances of termination; (4) the client's/patient's personal history; (5) the client's/patient's current mental status; (6) the likelihood of adverse impact on the client/patient; and (7) any statements or actions made by the therapist during the course of therapy suggesting or inviting the possibility of a posttermination sexual or romantic relationship with the client/patient. (See also Standard 3.05, Multiple Relationships.)

The American Psychiatric Association (2003) takes a categorical stance. Its code of ethics states:

A physician shall uphold the standards of professionalism, be honest in all professional interactions and strive to report physicians deficient in character or competence, or engaging in fraud or deception to appropriate entities.
(1) The requirement that the physician conduct himself/herself with propriety in his or her profession and in all the actions of his or her life is especially important in the case of the psychiatrist because the patient tends to model his or her behavior after that of his or her psychiatrist by identification. Further, the necessary intensity of the treatment relationship may tend to activate sexual and other needs and fantasies on the part of both patient and psychiatrist, while weakening the objectivity necessary for control. Additionally, the inherent inequality in the doctor–patient relationship may lead to exploitation of the patient. Sexual activity with a current or former patient is unethical.

The American Psychoanalytic Association (2001) is equally forthright on the topic. Its code of ethics states:

VI. Avoidance of Exploitation. In light of the vulnerability of patients and the inequality of the psychoanalyst–analysand dyad, the psychoanalyst should scrupulously avoid any and all forms of exploitation of patients and their families, current or former, and limit, as much as possible, the role of self-interest and personal desires. Sexual relations between psychoanalyst and patient or family member, current or former, are potentially harmful to both parties, and unethical. Financial dealings other than reimbursement for therapy are unethical.

Leaving aside that organized psychology prefers to leave a tiny loophole where the other major professions have established an outright ban on posttermination sexual relationships, we must note that the codes are silent about the concerns many therapists have about the propriety of far less transgressive contacts and relationships. The Codes leave therapists to their own good judgment about whether or not to accept or offer a dinner invitation or to take any other step to include the former patient or to be included in the former patient's social life. Patients are equally uncertain if they may, or ought to, take the initiative in this regard and are perhaps equally fearful about overstepping the not quite loosened bounds of the therapeutic situation and also possibly fearful of rejection.

To this point, I may seem to have taken for granted that all therapists and all patients look forward eagerly to continued contact and that therefore we need rules and sanctions to maintain propriety against the press of mutual attraction. Indeed, many patients (and some therapists) do desire a continuing relationship of some degree, but a perhaps silent minority seems quite willing to call it quits entirely or to maintain merely a conventional postprofessional relationship as one might with one's surgeon. After all, patient and analyst did not find each other as acquaintances who might become friends. They may be of quite disparate interests and tastes and have in common only this analysis. Still, I do not know of any psychoanalysis in which the termination phase did not include fantasies about the nature of the relationship between the parties afterward. These fantasies include not only a continuing or different relationship, but also often a wish to thank the analyst in some tangible way with a gift to express the gratitude the patient feels for the gains he has made and attributes to the analyst. Mostly, the patient obtains the therapeutic value of these fantasies, including those about a gift, by working them through during the phase of termination. What, then, of the supposed need for anticipatory regulation of posttherapy contact? Perhaps the several codes of ethics are correctly abstinent in leaving the areas to individual judgment.[2]

Rather than fretting about the possible misconduct of the former therapeutic partners, we would do better to consider the forces and factors that might interfere with the emergence of a comfortable relationship governed by the reality of their current situations and respectful of their previous professional engagement. Chief among the interfering factors are the very ones that likely interfered with analyzing and terminating—unanalyzed transference and countertransference in both parties as discussed in Chapter 7. A common, but mostly unremarked, example of

---

[2] The situation of the patient who is in a training analysis is complicated in this regard because, upon graduation, he is assured at least of a continuing professional relationship with his former analyst. This realistic expectation weakens the intensity of the patient's experience of separation and places a heavier demand on the skill of the analyst to extract the optimum benefit from the work in termination.

such interference can be seen most clearly in the professional circles of psychoanalysis, but they must exist elsewhere as well. The phenomenon of interest is that former patients[3] of certain therapists and analysts seem to develop a bond among themselves and with the former therapist and form themselves into what amounts to a support group for him. He becomes, in effect, the group's guru and his and their social life become inextricably entwined. Such groups may persist for many years and may even survive the death of the therapist. Some such groups want to maintain their identity and exclusiveness and so seek a new guru to replace the deceased analyst.

It is one of the general goals of psychoanalysis and psychotherapy to enhance or restore the freedom of patients that was impaired by neurosis. It would seem a violation of the spirit, if not the letter of the codes of ethics, for the therapist to encourage patients or former patients to organize in this way, or to accept any such efforts by them to do so. Doing so seems on its face to amount to exploitation of the transference.

We should not confuse these questionable practices with the occasions on which former patients assist elderly analysts who are long retired from practice and who have outlived their families, colleagues, and contemporaries. When younger colleagues, including former patients and supervisees, gather the resources to ensure the comfort of their former mentors, analysts, and colleagues, we can only applaud such humanitarian efforts, which also strengthen our sense of community.

## Self-Analysis

Although people seek analysis for many reasons, one of the main results of a successful analysis is one that was not explicitly sought in the first place but may prove to be the most useful outcome of all. The ability to self-analyze also permits a more comfortable relationship to oneself, one that is not based on self-deception. If one views clinical psychoanalysis as a process of self-analysis in the presence of, and with the guidance of, one's analyst (Ticho, 1967; Schlesinger, 2003), one can view the postanalytic phase as the former patient conducting the same process intermittently and as needed without the immediate presence of the analyst.[4]

---

[3] Perhaps also current patients.
[4] My late colleague Joan Fleming was fond of analogizing to the way a vessel drops the pilot who steered it out of the harbor while the captain of the vessel then navigates for the rest of the voyage.

A "good analysis" was once thought to be prophylactic, a sure way to ward off the effects of a future emotional onslaught that might otherwise lead to new neurotic difficulty. That belief is no longer widely held, but the occasional reference to the necessity of a "thorough analysis," perhaps on the model of a thorough house cleaning, reminds us of that former hope. But an analysis, thorough or not, no more guarantees immunity from future emotional problems than a thorough house cleaning guarantees a dust-free home. A knowledge of one's areas of vulnerability and the capacity to self-analyze, however, can help very much when matters, emotionally speaking, threaten to get out of hand. The capacity for self-analysis may also help a former patient to decide whether or not he ought return to the couch.

## Second Analyses

We recall that Freud (1937a, b, c) recognized that the results of analysis are not permanent; he recommended that analysts undergo reanalysis about every five years. I am not aware that any analyst has taken seriously the advice for periodic reanalysis, but many have sought additional analysis because of self-recognized need, generally with a different analyst, and some have done so several times. Some do so because events in life or difficulty in treating some patients have revealed that they were contributing to a patient's difficulty. If consultation proves insufficient, the responsible thing to do is to deal with it directly through additional personal analysis.

Others have a sense that, even though the training analysis did not look sufficiently into some areas of concern to them, the desire to graduate and put an end to student status was the governing concern. They resolved to return to analysis when more convenient, and some did. For others, the syncretism of training and personal analysis made it impossible for them to do all they thought they should do in analysis. Therefore, they resolved to do this analysis "for the institute" and the next one for themselves. Whatever the reason, if we tend to think cynically of second marriages as a triumph of hope over experience, we could reverse the aphorism to read that second analyses are best thought of as a triumph of experience over hope—we return to a method we know has helped when our hope to do without it proves unavailing.

I have no figures about the proportion of second analyses that are conducted with the same analyst. In my own experience, none was with a former patient although occasionally some former patients have returned for a brief consultation when they felt in difficulty. I know that, sometimes, when a former patient returns to his analyst for additional analysis, the analyst has suggested that the former patient try instead with another analyst. The analyst offered this advice when he recognized that the patient's current difficulty might have arisen because of insufficient attention to an area that the analyst recognized others might be better equipped to analyze.

# References

Akhtar, S. (1994), Object constancy and adult psychopathology. *Internat. J. Psycho-Anal.*, 75:441–455.

Alexander, F. (1958), A contribution to the theory of play. *Psychoanal. Quart.*, 27:175–193.

American Psychoanalytic Association (2001), *Principles and Standards of Ethics for Psychoanalysts*. New York: American Psychoanalytic Association.

American Psychological Association (2002), *Ethical Principles of Psychologists and Code of Conduct*. Washington, DC: American Psychological Association.

American Psychiatric Association (2003), *The Principles of Medical Ethics with Annotations Especially Applicable to Psychiatry*. Washington, DC: American Psychiatric Association.

Appelbaum, A. H. (1972), A critical re-examination of the concept, "Motivation for Change" in psychoanalytic treatment. *Internat. J. Psycho-Anal.*, 53:51–60.

——— (1996), Why traumatized borderline patients relapse. *Bull. Menninger Clin.*, 60:466–474.

Asch, S. (1976), Varieties of negative therapeutic reaction and problems of technique. *J. Amer. Psychoanal. Assn.*, 24:383–407.

Bachrach, H. M., Weber, J. J. & Solomon, M. (1985), Factors associated with the outcome of psychoanalysis (clinical and methodological considerations): Report of the Columbia Psychoanalytic Center Research Project (IV), *Internat. Rev. Psycho-Anal.*, 12:379–389.

Balter, L., Lothane, Z. & Spencer, J. H. (1980), On the analyzing instrument. *Psychoanal. Quart.*, 49:474–504.

Bemporad, J. (1994), The negative therapeutic reaction in severe characterological depression. *J. Amer. Acad. Psychoanal.*, 22:399–414.

Bergmann, M. S. (1997), Termination: The Achilles heel of psychoanalytic technique. *Psychoanal. Psychol.*, 14:163–174.

Blum, H. P. (1989), The concept of termination and the evolution of psychoanalytic thought. *J. Amer. Psychoanal. Assn.*, 37:275–295.

Bowlby, J. (1979), *The Making and Breaking of Affectional Bonds*. London: Tavistock.

Brenner, C. (1959), The masochistic character: Genesis and treatment. *J. Amer. Psychoanal. Assn.*, 7:197–226.

Campbell, R. J. (2004), *Campbell's Psychiatric Dictionary, 8th ed.* New York: Oxford University Press.

Castelnuovo-Tedesco, P. (1989), The fear of change and its consequences in analysis and psychotherapy, *Psychoanal. Inq.*, 9:101–118.

Coleridge, S. T. (1798), The Rime of the Ancient Mariner, In: *The Complete Poetical Works of Samuel Taylor Coleridge*, ed. E. H. Coleridge. London: Oxford University Press, 1912.

Cooper, A. (1986), Some limits on therapeutic effectiveness: The "burnout syndrome" in psychoanalysts. *Psychoanal. Quart.*, 55:576–578.

——— (1987), The transference neurosis: A concept ready for retirement. *Psychoanal. Inq.*, 7:569–585.

Davanloo, H. (1980), *Short-Term Dynamic Psychotherapy*. New York: Aronson.

Dewald, P. (1965), Reactions to the forced termination of therapy. *Psychoanal. Quart.*, 39:102–126.

Edelson, M. (1963), *The Termination of Intensive Psychotherapy*. Springfield, IL: Thomas.

Ekstein, R. (1965), Working through and termination of psychoanalysis. *J. Amer. Psychoanal. Assn.*, 13:57–78.

Erwin, E. (2002), *The Freud Encyclopedia: Theory, Therapy, and Culture*. New York: Routledge.

Fairbairn, W. R. D. (1952), *An Object Relations Theory of Personality*. New York: Basic Books.

Fenichel, O. (1934), On the psychology of boredom. In: *The Collected Papers of Otto Fenichel, 1st Ser.* New York: Norton, pp. 292–302, 1953.

Ferenczi, S. (1920), The further development of an active technique in psychoanalysis. In: *Further Contributions to the Theory and Technique of Psychoanalysis*, ed. J. Rickman. London: Karnac Books, 1980, pp. 198–216.

——— (1927), The problem of the termination of the analysis. In: *Final Contributions to the Problems and Methods of Psychoanalysis*, ed. M. Balint. London: Karnac Books, 1980, pp. 77–86.

——— & Rank, O. (1924), *The Development of Psychoanalyis*. Madison, CT: International Universities Press, 1986.

Fleming, J. (1969), Problems of termination in the analysis of adults. Panel, S. Firestein, Reporter. *J. Amer. Psychoanal. Assn.*, 17:222–227.

——— & Altschul, S. (1963), Activation of mourning and growth by psychoanalysis. *Internat. J. Psycho-Anal.*, 44:419–431.

Freud, S. (1896), The etiology of hysteria. *Standard Edition*, 3:189–221. London: Hogarth Press, 1962.

——— (1905), Three essays on the theory of sexuality. *Standard Edition*, 7:135–243. London: Hogarth Press, 1953.

——— (1908), Creative writers and day-dreaming. *Standard Edition*, 9:141–153. London: Hogarth Press, 1959.

——— (1911), Formulations on the two principles of mental functioning. *Standard Edition*, 12:213–226. London: Hogarth Press, 1958.

——— (1913), On beginning the treatment. *Standard Edition*, 12:121–144. London: Hogarth Press.

——— (1914), Remembering, repetition and working through. *Standard Edition*, 12:145–156. London: Hogarth Press, 1958.

———— (1916), Some character-types met with in psycho-analytic work. *Standard Edition*, 14:311–333. London: Hogarth Press, 1957.

———— (1917), Mourning and melacholia. *Standard Edition,* 14:243–258. London: Hogarth Press, 1957.

———— (1923), The ego and the id. *Standard Edition*, 19:6–63. London: Hogarth Press, 1961.

———— (1937a), Die Endliche und Die Unendliche Analyse. *Gesammelte Werke*, 11:57–99. London: Imago, 1950.

———— (1937b), Analysis terminable and interminable. In: *The Collected Papers of Sigmund Freud*, 5:316–357, ed. J. Strachey. London: Hogarth Press, 1950.

———— (1937c), Analysis terminable and interminable. *Standard Edition,* 23:216–243. London: Hogarth Press, 1961.

———— (1950), *The Collected Papers of Sigmund Freud*, ed. J. Strachey. London: Hogarth Press.

Garcia-Lawson, K. A. & Lang, R. C. (1997), Thoughts on termination. *Psychoanal. Psychol.*, 14:239–257.

Gerson, B., ed. (1996), *The Therapist as a Person: Life Experiences and the Effects on Treatment.* Hillsdale, NJ: The Analytic Press, 2001.

Gill, M. M. (1982), *Analysis of the Transference Vol. 1. Theory and Technique*. Madison, CT: International Universities Press.

Glenn, M. (1971), Separation anxiety: When the therapist leaves the patient. *Amer. J. Psychother.*, 25:437–446.

Glover, E. (1955), *The Technique of Psychoanalysis*. New York: International Universities Press, 1971.

———— & Brierley, M. (1940), *An Investigation of the Technique of Psychoanalysis*. London: Balliere, Tindall & Cox.

Goldberg, A. & Marcus, D. (1985), "Natural termination": Some comments on ending analysis without setting a date. *Psychoanal. Quart.*, 54:46–65.

Greenacre, P. (1959), Play in relation to creative imagination. *The Psychoanalytic Study of the Child*, 14:61–80. New Haven, CT: Yale University Press.

Greenson, R. R. (1949), The psychology of apathy. *Psychoanal. Quart.*, 18:290–302.

———— (1954), The struggle against identification. *J. Amer. Psychoanal. Assn.*, 2:200–217.

———— (1992), Problems of termination: In: *The Technique and Practice of Psychoanalysis, Vol. II,* ed. A. Sugarman, R. Nemeroff & D. P. Greenson. Madison, CT: International Universities Press, pp. 341–342.

Gunderson, J. G. (1996), The borderline patient's intolerance of aloneness: Insecure attachments and therapist availability. *Amer. J. Psychiat.*, 153:752–758.

Hinsie, L. E. & Schatsky, S. (1940), *Psychiatric Dictionary*. New York: Oxford University Press.

Hoffer, W. (1950), Three psychological criteria for the termination of treatment. *Internat. J. Psycho-Anal.*, 31:194–195.

Kantrowitz, J. L., Katz, A.L., Greenman, D.A., Morris, H., Paolitto, F., Sashin, J. & Solomon, L. (1989), The patient–analyst match and outcome of psychoanalysis: A pilot study. *J. Amer. Psychoanal. Assn.*, 37:893–920.

Keith, C. (1966), Multiple transfers of psychotherapy patients. *Arch. General Psychiat.*, 14:185–189.

Kernberg, O. (1974), Barriers to falling and remaining in love. *J. Amer. Psychoanal. Assn.*, 22:486–511.

——— (1975), *Borderline Conditions and Pathological Narcissism.* New York: Aronson.

Klauber, J. (1977), Analyses that cannot be terminated. *Internat. J. Psycho-Anal.*, 58:473–477.

Knight, R. (1953), Borderline states. *Bull. Menn. Clin.*, 17:1–12.

——— (1954), Management and psychotherapy of the borderline schizophrenic patient. *Bull. Menn. Clin.*, 17:139–150.

Kohut, H. (1971), *The Analysis of the Self.* New York: International Universities Press.

Kramer, M. K. (1959), On the continuation of the analytic process after psycho-analysis (a self-observation). *Internat. J. Psycho-Anal.*, 40:17–25.

Kris, E. (1956), On some vicissitudes of insight in psychoanalysis. *Internat. J. Psycho-Anal.*, 37:445–455.

Kubie, L. S. (1968), Unsolved problems in the resolution of the transference. *Psychoanal. Quart.*, 37:331–352.

Kubler-Ross, E. (1969), *On Death and Dying.* New York: Macmillan.

Lehrer, T. (1953), The hunting song. *Songs by Tom Lehrer.* Reprise, 1996.

Leupold-Lowenthal, H. (1988), Notes on Sigmund Freud's "Analysis Terminable and Interminable." *Internat. J. Psycho-Anal.*, 69:261–272.

Loewald, H. (1972), Freud's conception of the negative therapeutic reaction, with comments on instinct theory. *J. Amer. Psychoanal. Assn.*, 20:235–245.

——— (1988), Termination analyzable and unanalyzable. *The Psychoanalytic Study of the Child*, 43:155–166. New Haven, CT: Yale University Press.

Loewenberg, P. (1988), An historical, biographical, literary, and clinical consideration of Freud's "Analysis Terminable and Interminable" on its fiftieth birthday. *Internat. J. Psycho-Anal.*, 69:273–281.

Luborsky, L. (1976), Helping alliances in psychotherapy. In: *Successful Psychotherapy*, ed. J. Claghorn. New York: Brunner-Mazel.

——— McClellan, A. T., Woody, G. E., O'Brien, C. P. & Auerbach, A. (1985), Therapist success and its determinants. *Arch. Gen. Psychiat.*, 42:602–611.

Mahler, M. S. (1961), On sadness and grief in infancy and childhood—Loss and restoration of the symbiotic love object. *The Psychoanalytic Study of the Child*, 16:332–351. New York: International Universities Press.

——— (1972), On the first three subphases of the separation-individuation process. *Internat. J. Psycho-Anal.*, 53:333–338.

Malan, D. (1963), *A Study of Brief Psychotherapy.* New York: Plenum Press.

——— (1976), *Frontier of Brief Psychotherapy.* New York: Plenum Press.

Mann, J. (1976), *Time-Limited Psychotherapy.* Cambridge, MA: Harvard University Press.

Martinez, D. (1989), Pains and gains: A study of forced terminations. *J. Amer. Psychoanal. Assn.*, 37:89–115.

Marzio, P. C. (1973), *Rube Goldberg: His Life and Work.* New York, Harper & Row.

McWilliams, N. (1994), *Psychoanalytic Diagnosis.* New York: Guilford Press.

Menninger, K. A. & Holzman. P. S. (1973), *Theory of Psychoanalytic Technique*. New York: Basic Books.

Miller, I. (1965), On the return of symptoms during the terminal phase of psychoanalysis. *Internat. J. Psycho-Anal*, 46:487–501.

Mitchell, S. A. (1995), Interaction in the Kleinian and interpersonal traditions. *Contemp. Psychoanal.*, 31:65–91.

Novick, J. (1982), Termination: Themes and issues. *Psychoanal. Inq.*, 2:329–365.

Person, E. (1988), *Dreams of Love and Fateful Encounters*. NY: Penguin Books.

Pfeffer, A. Z. (1993), After the analysis: Analyst as both old and new object. *J. Amer. Psychoanal. Assn.*, 41:323–337.

Pumpian-Mindlin, E. (1958), Comments on techniques of termination and transfer in a clinic setting. *Amer. J. Psychother.*, 12:455–464.

Rangell, L. (1982), Some thoughts on termination. *Psychoanal. Inq.*, 2:367–392.

Reider, N. (1953), A type of transference to institutions. *Bull. Menn. Clin.*, 17:58–63.

Richards, A. D. & Richards, A. (2002), Psychoanalytic technique and process. In: *The Freud Encyclopedia: Theory, Therapy and Culture*, ed. E. Erwin. New York: Routledge, pp. 446–454.

Rickman, J. (1950), On the criteria for the termination of an analysis. *Internat. J. Psycho-Anal.*, 31:200–201.

Rothstein, A. (1984), *The Narcissistic Pursuit of Perfection*, New York: International Universities Press.

Safran, J. D., McMain, S., Crocker, P. & Murray, P. (1990), Therapeutic alliance rupture as a therapy-event for empirical investigation. *Psychother.*, 27:154–164.

Schafer, R. (1982), *The Analytic Attitude*. New York: Basic Books.

Schlesinger, H. J. (1969), Diagnosis and prescription for psychotherapy. *Bull. Menninger Clin.*, 33:269–278.

———— (1973), Interaction of dynamic and reality factors in the diagnostic testing interview. *Bull. Menninger Clin.*, 37:495–517.

———— (1978), A contribution to a theory of promising: I. Developmental and regressive aspects of the making of promises. In: *The Human Mind Revisited: Essays in Honor of Karl Menninger*, ed. S. Smith. New York: International Universities Press, pp. 21–50.

———— (1981), The process of empathic response. *Psychoanal. Inq.*, 1:393–415.

———— (1988), Case discussion and position statement on case presentation. *Psychoanal. Inq.*, 8:524–560.

———— (1992), What does psychoanalysis have to contribute to the understanding of character? *The Psychoanalytic Study of the Child*, 47:225–234. New Haven, CT: Yale University Press.

———— (1993), In defense of denial. Unpublished manuscript.

———— (1994a), The role of the intellect in the process of defense. *Bull. Menn. Clin.*, 58:15–36.

———— (1994b), How the analyst listens: The pre-stages of interpretation. *Internat. J. Psycho-Anal.*, 75:31–37.

———— (1995a), The process of interpretation and the moment of change. *J. Amer. Psychoanal. Assn.*, 43:662–685.

——— (1995b), Supervision for fun and profit: Or how do you know if the fun is profitable? *Psychoanal. Inq.*, 15:190–210.

——— (1996), The fear of being left half-cured. *Bull. Menn. Clin.*, 60:428–448.

——— (2003), *The Texture of Treatment: On the Matter of Psychoanalytic Technique.* Hillsdale, NJ: The Analytic Press.

——— & Schuker, E. (1990), Effects of theory on psychoanalytic technique and on the development of psychoanalytic process. *J. Amer. Psychoanal. Assn.*, 38:221–233.

Schlessinger, N. & Robbins, F. (1974), Assessment and follow-up in psychoanalysis. *J. Amer. Psychoanal. Assn.*, 22:542–567.

Searles, H. (1985), Separation and loss in psychoanalytic therapy with borderline patients: Further remarks. *Amer. J. Psychoanal.*, 45:9–27.

Shectman, F. (1968), Time and the practice of psychotherapy. *Psychother.*, 23: 521–525.

Shengold, L. (2002), "What do I know?" Perspectives on what must not be known when change means loss. *Psychoanal. Quart.*, 71:699–724.

Sifneos, P. (1972), *Short-term Psychotherapy and Emotional Crisis.* Cambridge, MA: Harvard University Press.

Skinner, B. F. (1938), *The Behavior of Organisms: An Experimental Analysis.* New York: Appleton-Century-Crofts.

Solnit, A. (1987), A psychoanalytic view of play. *The Psychoanalytic Study of the Child*, 42:205–219. New Haven, CT: Yale University Press.

Spitz, R. A. (1955), The primal cavity: A contribution to the genesis of perception and its role for psychoanalytic theory. *The Psychoanalytic Study of the Child*, 10:215–240. New York: International Universities Press.

Sterba, R. (1934), The fate of the ego in analytic therapy. *Internat. J. Psycho-Anal.*, 15:117–126.

Stone, L. (1961), *The Psychoanalytic Situation: An Examination of Its Development and Essential Nature.* New York: International Universities Press.

Ticho, G. (1967), On self-analysis. *Internat. J. Psycho-Anal.*, 48:308–318.

——— (1972), Termination of psychoanalysis: Treatment goals, life goals. *Psychoanal. Quart.*, 41:315–333.

Viorst, J. (1982), Experiences of loss at the end of analysis: The analyst's response to termination. *Psychoanal. Inq.*, 2:399–418.

Waelder, R. (1933), The psychoanalytic theory of play. *Psychoanal. Quart.*, 2:208–224.

Wallerstein, R. (1967), Reconstruction and mastery in the transference psychosis. *J. Amer. Psychoanal. Assn..*, 15:531–583.

——— & Coen, S. J. (1994), Impasses in psychoanalysis. *J. Amer. Psychoanal. Assn.*, 42:1225–1235.

Winnicott, D. W. (1968), Playing: Its theoretical status in the clinical situation. *Internat. J. Psycho-Anal.*, 49:591–599.

——— (1971), *Playing and Reality.* New York: Routledge.

Zetzel, E. R. (1949), Anxiety and the capacity to bear it. *Internat. J. Psycho-Anal.*, 30:1–12.

# Index

233